4 or 5% p. 25

# The Managerial Revolution
# Reassessed

# The Managerial Revolution Reassessed

**Family Control in America's Large Corporations**

Philip H. Burch, Jr.
Rutgers University

**Lexington Books**
D.C. Heath and Company
Lexington, Massachusetts
Toronto          London

To Carol, David, Terry,
and Ellen

# Contents

# List of Tables

# Preface

This book represents an attempt to correct certain commonly held notions about the magnitude of the managerial revolution in the United States. In this endeavor, I have examined and analyzed all major English-language works dealing with the separation of ownership and the effective control of corporations. Two fairly recent books—one French, one Russian—have been brought to the author's attention too late, unfortunately, for inclusion in this study: J-M. Chevalier, *La structure financiere de l'industrie americaine et le probleme du controle dans les grandes societes americaines* (E. Cujas, 1970) and Stanislov M. Menshikov, *Millionerii i Menedzherii, sovremennaya structura financovoye oligarchii CSHA* (Moscow: Muisl publishers, 1965).

In the preparation of this monograph, I have been helped considerably by the support provided by the staff and facilities of the Rutgers University library. In particular, I would like to thank Mr. H. Gilbert Kelley and other members of the Reference Department for their frequent and unfailing assistance, and Mr. Francois-Xavier Grondin and his able staff in the Government Publications Department for their very substantial efforts over the years. I would also like to show my appreciation to the Rutgers University Research Council for its financial aid, and to Dr. Dorothy S. Redden for her very generous and capable help in editing the manuscript. And finally I want to express my gratitude to Prof. Earl Cheit and Mr. Paul R. Booth for their substantive review and commentary, and to Prof. Ernest C. Reock, Director of the Bureau of Government Research, for his support and encouragement of this undertaking. Any errors that still remain, of course, are my responsibility.

# 1

## "The Managerial Revolution": A Survey of the Pertinent Literature

Since the early depression days, many Americans have been led to believe that control of most of the nation's largest corporations has passed from the hands of various wealthy families to those of a rather sizable number of professionally trained managers and administrators who have very little stock ownership interest in these concerns. From an academic point of view in particular, this line of thinking dates back to 1932, when Berle and Means published their now landmark study on *The Modern Corporation and Private Property*.[1] This book was the first to direct close scholarly attention to the growing dispersion of stock ownership in the United States and to argue that, largely as a result, effective control of most of the big companies in the country had shifted to a managerial class which held no major blocks of stock in these firms and which, furthermore, often held divergent views from those of their many shareholders, large and small. To back up this assertion, the authors assembled a considerable amount of data which, they maintained, showed that of the 200 largest nonfinancial corporations (ranked according to assets as of around January 1930) only about 34 percent were actually under the ultimate control of family or various other outside (that is, nonmanagerial) interests.[2] As one might expect, Berle and Means also found that the nature of control varied a good deal with the type of industry or economic activity. According to their rather involved calculations, approximately 46 percent of the 106 largest industrial concerns were dominated

[1] See Adolf A. Berle, Jr. and Gardiner C. Means, *The Modern Corporation and Private Property* (New York: The Macmillan Co., 1932). A revised edition, published in 1968, contains the authors' latest views on this important subject.

[2] Berle and Means, it should be noted, did not specifically classify corporations in this manner, but rather in terms of such categories as private ownership, majority ownership, minority control, joint control, management control, and control by a legal device (with the latter two considered virtually identical and the first three viewed ultimately as control exercised by certain family or outside interests). In their study, private ownership was defined as the holding of 80 percent or more of the voting stock in a concern, majority ownership generally as the ownership of from 50 to 80 percent of such stock, and minority ownership with but few exceptions as the holding of from 20 to 50 percent of the voting shares, while the 5-to-20 percent stock ownership range was viewed as something of a twilight zone and treated in a rather ambiguous manner. The authors claimed that in none of the companies classified as under management control was the dominant stock interest *known* (and this is a key word here) to be greater than 5 percent of the voting stock. Control by a legal device was regarded essentially as a pyramiding arrangement which led to a very considerable separation of ownership and control. According to another separate set of calculations, Berle and Means also found that only about 20 percent of the overall assets of the top 200 nonfinancial firms were controlled by various family or outside interests, but this, in the author's estimation, is not as significant or meaningful a finding as that based on the actual number of big business concerns.

1

by family or other minority interests, whereas only about 18 percent of the top 42 railroads and 24 percent of the 52 biggest public utilities were so controlled. Thus the latter two percentage figures in particular indicated that at least these essential governmentally regulated public services were very much under management control.[3]

Yet a closer look at this pioneering study by Berle and Means reveals that, although it was undoubtedly a laudable effort for its time, much of its data and procedures are open to serious challenge, and a sizable number of firms seem to have been placed in the wrong control category. Aside from the railroads (these were analyzed on the basis of the so-called Splawn report, which is treated in Appendix A), the bulk of Berle and Means' data was taken from various 1929-31 issues of Standard's *Corporation Records* (now Standard & Poor's *Corporation Records*), the appropriate 1930 *Moody's* manuals, and *The New York Times* and *The Wall Street Journal* from 1928 through 1930. These sources of information, while certainly good in some respects, are still far from adequate, and thus, though the fact is apparently not widely recognized or conceded in academic circles, many of Berle and Means' stock ownership and control findings are of a questionable nature.[4]

Nonetheless, in the last few decades the concept of managerial supremacy has been given even greater currency through the writings of a number of noted economic observers and authorities. From the standpoint of the general reading public, the term "managerial revolution" was transformed into something approaching a household word by James Burnham, who coined and first popularized this phrase through the publication in 1941 of his much-heralded book with that rather sweeping title.[5] Since then this theory has received additional academic support and promotion through the works of such distinguished commentators as Robert A. Gordon, Daniel Bell, Edward S. Mason, and John Ken-

---

[3]The above statistics actually give a rather deceptive picture of the extent to which these companies were controlled by various wealthy families (in contrast to groups of unrelated outsiders). On the basis of the evidence presented, it would appear that only about 16 percent of the above 106 industrial firms—and only about 14 percent of the overall total of 200 concerns—were controlled by families which were clearly identified as such by Berle and Means. For a more detailed analysis and criticism of these data, see Appendix A, which also contains a breakdown of the individual corporations and control status determinations made by Berle and Means and the author's critical evaluation of this work.

[4]Indeed the authors freely admitted that their inferences were often drawn from fragmentary data (Berle and Means, *Modern Corporation*, p. 84). In light of these facts, it is rather curious, as Robert Lekachman recently pointed out (see *New York Times*, 15 September 1968, Sect. VII, p. 8), that most economists have chosen to emphasize that portion of Berle and Means' work dealing with the dispersion of stock ownership and the concomitant growth of managerial control in corporate affairs, while striving to refute or ignore their then equally controversial findings (in Chapter 3 of *The Modern Corporation and Private Property*) concerning the marked trend toward a perhaps dangerous concentration of economic power in the United States.

[5]See James Burnham, *The Managerial Revolution* (New York: The John Day Co., 1941).

neth Galbraith, in addition to the aforementioned Adolf Berle.[6] In 1959, for instance, Mason no doubt accurately expressed the thinking of the vast majority of economists in this country when he asserted that almost everyone now agreed that in the large corporation the stockholders are, as a rule, a distinctly passive, if not impotent body, and that control generally lies in the hands of management forces, which are usually able even to pick their own successors in office.[7] And in 1965 Berle himself (by then, unknown to many, a long-established corporate executive) went so far as to say that in all but an atypical few of the largest corporations in America—and in a good many lesser companies too—the old ownership form of control was now atomized among thousands of stockholders, most of whom were very small.[8] Indeed the noted Harvard economist, John Kenneth Galbraith, has artfully erected a rather elaborate theory of modern industrial organization, succinctly described in his widely acclaimed book, *The New Industrial State*, as the technostructure, which is based in considerable part on the reported separation of corporate ownership and control.[9] But in none of these works, unfortunately, have any really new factual (in particular, quantitative) data been presented to buttress or substantiate this oft-repeated claim. Except for the 1932 Berle and Means study, learned and laymen alike have, until recently, just had to accept the tenet of managerial supremacy or less as an article of faith—all this, curiously enough, despite the publication prior to World War II of a major Congressional report which seemed to cast considerable doubt on this thesis.[10]

[6]See Robert A. Gordon's rather impressive and ably organized book, *Business Leadership in the Large Corporation* (Washington: The Brookings Institution, 1945), pp. 30-45; Daniel Bell's chapter entitled "The Breakup of Family Capitalism" in *The End of Ideology* (New York: Crowell-Collier Publishing Co., 1961), pp. 39-46; and three of Berle's later works—*The 20th Century Capitalist Revolution* (New York: Harcourt, Brace & Co., 1954), *Power Without Property* (New York: Harcourt, Brace & World, Inc., 1959), and *The American Economic Republic* (New York: Harcourt, Brace & World, Inc., 1963). Even some prominent Marxist scholars have come to the point where they too now subscribe to the concept of the managerial revolution. See, for instance, Paul A. Baran and Paul M. Sweezy, *Monopoly Capital* (New York: Monthly Review Press, 1966), pp. 15-17.

[7]See Edward S. Mason, ed., *The Corporation in Modern Society* (New York: Atheneum Publishers, 1959), p. 4.

[8]See Adolf A. Berle, "The Impact of the Corporation on Classical Economic Theory," *Quarterly Journal of Economics* (February 1965), pp. 27-28. Following a number of years of service as, first, director and then treasurer, Berle was appointed board chairman of the family controlled American Molasses Co. (or as it was known after 1961, Sucrest Corp.) and held this post until 1965, at which time he resumed his former status of corporate director (for more on this point, see *Forbes*, 15 February 1958, p. 24). In the mid and late thirties, he also served on the board of directors of the Institutional Securities Corp. and Savings Bank Trust Co. of New York City, both fairly small concerns.

[9]See John Kenneth Galbraith, *The New Industrial State* (Boston: Houghton Mifflin Co., 1967), especially pp. 81 and 309.

[10]In the author's estimation, the most thorough study of this critical and controversial subject was that conducted by the U.S. Temporary National Economic Committee (TNEC) back in the late thirties (see its very detailed and lengthy Monograph No. 29 entitled *The Distribution of Ownership in the 200 Largest Nonfinancial Corporations*). Though now of course quite dated, it raised (or should have raised) a great deal of doubt about the validity of Berle and Means' stock ownership data and summary findings. In contrast to their rather restricted research effort, the TNEC was able, because of its official governmental status, to

More concrete corporate control data, however, have been presented in two fairly recent articles devoted to this important topic. The first of these brief surveys, Robert Larner's analysis of the current stage of the separation of ownership and management in the nation's 200 largest nonfinancial concerns, was an acknowledged attempt to update the original Berle and Means study.[11] Larner, who was at that time a graduate student in economics at the University of Wisconsin, relied largely on corporate proxy statements and selected annual reports submitted to various federal agencies to arrive at his stock ownership totals and control status determinations. His carefully collected data indicated that only about 18 percent of the top 108 manufacturing and mining companies (ranked according to assets as of 1963) could be considered family or entrepreneurially controlled firms (control here being defined, as a rule, as the holding of 10 percent or more of the voting stock in a corporation).[12] All told, Larner found that

gather accurate information as to the amount of stock owned by the officers, directors, and 20 largest shareholders of the then top 200 nonfinancial concerns (which were ranked according to their total assets as of about December 31, 1937). Also unlike Berle and Means, the TNEC research staff used a generally much more realistic stock ownership standard of 10 percent (and in some cases even less) as its primary means of determining the locus of control in a corporation, together with selected supplementary data on family and interest group representation on these particular boards of directors (a form of evidence, it should be noted, which Berle and Means chose not to employ). Overall, this TNEC monograph found that close to two-thirds of the top 200 nonfinancial corporations in the country were under the control of family or various outside interests, with almost the same percentage holding for the 120 biggest industrial concerns. Furthermore, when viewed solely in family terms, it would appear that, according to the author's slight modification of the TNEC data, at least 37 percent of the nation's 200 largest nonfinancial corporations could then be described as probably under family control and that about 52 percent of the aforementioned 120 industrial firms could be so classified. These totals, it is plain to see, represent a far different set of figures from those arrived at nearly ten years earlier by Berle and Means. (See the latter part of Appendix A for a detailed analysis and breakdown of the TNEC's stock ownership statistics and corporate control findings and the author's use and interpretation of these data, including, for purposes of comparison with Berle and Means, a shift in classification of six communications companies to the public utilities category.)

[11] See Robert J. Larner, "Ownership and Control in the 200 Largest Nonfinancial Corporations: 1929 and 1963," *American Economic Review* (September 1966), pp. 777-87.

[12] These 19 manufacturing and mining concerns represented about 19 percent of the overall assets of the above 108 concerns. Actually, Larner did not classify corporations on the basis of family versus managerial control, but on the basis of the same categories used by Berle and Means, most of which represent various outside interests. However, in the author's judgment outside interests must ultimately represent either family or management forces. This rather superficial emphasis on outside control represents one of the many serious errors involved in Larner's work (also that of Berle and Means and to some extent the TNEC), for a number of firms described as under outside (majority, minority or pyramiding) control were actually dominated, albeit indirectly, by management interests. Fortunately, with the aid of a mimeographed, detailed appendix—a company-by-company breakdown which was not incorporated in his *American Economic Review* article, but which Mr. Larner very kindly made available—the author was able to convert Larner's findings into family versus management terms. The above figure of about 18 percent is only approximate, because of some apparent discrepancies in Larner's tabulations or totals, particularly when one views them from the standpoint of family control. For more on this point, see Appendix B, which includes a list of the manufacturing and mining concerns described by Larner as being under family (or majority or minority interest) control. In addition, it should be noted, Mr. Larner made a control-type analysis of the 9 largest merchandising firms in the country (three of

about 14 percent of the nation's 200 largest nonfinancial concerns (ranked according to 1963 assets) were dominated by family or other outside interests. As a result of these findings, Larner came, quite understandably perhaps, to the conclusion that the managerial revolution now seemed close to complete in America.[13]

The second article on the subject, which was written by Robert Sheehan of *Fortune* magazine, was not of an academic nature. Sheehan, using presumably reliable but unrevealed data, came to a somewhat different conclusion, namely that family ownership and control of large corporations was still quite significant—a rather interesting observation in view of *Fortune's* pronounced pro-management and big business orientation.[14] This statement notwithstanding, however, Sheehan still managed to lend considerable support to the concept of managerial supremacy, finding as he did that only 11 percent of the top 100,[15] 17 percent of the top 200, and about 24 percent of the top 300 industrial firms (ranked according to volume of sales as of 1966) were controlled by various wealthy families or individuals (control again being defined here as the holding of 10 percent or more of the voting stock in a concern, a yardstick which even this economic spokesman freely admitted was "very conservative"). Thus, despite certain differences, both Sheehan and Larner seemed, in essence, to be saying pretty much the same thing—namely, that the widely acclaimed corporate

which he described as being dominated by nonmanagerial interests), the 24 largest transportation corporations (four of which he claimed were controlled by outside interests), and the 59 largest public utilities (only one of which he found to be under outside control). These various companies are also treated in Appendix B. In his September 1966 article, Larner classified the above 9 merchandising companies as industrial enterprises, but the author has deleted these concerns from this particular tabulation in order to make it categorically comparable with the *Fortune* ranking and analysis treated in the next paragraph of the text.

[13]Indeed, in the latter part of 1970, a highly technical (though in some respects substantively questionable) work was published on this subject which made almost no reference to the possible existence of entrepreneurial, family or other outside forces, apparently assuming instead that the only significant types of corporate control today were two species of managerial control which were described as unitary form corporations and multidivision form enterprises. See Oliver E. Williamson, *Corporate Control and Business Behavior* (Englewood Cliffs, N.J.: Prentice-Hall, Inc., 1970).

[14]See Robert Sheehan, "Proprietors in the World of Big Business," *Fortune* (15 June 1967), pp. 178-83. Unfortunately, no sources of information are identified in this article, and *Fortune* claims (in a letter, dated October 4, 1967, to Prof. Stanley W. Ackley of the Rutgers University Economics Department) that its data, for other than the top 100 industrial concerns, are in no form to release or make public. While the author has no reason to doubt the accuracy of many of the individual corporate stockownership percentages contained in this article, some figures nevertheless seem to be in error. Mr. Sheehan, for example, asserted that the Pew family owned 44 percent of the stock of the Sun Oil Co. (see p. 181). Yet *Forbes* maintained just four months later (15 October 1967, p. 28) that this particular family had a total of 56.5 percent of the stock. Given the brief intervening time period, the difference is difficult to explain.

[15]Ibid., p. 179. For a list of these eleven giant companies described as being under single family or individual control, see Appendix B. Sheehan, it should be observed, did not include any large firms under multiple family control in his corporate ownership aggregate, which may account for some of the difference between his findings and those of Mr. Larner, who chose to count such concerns and arrived at a family control total of about 18 percent for the top 100 industrials.

takeover by professional managers or administrators has now reached the point of undisputed dominance (if indeed Berle and Means did not so demonstrate many years ago).

Additional evidence of a more detailed nature concerning the control status of America's major nonfinancial concerns was provided in December 1970 when Larner published a revised version of his dissertation entitled *Management Control and the Large Corporation.*[16] In this book Larner made no effort to update his data and did little to improve upon his study methodology and sources of share ownership information (both of which, it will be shown, leave much to be desired). Instead he adhered very closely to his earlier line of economic analysis, which was based largely on corporate proxy statements and selected annual reports submitted to various federal agencies, and also on a concept of working control generally defined as the ownership of 10 percent or more of the voting stock in a concern.[17] However, in this lengthier work, Larner did expand the numerical scope of his study to encompass the top 500 nonfinancial firms in the country (which were ranked again according to assets as of 1963). And for the first time he now included in an appendix a company-by-company breakdown of his control status findings and sources of information. Indeed, from the standpoint of the locus of economic control, this probably represents the only really significant addition to Larner's corporate research analysis.[18]

Overall, Larner found that about 27 percent of the top 290 manufacturing and mining firms, a little over 39 percent of the 33 largest merchandising concerns, no more than 13 percent of the 45 biggest transportation companies, and just 2 percent of the 120 largest public utilities were dominated by nonmanagerial interests.[19] Furthermore, Larner went on to assert that this evidence suggests

[16]See Robert J. Larner, *Management Control and the Large Corporation* (New York: Dunellen Publishing Co., 1970).

[17]In five cases, Larner deviated from his 10 percent or more stock ownership rule of working control. He classified the Transcontinental Gas Pipe Line Co. as management controlled, even though the probably family dominated Stone & Webster, Inc. (which was not represented on the former's board of directors) held an 11 percent stock ownership interest. Conversely, he treated the Mead Corp., May Department Stores Co., Pittston Co., and Spiegel, Inc. as minority controlled firms, apparently because of certain directorship data, notwithstanding the fact that these particular family holdings ranged from less than 4 percent to a little over 8 percent of the voting stock in these concerns. See Larner, *Management Control*, pp. 78-79, 84-85, 88-91, and 102-03.

[18]As a matter of fact, there are only about 7 pages of text devoted to this extremely important topic, all in Chapter 2, which is essentially a reproduction of his 1966 *American Economic Review* article, except for the insertion of some additional summary statistics to extend his coverage from the top 200 to the top 500 nonfinancial concerns. Oddly enough, Larner made no reference in his 1970 monograph to Sheehan's June 15, 1967 analysis of the subject in *Fortune*, although he saw fit to cite a much less pertinent article on mutual funds by Arthur M. Louis in the May 1967 issue of *Fortune*.

[19]The above companies add up to a total of 488, 12 short of the 500 found on Larner's list. The reason for this discrepancy is that the author deleted a dozen miscellaneous or service concerns (at least six of which were probably family controlled) from these computations to make them categorically comparable to the *Fortune* ranking used elsewhere in this study. The author also took the 33 merchandising concerns out of Larner's aggregate of industrial

that "... a corporation may reach a size so great that, with a few exceptions, its control is beyond the financial means of any individual or interest group."[20] In other words, Larner apparently takes the position that it is almost impossible for any outside interests, no matter how wealthy, to either gain or retain working control of large corporations in the United States, which are of such size today that managerial forces must inevitably predominate. It would be hard to find a more strongly worded statement of the doctrine of managerial supremacy.

enterprises for the same reason. If all 500 firms were lumped together, the family or outside control total would be about 21 percent. Computations on the basis of assets, it should be noted, result in slightly lower majority and minority control findings.

With the exception of the public utility category, the above figures do not coincide with those contained in Larner's book because the author is convinced that some of the corporations described by Larner as majority or minority controlled are actually dominated by managerial interests. The General Aniline and Film Corp., for example, was classified as privately controlled because 98 percent of the voting stock was held by the federal government (this being a former German firm seized by the Roosevelt administration during World War II), but, as far as the author can determine, the men placed in charge of this concern by the U.S. Attorney-General have been professionally trained managers or administrators. In like manner, the Soo Line RR Co. was categorized as being majority controlled because the Canadian Pacific Rwy. Co. owned about 56 percent of the outstanding common stock. However, the latter company appears to have been management dominated. Similarly, although Trans World Airlines, Inc. was described as majority controlled, even Larner admitted (on page 11) that an equally cogent argument could be made for classifying it as indirectly controlled by a legal device (and ultimately, in the author's opinion, by management forces) since in 1963, Howard Hughes' 78 percent stock ownership interest was, at least temporarily, being held in trust by a group of banks and insurance companies. Because of this important distinction in economic status, all figures used in the above computations are quite logically based on Larner's determinations (where accurate) as to the locus of ultimate, rather than immediate, control. For a more detailed analysis and critique of Larner's corporate control findings and methodology, see the latter part of Appendix B. Certain other major aspects of Larner's work, such as his investigation of the profitability and performance of management dominated and owner controlled companies, will be discussed in Chapter 5.

[20] Larner, *Management Control*, p. 20. He also asserted in the very next sentence that "this point appears to have been reached only by the larger of the 200 firms on the 1929 list [of Berle and Means], but by *all* 500 corporations ..." on his 1963 list (italics added). Given the evidence that Larner has compiled (an absolute minimum of 103 big companies controlled by nonmanagerial interests), this can only be described as an extremely contradictory or erroneous statement.

# 2

## Selection of Firms for Study and Sources of Corporate Control Data

One very good reason why the concept of the managerial revolution has taken such a pervasive hold on professional and public thinking in America is that, Larner's research notwithstanding, there has been little reliable stock ownership or other evidence presented since the days of the depression with which to challenge or refute this rather appealing notion. Aside from the aforementioned TNEC study (which has not received much popular or academic recognition over the years, although it was actually a fairly thorough and revealing report), there have been only two other works published in the post-1930 period which have shed any light on the subject, and neither of these could be considered very convincing.[1] What's more, and this is most important, it is difficult to get any kind of sound, systematic data on the amount of family control or stock ownership (the usual means of determining the locus of corporate power) in most of America's large business concerns. Such information is simply not published or released in any permanent or regular form. For example, the famous *Moody's* manuals, which are undoubtedly the best-known and most complete source of pertinent corporate data readily available, rarely list any figures on overall family (or individual) shareholdings in the stock section found ordinarily at the end of each corporate entry.[2] The official reports submitted to responsible governmental authorities, in conformance with various legal or administrative requirements, are not much better as a rule, for they are not primarily concerned with ascertaining the extent of family-versus-management control of large corporations. The rather elaborately prepared annual reports put out each year by all major (publicly owned) corporations almost never include any stock ownership statistics. In fact, they often don't even identify the members of their board of direc-

---

[1] One of these studies was undertaken by Don Villarejo and published in the autumn 1961 issue of *New University Thought*, a rather radical journal with an extremely limited circulation. (A summary of Villarejo's findings is contained in Earl Cheit's *The Business Establishment*, John Wiley & Sons, Inc., 1964, pp. 172-73.) The other is Ferdinand Lundberg's recent best-seller *The Rich and the Super-Rich* (New York: Lyle Stuart, Inc., 1968). The author, however, does not consider either of these works to be of much real value or substance, for reasons indicated in the latter part of Appendix B. Gabriel Kolko's *Wealth and Power in America* (New York: Frederick A. Praeger, Inc., 1962), also touches on this topic very briefly (see pp. 60-68).

[2] There are, of course, several other similar sources of corporate data, such as Standard & Poor's *Corporation Records* and its less widely known *Standard Listed Stock Reports*, but both of these directories are published in loose-leaf form, with new entries being added regularly to replace various dated sections (which are then usually discarded), so that it is impossible to check back over any extended period of time on some particular stockownership statistic.

9

tors other than by name. (A listing of all institutional affiliations might reveal, for instance, the existence of a family holding company.) And finally it should be pointed out that although corporate proxy statements (which are distributed to all shareholders in a company before its regular annual meeting) do contain in a number of cases some family or outside stock ownership figures, these special statements are not collected at any central point other than the national or regional offices of the Securities and Exchange Commission and certain select business libraries, and are thus not accessible to most persons. Moreover, no permanent record of proxy data is maintained or made public by any government or private agency. Given these facts, it is not at all surprising then that the vast majority of people in the country have come to believe that managerial interests now reign supreme in the world of big business.

Yet a close look at the situation reveals that such is not really the case. Both Sheehan and Larner seriously understate, because of certain data and definitional problems (see Appendix B), the actual extent of family ownership and control of large corporations today. Contrary to most professional and popular opinion, family interests still play a fairly prominent role in the conduct of big business affairs in the United States. This assertion can and will be demonstrated, using a different approach based largely on other reliable sources of information, the vast majority of which have not been systematically exploited up to the present time. The data generated by these sources include stock ownership figures collected over a period of many years, as well as evidence of family representation as either directors or high administrative officials of large corporations.

As a basis for proceeding, this study has used in its selection and identification of the nation's largest business firms the 1965 *Fortune* list of the top 500 industrials, although it has concentrated primarily on the first 300 such concerns (which like the other 200 were ranked according to volume of sales).[3] In addition, it appraised the top 50 merchandising firms (again arranged according to volume of sales), the top 50 transportation companies (ranked on the basis of operating revenues), and the top 50 commercial banks (listed according to their officially stated assets or resources).[4]

---

[3]See "The Fortune Directory," *Fortune* (July 1965), pp. 149-68. The author chose the year 1965 because it fell between the dates of the Larner and Sheehan articles and also because it represented the midpoint of the decade. The decision to confine the basic analytical scope of this study to the first 300 industrial concerns was made largely because these particular companies took in almost all (nearly 90 percent) of the sales dollars collected by the 500 biggest manufacturing and mining firms in 1964. Indeed, many might argue that the cut-off point could even have been established at some prior point since the 200 largest corporations accounted for about 80 percent of the (top 500) volume of sales in 1964. A breakdown of the author's corporate control findings for the less important (and often lesser known) companies ranked from 301 to 500 on *Fortune's* 1965 list is contained in Appendix C.

[4]See "The Fortune Directory," *Fortune* (August 1965), pp. 174-80. No data have been compiled in this study concerning savings banks, property and casualty insurance companies, investment banking firms (many of which are family dominated), savings and loan

While the 1965 *Fortune* lists were by far the most reliable and useful rankings available for purposes of this study, they nevertheless do have certain limitations. For example, their fourfold selection of large corporations was compiled on three different bases, and some might argue that it would have been preferable to utilize a single fiscal standard, as Larner did.[5] However, there is no per-

---

associations (a number of the bigger ones in California being under family control), mutual funds (some very sizable ones, including the nation's first-ranked Investors Diversified Services complex, being under family control), and other financial institutions such as (closed-end) investment companies. Moreover, the author has not presented any control data concerning the top 50 utility companies and the top 50 life insurance companies on *Fortune's* 1965 list. In the case of public utilities, he did not do so because, to the best of his knowledge, only a few—notably the Duke Power Co., the Brown-dominated Texas Eastern Transmission Corp., and very possibly the Pacific Lighting Corp.—have been under the control of family interests in recent years. In this respect the author agrees pretty much with Larner, who found just one utility company (Duke Power) in his top 59 to be under outside control. The life insurance companies are not included for a number of reasons. Since more than half of these companies are mutual firms (that is, ones in which there is no stock ownership), the determination of the locus of control becomes a much more difficult and tenuous process, and one which is not, from a methodological point of view, truly comparable to that employed elsewhere in this study. (See, for instance, *Forbes*, 15 February 1971, p. 43 with regard to the Lumbermans Mutual Casualty Co., one of the nation's largest mutual casualty companies, which this magazine claims is dominated by the Kemper family in part through its control of the corporate proxy mechanism.) In addition, the life insurance industry is very badly skewed from the standpoint of size. The 15 largest companies come close to dominating this field, accounting for well over 50 percent of the total business, and in this sense represent a rather atypical condition. In all, the author would place twelve of the 50 largest life insurance companies in the probably family-controlled category (with a few others viewed as possibly under family control). However, only one of these twelve companies ranks in the top 15 in the field, this concern being the Aetna Life Insurance Co., which has, since its inception, been dominated by the Bulkeley-Brainard family interests (see *Finance*, February 1968, pp. 9-12).

Because of its reliance on the above *Fortune* top 500 and 50 rankings, and the fact that some family-controlled business complexes are run through a number of companies of various sizes (rather than as a single corporate unit), this study does not take into account certain other huge economic empires which cut across the above standard lines of business activity. For one such case involving the Jessie Ball du Pont industrial, transportation and banking enterprise in Florida (which probably had overall assets of at least roughly $1 billion in 1964), see *Business Week*, 27 August 1960, p. 67 and *Finance*, May 1967, pp. 23-25 and also June 1967, p. 30.

[5] Larner, for instance, claims that the use of assets as a corporate yardstick overstates the size of transportation and utility companies in relation to firms in other industries, while the utilization of total sales results in an even larger bias in the opposite direction. Overall, Larner felt that the best measure of size is value added, but such data are not generally available for individual concerns (see Larner, *Management Control*, p. 10). *Forbes*, by the way, recently came out with a multiple listing of the top 500 concerns in the country, these corporations being ranked first on the basis of revenues, then market value, followed by assets, and finally net profits (see *Forbes*, 15 May 1969, pp. 63-171). In each case commercial banks, stock insurance companies, merchandising firms, transportation companies, and public utilities were mixed in with industrial concerns, and thus this arrangement is not comparable with the better known *Fortune* 500 or 50 rankings. The top 20 mutual life insurance companies were also included in a separate tabulation by *Forbes* (see p. 195). The author, however, chose not to rely on any of these *Forbes* lists because he preferred a 1965 date for corporate ranking purposes.

fect measure of economic size or importance.[6] For instance, the use of sales as the yardstick for determining the 500 largest industrials has resulted in the exclusion of certain very sizable companies which happen to have suffered a temporary decline in business (such as the Freeport Sulphur Co.—a probably family controlled firm with 1964 sales of $79 million, but with total assets of $227 million).[7]

Furthermore, it should be noted, particularly from the standpoint of assessing the overall magnitude of family firms in the American economy, that a number of other big entrepreneurially controlled corporations were not included in *Fortune's* top 50 or 500 lists. One group of companies was omitted apparently because they fell into what is commonly considered a miscellaneous or service category.[8] Some of the most prominent such concerns are as follows:[9]

[6]The ranking of commercial banks in this study is on the basis of their officially stated assets or resources and does not include trust department funds, which, as far as the very big commercial banks are concerned, often run into billions of dollars. For example, the United States Trust Co. of New York City was not listed by *Fortune* as among the top 50 banks, having "official" assets of only about $309 million in 1965. Yet at the same time, it also had trust department assets of another $6 billion (see *Trusts and Estates*, February 1965, p. 161), which, if counted, would easily place it in this select category. If all commercial banks were ranked on the basis of their total true assets (that is, including their trust department funds), it would still not significantly alter the overall family control findings arrived at in this study with regard to such banks.

[7]Another minor defect of the *Fortune* lists is that in several instances companies are included which are, for all practical purposes, subsidiaries of other generally larger concerns already incorporated in these rankings. For example, both the Kaiser Steel Corp. and the Kaiser Aluminum & Chemical Corp. are actually effectively controlled by the Kaiser Industries Corp. (all of which are listed in the top 300 category). In like manner, the American Smelting & Refining Co. (#101) would appear to control both the General Cable Corp. (#242) and Revere Copper & Brass, Inc. (#231). Up to January 1966, the Richfield Oil Corp. presented a somewhat different set of circumstances, being dominated jointly by the Cities Service Co. and the Sinclair Oil Corp. And in the transportation field, the Pennsylvania Railroad held 56 percent of the stock of the Norfolk & Western Rwy.; the Atlantic Coast Line RR Co. had 33 percent of the stock of the Louisville & Nashville RR; while the Chesapeake & Ohio Rwy. was found to control the Baltimore & Ohio RR, which in turn owned over 38 percent of the Reading Co. Moreover, the Chicago, Burlington & Quincy RR was controlled jointly by the Great Northern Rwy. and the Northern Pacific Rwy. If, later in this study, one were to attempt to adjust for these minor discrepancies by reaching down a little further on one or the other list, the overall corporate control percentages would still probably remain close to the totals arrived at in the latter parts of Chapters 3 and 4.

[8]There were also apparently a few outright omissions from *Fortune's* 1965 first 500 industrial list, mostly at the lower end of the scale (the 400-500 range). There is, of course, no way of knowing just how many companies were inadvertently missed in the compilation of this tabulation (without expending an inordinate amount of time and energy), but, judging from an examination of various business directories, the number was probably very small, and the *Fortune* 500 was undoubtedly the best ranking readily available at this particular time. By thumbing through the 1964 *Poor's Register of Corporations, Directors, and Executives*, the author found two large industrial concerns which should have been included in the first 500 category. Both were, by chance, family-dominated firms. These corporations were Publicker Industries, Inc. (a Philadelphia chemical and liquor company with 1964 sales of about $153 million), which was controlled by the Publicker-Neuman interests (see the 1965 *Moody's Industrial Manual*, p. 554, the SEC *Official Summary*, December 1963, and *Forbes*, 1 June 1969, p. 26), and Heublein, Inc. (a Connecticut liquor company with 1964 sales of almost $136 million), which was controlled by the Heublein-Martin family (*Time*, 1 January 1965, p. 64).

[9]All of the above companies (other than the Sheraton Corp. of America) are listed in a

Columbia Broadcasting System, Inc. (1964 revenues of $638 million and assets of $409 million)—probably controlled by the Paley family (*New York Times*, 19 July 1965, p. 51); such control is also reflected in the make-up of the board of directors, including both management and outside members, over the years.

American Broadcasting Companies, Inc. (1964 revenues of $421 million and assets of $227 million)—probably controlled by the E.J. Noble family interests (*New York Times*, 19 July 1965, p. 51 and *Fortune*, March 1969, p. 134); such control is also reflected in either the inside or outside make-up of the board of directors over the years.

Hilton Hotels Corp. (1964 revenues of $226 million and assets of $296 million)—probably controlled primarily by the Hilton family (*Fortune*, January 1961, p. 166); such control is also reflected in the inside make-up of the board of directors over the years.

Sheraton Corp. of America (1964 revenues of $233 million and assets of $264 million)—up to 1967 (when it was merged into I.T.&T.) most likely controlled by the Moore and Henderson families of Boston (*Fortune*, January 1961, p. 166); such control is also reflected in both the inside and outside make-up of the board of directors over the years.

Pittston Co. (1964 revenues of $257 million and assets of $214 million)—probably controlled by the Routh family (*Forbes*, 1 April 1967, p. 71); such control is also reflected in the inside make-up of the board of directors over the years.

In addition, the *Fortune* lists cover only publicly owned concerns. Yet there are more than a few very large essentially privately owned firms (companies owned outright by some individual or with, as a rule, 80 percent or more of the stock family owned) which should be given due consideration in any appraisal of the role of family controlled corporations in today's business world. According to two mid-decade surveys on the subject and one conducted in 1969, there were at least 13 such sizable concerns (10 industrial and 3 merchandising firms) which should really be included in the top 300 industrial and top 50 merchandis-

ranking of miscellaneous firms which *Fortune* has put together since 1969 (see either its 15 May 1969 or May 1970 issue). With but three exceptions, the other companies in this recently established miscellaneous category were either included in one or the other of *Fortune's* 1965 lists or were too small as of that time to warrant such ranking. (Actually, the Columbia Broadcasting System and the American Broadcasting Companies would not be large enough either if treated as public utilities, which were ranked according to assets, rather than as manufacturing concerns; they are mentioned here simply to point up the fact that there are a rather sizable number of other big family firms in the United States which do not appear on any of the famous *Fortune* lists.) The three exceptions were the Halliburton Co. (a Texas oil equipment and construction company), the United Fruit Co. (a wholesale trading concern), and the Railway Express Agency, all of which were probably management dominated. For the necessary directorship data on each company cited here, see the pertinent corporate entry in various 1955 to 1965 annual issues of either (Standard &) Poor's *Register of Corporations, Directors, and Executives* or the appropriate *Moody's* manual.

ing categories. These companies, together with their estimated sales figures (their finances are rarely made public), are shown in Table 2 1.[10]

Furthermore, it should be pointed out that, from a family control standpoint, there were several significant omissions from *Fortune's* top 50 transportation list in 1965. For one thing, the big truck hauling and rental firm, Ryder System, Inc., which had operating revenues of $119 million in 1964 and 21 percent of whose stock was then owned by its founder, J.A. Ryder (see 1965 *Moody's Transportation Manual*, p. 998), was not included in the first 50 transportation ranking.[11] But even more important was the fact that certain other huge transportation enterprises were overlooked by *Fortune's* researchers because they were completely privately owned affairs. The well over a billion dollar (oil tanker) shipping empire of Daniel K. Ludwig, for example, should certainly be counted as one of the top 50 transportation concerns in the country, for Ludwig is generally acknowledged to be the largest independent ship operator in the world.[12] For like reasons the family dominated States Marine Lines was not

---

[10]See "Behind Closed Doors," *Forbes* (1 February 1965), pp. 33-35; Robert Sheehan, "There's Plenty of Privacy Left in Private Enterprise," *Fortune* (15 July 1966), pp. 224-25 and 327-48; "The Luxury of Privacy," *Forbes* (15 May 1969), pp. 186-92. The blanks in the above table reflect omissions in these articles. For the most part, the sales figures reported here seem accurate and consistent. There are, however, a few discrepancies, such as the difference between the Bechtel Corp.'s 1964 and 1968 revenues, which are difficult to account for. Similarly, the above over-$100 million figure given by *Fortune* for Mars, Inc. would certainly seem to be in error, for shortly thereafter this journal stated that the company had sales in excess of $350 million in 1966 (Harold B. Meyers, "The Sweet, Secret World of Forrest Mars," *Fortune*, May 1967, p. 155), and two years later *Forbes* put it at $375 million. (On the other hand, additional evidence that the sales figures for the Sperry & Hutchinson Co., Cargill, Inc., and Continental Grain Co. are fairly accurate can be found in *Fortune*, November 1964, p. 157, *New York Times*, 31 October 1969, p. 67, ibid., 12 January 1964, Sect. 3, p. 3, and the 1966 *Moody's Industrial Manual*, p. 1482.)

In any event, all of these 13 companies appear to be large enough to be included among the top 300 industrial or top 50 merchandising firms. This can be seen from the fact that the 300th-ranked industrial concern on *Fortune's* 1965 list had total (1964) sales of $192 million, in 1966 total (1965) sales of $216 million, and in 1969 total (1968) sales of $283 million. The 50th largest merchandising firm in 1965 had total (1964) sales of $266 million. In this listing of private companies large enough to be ranked in the top 300 industrial or top 50 merchandising category, the author has chosen to be rather conservative and has not included, as he might well have, three other big privately owned concerns—namely, the Reader's Digest Assn., Inc., the E.W. Scripps Co. (Scripps-Howard newspapers), and the Peter Kiewit Sons Inc. (a Nebraska general contractor). In fact, there may be other large privately owned companies which were missed by *Forbes* and *Fortune*; in both of its articles *Forbes* readily acknowledged that, because of the immense difficulties involved in gathering the pertinent data (most of the above companies, for example, are not listed in *Moody's Industrial Manual*), their lists were still probably incomplete.

[11]The Railway Express Agency, which had total revenue and income of $422 million in 1964, was also excluded from this tabulation, but was not listed above because it was, in effect, a management dominated subsidiary of 58 participating railroads which exercise control through substantial stock ownership (the bulk of which was held by the nation's seven largest railroads).

[12]See *Business Week*, (16 March 1957), pp. 105-08; ibid., (23 November 1963), pp. 88-92; *Forbes* (1 August 1970), p. 23.

**Table 2-1**
**Privately Owned Companies Large Enough to be Incorporated in the First 300 Range of the 1965 *Fortune* Industrial Ranking**

| Name, Type and Location of Company | Estimated 1964 Sales according to *Forbes* (1 February 1965) | Estimated 1965 Sales according to *Fortune* (15 July 1966) | Estimated 1968 Sales according to *Forbes* (15 May 1969) |
|---|---|---|---|
| Cargill, Inc. (a Minneapolis-based grain trading company controlled by the Cargill MacMillan interests) | $1,800,000,000 | | $2,000,000,000 |
| Continental Grain Co. (a NYC-based trading company controlled by the Fribourg family of France) | $1,000,000,000 | | $1,500,000,000 |
| Deering Milliken, Inc. (a textile company controlled by the Milliken family of NYC and South Carolina) | $400,000,000 | $500,000,000 | $600,000,000 |
| Hearst Corp. (a newspaper publishing company controlled by the Hearst family of NYC and California) | $500,000,000 | $350,000,000 | $500,000,000 |
| Hughes Aircraft Co. (a Calif.-based company controlled by Howard Hughes) | $500,000,000 | $500,000,000 | $500,000,000 |
| Hughes Tool Co. (a Texas-based company controlled by Howard Hughes) | $400,000,000 | $500,000,000 | $500,000,000 |
| Bechtel Corp. (a West Coast construction firm controlled by the Bechtel family of San Francisco) | $250,000,000 | | $1,500,000,000 |
| Tribune Co. (a Chicago newspaper publishing company controlled by the McCormick family, an arm of the McCormick family of the International Harvester Co.) | | $320,000,000 | $475,000,000 |
| Sperry & Hutchinson Co. (a NYC-based trading company controlled by the Beinecke family) | $330,000,000 | | |

**Table 2-1** *(Cont.)*

| Name, Type and Location of Company | Estimated 1964 Sales according to *Forbes* (1 February 1965) | Estimated 1965 Sales according to *Fortune* (15 July 1966) | Estimated 1968 Sales according to *Forbes* (15 May 1969) |
|---|---|---|---|
| Gates Rubber Co. (a Denver-based company controlled by the Gates family) | | $228,000,000 | $450,000,000 |
| Mars, Inc. (a big Chicago-based candy company controlled by the Mars family) | | Well over $100,000,000 (but in 1967 revised to more than $350,000,000) | $375,000,000 |
| Dubuque Packing Co. (an Iowa company owned largely by the Wahlert interests) | | Over $250,000,000 | $300,000,000 |
| Field Enterprises, Inc. (a Chicago-based newspaper publishing enterprise controlled by the Marshall Field family) | $200,000,000 | $200,000,000 | $280,000,000 |

ranked in the first 50 transportation category, although it had as of the late 1950s (and presumably early and mid-1960s) many more ships under its control than either the United States Lines or the Moore-McCormack Lines, both of which were on the top 50 transportation list in 1965.[13]

Finally it should be borne in mind that the findings arrived at in this study do not really take into account the now truly vast blocks of corporate stock held by the big institutional investors, particularly the top 50 commercial banks and trust companies, a number of which are controlled by various wealthy families (see the last section of Table 4-1). The major reason for this omission is that detailed, accurate information on this subject (on a company-by-company basis) has been, for the most part, simply not available until very recently.[14] In fact, as far as the great commercial banks were concerned, this information was a rather closely guarded secret. And yet their holdings over the years are believed to have been quite substantial (as has, no doubt, sometimes been their influence over certain aspects of corporate affairs).[15] For instance, to the best of the author's knowledge, the only bank trust fund figures published prior to 1968 were contained in an article which appeared in a 1967 issue of *Forbes*, showing that the Cleveland Trust Co. controlled (for some unnamed beneficiaries) 16 percent of the outstanding stock of the Island Creek Coal Co., 18 percent of that of the Medusa Portland Cement Co., 14 percent of all shares of the Reliance Electric & Engineering Co., 12.3 percent of the outstanding stock of the Sherwin-Williams Co., and 12 percent of that of the Cleveland-Cliffs Iron Co.[16] However, the significance of such relationships is still not at all clear in many cases, and for

[13]See *Business Week* (6 September 1958), p. 141 and *New York Times* (4 February 1969), p. 47. The aforementioned 1965 *Forbes* survey of big privately owned companies claimed that the States Marine Lines had overall revenues of $93 million as of 1964 (the 50th-ranked transportation company had a total of only $79 million) and also included Daniel Ludwig's National Bulk Carriers, but said that its income figures were not available. See *Forbes* (1 February 1965), p. 34.

[14]This state of affairs was largely corrected in 1968 with the release of a staff report of the Subcommittee on Domestic Finance, House Committee on Banking and Currency, entitled *Commercial Banks and their Trust Activities: Emerging Influence on the American Economy*. All told, according to one recent report, the commercial banks (through their trust departments) held a little over 19 percent of all outstanding common and preferred stock in 1968 (most of this being concentrated in large corporations, over which stock these banks often exercise considerable voting rights). See *New York Times* (20 April 1970), p. 57.

[15]For more on this point, see Daniel J. Baum and Ned B. Stiles, *The Silent Partners: Institutional Investors and Corporate Control* (Syracuse University Press, 1965) and, with regard to mutual funds, Arthur M. Louis, "The Mutual Funds Have The Votes," *Fortune* (May 1967), pp. 150-53 and 205-07.

[16]See *Forbes* (15 April 1967), pp. 26-27. By way of showing that such stockholdings may lead to the exercise of corporate influence or control, it should be pointed out that three of the seven outside directors of the Island Creek Coal Co. in 1967 were also directors of the Cleveland Trust Co., one of them being a former high bank official (now retired). In addition, this executive, I.F. Freiberger, served as both Board Chairman of the Cleveland Trust Co. and Board Chairman (or Chairman of the Executive Committee) of the Island Creek Coal Co. from at least 1957 to 1963. Perhaps not coincidentally, the federal government has recently taken unprecedented legal action against the Cleveland Trust Co., charging that it has violated the Clayton Antitrust Act in holding (as a trustee) substantial blocks of stock in large competing machine tool companies in the Cleveland area (*New York Times*, 27 March 1970, p. 1).

this and other reasons (the most important being the paucity of pertinent reliable data at the time), these various institutional shareholdings have not been included as a part of this study.[17]

Now control of a corporation can be exercised through either inside (i.e., management) or outside representation on the board of directors, or through owning a very sizable block of stock in a company (other than a mutual concern), and, many would contend, even more authoritatively through a combination of these corporate devices.[18] Control manifested through occupancy of the top management posts in a company (especially those of president and/or board chairman) is undoubtedly the most direct form of control that can be wielded by a person, family, or close-knit group of families. As a rule, this state of affairs can be ascertained by a careful, systematic look at the names of the various individuals who have held these key posts over a period of years.[19] If one or

[17]Quite clearly, there are also other forms of outside control of a nonfamily institutional nature, such as the United Mine Workers' control of the National Bank of Washington and the Mormon Church's control of a substantial set of big business enterprises in Utah, but such holdings are not of sufficient size to warrant inclusion and discussion in this study. For more on these two cases of outside influence, see *Business Week* (23 November 1957), pp. 108-16; *Fortune* (April 1964), pp. 136-39 and 166-72; U.S. House Select Committee on Small Business report, *Chain Banking* (Washington, D.C.: U.S. Government Printing Office, 1963), p. 179; and *New York Times* (29 April 1971), p. 1.

[18]By control, it should be noted, the author means the ultimate overall economic power to decisively affect corporate policy and management, whenever need be, rather than the immediate day-to-day direction of company operations. In this study, the term inside (or management) director is applied to anyone (including any member of a family with controlling stock ownership interest) who is presently serving as an executive of the company in question or who has previously served in such capacity and is now retired. The term outside director, on the other hand, refers to any individual (again including any member of a family with controlling stock ownership interest) serving on a board of directors who has never held a management post with this corporation.

Occasionally, there are certain difficulties involved in deciding whether a person is an inside or outside director of a company. This problem usually arises with regard to the position of board chairman or general counsel, one of which may be occupied by a person who is also actually (and perhaps even more importantly) an official in a major financial institution or a senior partner in a corporate law firm. In the early sixties, for example, the Board Chairman of the United Fruit Co. was George P. Gardner, Jr., a partner in the investment securities concern of Paine, Webber, Jackson & Curtis. Fortunately, however, such situations are relatively rare and probably not of sufficient significance to invalidate any corporate control judgments made in this study.

[19]If a company has been dominated over the years by a single affluent individual (quite often the firm's founder), it is sometimes difficult to discern this condition using the above approach or procedure. But the author does not know of any analytical way to get around this problem and, as a result, may have made several errors in his corporate control classifications. Thus in this study, there may be some companies described as management dominated concerns which are actually controlled by a corporate executive with a major stock ownership interest, though the author suspects that the number is fairly small.

The author has generally avoided using the term "entrepreneurial control," which some observers believe can be employed to cover all forms of stock ownership control, because

more family names appear frequently in the upper managerial (vice-president or above) echelons of a concern—a condition determined nonquantitatively but as objectively as possible by the author—it is probably a good indication that this company is under family control. A less direct, though still important form of control is that manifested through substantial outside representation on the board of directors of a firm.[20] This phenomenon can usually be detected in the same manner as described above. In many cases, of course, family control is exercised through the occupany of both high management (inside directorship) posts and outside representation on the board of directors, a set of circumstances which, it could be argued, makes family control quite secure.

In this study the author did not adhere to any rigorous requirement that the family representatives on a board of directors constitute a majority of the membership of either the outsiders or the overall board over some specified period of time, because control can and frequently has been wielded by family interests which hold considerably less than a majority of the board membership.[21] In 1968, for example, *Forbes* stated that the Di Giorgio Corp. (a California-based fruit company that ranks well up in the *Fortune* 500) was controlled by the Di Giorgio family, even though they held just 4 of the 16 seats on the board of directors—their control really resting, according to this account, on their very sizable stock ownership.[22] Therefore, the author has taken the position that if there has been a significant amount of family representation on a firm's board of

the word "entrepreneur" has to do with the establishment and early development of a business concern, and many of the companies in this study have been dominated by family interests for 40-50 years or more. If pressed for another way of describing the nonmanagerial firms identified in this study, the author would probably pick the term "owner control," a phrase which many might find confusing because of the stress frequently placed by professional and popular writers on the separation of ownership and control.

[20]The absence of family figures in the managerial echelons of a company does not necessarily indicate that a certain family is no longer in control. In some cases, the particular family may merely have run out (perhaps just temporarily for lack of entrepreneurial interest) of male members to direct or help in the management of a concern, or it may be that the dominant members of an enormously wealthy family really prefer to have well-qualified administrators run a business for them, albeit under their indirect supervision. Indeed, there has probably been a very significant shift in the familial make-up of many a large corporation's executive ranks over the years, which various authorities may choose to describe as some kind of managerial revolution. If so, the author would not attempt to challenge or refute this contention (he has accumulated no real data on the subject), but would simply point out that this is a different sort of managerial revolution from that depicted by Berle and Means and other later economic observers. In any event, a dominant family can almost always remove a professional corporate executive (even one of very high rank) with relative ease. Witness the recent deposal of technocrat Simon Knudsen as President of the Ford Motor Co., an action which would seem to run counter to John Kenneth Galbraith's view of this company (see *The New Industrial State*, p. 102 and *New York Times*, 12 September 1969, p. 1).

[21]In this respect the author differs decidedly with certain other academicians and economic observers, such as Peter Dooley, who, for instance, maintained in a recent *American Economic Review* article that management control of a corporation could be determined by the proportion of administrative officers found on a board of directors (though in this case the exact percentage was left unspecified). See Peter G. Dooley, "The Interlocking Directorate," *American Economic Review* (June 1969), p. 316.

[22]See *Forbes* (1 August 1968), p. 48.

directors, this is in itself a good indication that the company in question may be under family control.

The identification of family representatives in either managerial or outside directorship posts, it should be observed, is not always as easy as one might think. For instance, in 1955 two of the three top executives of Deere & Co. (which had at that time a completely inside board of directors) were Charles D. (for Deere) Wiman, who served as president of the firm, and William A. Hewitt, the executive vice-president, who had married Wiman's daughter. Similarly, three of the nine outside directors of W.R. Grace & Co. in 1960 (which was then headed by J. Peter Grace) were members (through marriage ties) of the Grace family—these three individuals being Michael G. (for Grace) Phipps, his brother John H. Phipps, and Eben W. Pyne (who wed a great granddaughter of the original W.R. Grace). In addition, family interests are occasionally represented indirectly on a board of directors by certain lawyers or other trusted figures.[23] Conversely, a person can easily be misled by the appearance on some company boards of a number of people with a common last name, but who, in fact, may not even be remotely related. In 1970, for example, three of the nine outside members of the board of directors of the Public Service Electric & Gas Co. (of New Jersey) had the same last name (Davis), but this was not a sign that the firm was under family control, for, as subsequent investigation plainly showed, the three men were unrelated and represented various institutional enterprises in the state of New Jersey—C. Malcolm Davis being head of the Fidelity Union Trust Co. of Newark, W. Robert Davis President of the Camden Trust Co., and Jess H. Davis President of the Stevens Institute of Technology.

Control of a corporation through ownership of a sizable block of (voting) stock is obviously of a different nature from that exercised through occupancy of key managerial or directorship posts, and is often much more difficult to determine in any precise fashion. Yet it undoubtedly represents the ultimate source of power in a corporation (other than a mutual concern), for in the event of a major struggle for control of a company, the issue is almost always resolved in favor of the individual or faction that can muster the most (shareholder) votes.[24]

Unfortunately, however, there are many serious problems involved in trying

---

[23]For example, with regard to the Great Altantic & Pacific Tea Co. in recent years, see *Fortune* (1 September 1968), p. 144 and, with reference to the role of a representative of the powerful Loeb Rhoades interests, see *Forbes* (15 July 1962), p. 34.

[24]Perhaps the most famous instance of such power being exercised in the last half-century occurred back in the late twenties when the Rockefeller interests, though not represented in any manner on the board of directors, waged a very costly and successful proxy battle to oust Colonel Robert W. Stewart as Board Chairman of the Standard Oil Co. of Indiana. More recent evidence of this kind can be found in the forceful testimony of William P. Lear, the Board Chairman of Lear, Inc. (now Lear Siegler, Inc.), who, although he owned no more than 18 percent of the voting stock and was apparently the only member of his family represented on the 9-man board of directors, stated flatly in 1960 that there ". . . never has been a director [of this company] that I didn't elect." See *Business Week*, (3 December 1960), pp. 119 and 125.

to get accurate, up-to-date information on the distribution of stock ownership in American big business. Generally speaking, there are only two sources of periodically compiled pertinent data—the corporate proxy statement, which is mailed to all stockholders before the company's annual meeting, in addition to being filed with the Securities and Exchange Commission (SEC), and the SEC's *Official Summary of Securities Transactions and Holdings* (hereafter referred to as the SEC *Official Summary*), which is published each month in an effort to curb possibly unethical dealings by corporate officers, directors, and huge ownership interests. But both are of rather limited value in attempting to determine the locus of economic control in a large corporation. Proxy statements, for example, usually list only the stockholdings of the current directors of a company and their immediate families, plus occasionally the number of shares owned by certain big trusts or other concerns, and therefore frequently fail to reveal the existence of sizable blocks of stock held by other family or economic interests.[25]

The data contained in the SEC's *Official Summary* or "insider" report (as it is more popularly known) also leave much to be desired. For one thing, no officer, director, or big corporate investor is required to report his holdings in a company to the SEC other than when he either buys or sells stock, and since many wealthy figures keep their large blocks of stock intact for long periods of time, such shareholdings often go unrecorded for as much as one, two or even three decades. In addition, this SEC publication lists only the number of shares of that class of stock traded in the course of a month, and not a person's overall holdings, so that an individual's common stock may be recorded without any mention being made of his or her preferred shareholdings, which in some cases have equal, if not even proportionately greater, voting rights.[26] No entry, further-

---

[25]Though filed annually with the SEC, these proxy statements are not compiled in any systematic manner and published by the government as a public service, so that one is not ordinarily able to find anything like a complete set of such statements at even a good municipal or university library, but must go instead to either the SEC in Washington or one of its nine regional offices (or to a special business library). This being the case, the author went to the New York City regional office of the SEC in early 1969 and carefully looked over the proxy statements of most of the companies listed in Tables 3-1 and 4-1 as possibly under family control (exclusive of commercial banks, whose proxy records were not on file there), but came across only one which provided control data not otherwise found in the other, frequently better sources of information used in this study (which are discussed in some detail at a later point). As an alternative procedure, the author also examined, thanks to the generosity and cooperation of Gabriel Kolko, the rather substantial set of 1957 proxy data gathered by this researcher in conjunction with his well-known analysis, *Wealth and Power in America*. However, for the most part all these stock ownership figures simply point up the limitations of corporate proxy statements as a means of locating control blocks of stock in a big business concern. For additional comment concerning this and other pertinent sources of information used by Larner in his 1966 article and 1970 book on the subject, see Appendix B.

[26]Moreover, these SEC records sometimes show only the number of directly personally owned shares rather than any indirect (though still effectively controlled) holdings which may well, in fact, loom much larger in the overall stock ownership picture. In March 1969, for instance, an SEC "insider" report revealed that Edgar Kaiser and his wife had each recently disposed of approximately 30,000 shares of the family-dominated Kaiser Industries

more, is made if the transaction involves less than 100 shares, an administrative policy decision made understandably in the interests of simplification and economy, but one which still further reduces the chances of revealing concentrated stock ownership in a corporation.

Another major deficiency in the definitions and procedures used by the SEC lies in the fact that only those relatives of an officer or director living at the same home address are required to report their shareholdings. Thus a wealthy uncle, brother or sister with whom an officer or director has a close working relationship—in effect, one might say, an informal economic partnership—need not report the amount of stock he or she owns in a company to the SEC (unless of course, it represents more than 10 percent of the total stock). It is most likely for this reason that the holdings of the Mellon family in the Koppers Co. have never been recorded in the SEC *Official Summary* as totaling more than about 5 percent in recent years (this being the amount owned personally and reported by director Richard K. Mellon in 1956), although *Fortune* magazine stated in late 1967 that, overall, the family controlled at least 20 percent of the company's voting stock.[27] To get some idea of how really difficult it often is to determine the magnitude of a family's holdings in a firm, one need only turn to the February 1969 issue of *Fortune*, which noted that approximately 200 members of the Oscar Mayer family owned stock (amounting, in toto, to roughly 80 percent of the voting stock) in the big Chicago meat-packing concern with that name.[28] Not only, therefore, would one be faced with the formidable job of identifying all the various members of a corporate family (including many with different surnames), but, given the relative infrequency with which such holdings are usually reported to the SEC after a purchase or sale of stock, it would probably take so long to arrive at the overall family total that a number of shareownership figures (and thus in some measure the overall finding) would be of questionable validity.[29]

Corp., thereby reducing their personal holdings to somewhere around 20,000 or 25,000 shares apiece. Yet *Forbes* claimed (on the basis of presumably reliable data) that through various trust arrangements Edgar and Sue Kaiser actually owned almost 3,000,000 shares, nearly 60 times the amount officially recorded by the SEC. See *Forbes* (15 April 1969), p. 79. (This article erroneously refers to a December 1968 SEC report instead of the above-mentioned March 1969 summary; also note that there is some discrepancy in the personal stock ownership and sales figures listed in the *Forbes* and SEC accounts.)

[27]See the SEC *Official Summary* (March 1956) and Charles J.V. Murphy, "The Mellons of Pittsburgh," *Fortune* (October 1967), p. 122.

[28]See Harold B. Meyers,"For the Old Meatpackers, Things Are Tough All Over," *Fortune* (February 1969), p. 136. In much the same vein, *Forbes* noted back in 1955 that although the Luke family held a substantial interest in the West Virginia Pulp and Paper Co. (perhaps as much as 30 percent or more, according to the data in Table 3-1), no one member of the family owned over 2.4 percent of the shares, and thus the overall family holdings have never apparently been reported to the SEC. See *Forbes* (15 March 1955), p. 25.

[29]Since, unfortunately, no annual summation of stockholdings is provided in the SEC *Official Summary*, a person must laboriously thumb through a very substantial number of monthly reports (extending most likely over a decade or more) if he wants to ascertain which officers and directors, together sometimes with their associates, are the dominant stockholders in a concern. This obviously requires a great deal of time and patience.

Another important defect in the SEC's stock ownership data concerns the holdings of an officer's or director's business associates (or subordinates).[30] The problem here is not only in the definition of the term "associate," but also (until at least the late 1960s) to a very considerable extent in the SEC's inadequate enforcement measures. In September 1963, for example, F. William Harder and Charles Allen, Jr. were listed as directors and substantial stockholders of the American Bosch Arma Corp. (a concern then in the *Fortune* 500), but neither was identified as having any association with the other. Yet a look at (Standard &) Poor's *Register of Corporations, Directors and Executives* plainly reveals that Harder was an official in the investment securities firm of Allen & Co. (of which Charles Allen, Jr. was a senior and probably dominant partner) and that both were members of the board of directors of the Ogden Corp., Teleregister Corp., and Allied Supermarkets, Inc. Similarly, in July 1960 Cyrus S. Eaton and William R. Daley were reported in the SEC *Official Summary* as being very sizable stockholders in the Detroit Steel Corp. (a *Fortune* 500 company), but again no mention was made of any corporate connection between them.[31] That this was a most conspicuous omission in the SEC's records may be seen in the following 1960 tabulation of their major managerial and directorship positions.[32]

---

[30] The author is referring here mainly to the business associate who serves largely as the agent or representative of some very wealthy family or economic notable. There are, of course, many other types of (nonfamily) business relationships. Though not of primary concern in this study, there are, for example, still a number of entrepreneurial syndicates in operation today, informal groups of often unrelated individuals who may constitute a powerful and close-knit voting bloc on a board of directors. Unfortunately, such groups, which are sometimes based in part on family ties, are usually difficult to detect, much less identify in any precise and consistent manner. In 1956, to give just one illustration, the two highest management officials and four of the seven outside directors of the Automatic Canteen Co. of America (which just made *Fortune's* top 50 merchandising list in 1965) were described as being part of a network of friends or investment allies headed by Chicago financier J. Patrick Lannan, though they have never been designated in any of the SEC's "insider" records as being linked in any way (there being no legal or administrative provisions dealing with this admittedly very loose type of relationship). According to *Fortune*, the four outside directors were Lannan, Chicago business figure Arthur Bowes, Chicago lawyer J. Arthur Friedlund, and Dan Topping (then a co-owner of the New York Yankees), while the two management officials were the company's founder, Nathaniel Leverone, and Arnold M. Johnson (of the old Kansas City Athletics). All told, they made up six out of a total of twelve directors. See Dero A. Saunders, "How Managements Get Tipped Over," *Fortune* (October 1955), p. 125; Thomas P. Murphy, "Pat Lannan: Kid-Glove Raider," *Fortune* (August 1956), pp. 122 and 190; and *Forbes* (15 November 1959), p. 19.

[31] For more on this affiliation, see *Finance* (April 1966), p. 10.

[32] As recently as 1959 *Forbes* termed the SEC's recording of securities transactions a "weak operation," claiming that there were only about seven persons then assigned to checking into these forms and figures. It also later noted that one October 1957 transaction was not reported to the SEC until December 1961, although the law calls for federal notification of such exchanges within ten days of the end of the month in which the transaction took place. And again, with reference to the many longstanding gaps and deficiencies in the SEC's "insider" records, *Forbes* went so far as to declare in March 1968 that threre were still "... holes you could drive a truck through." See *Forbes* (1 January 1959), p. 18; (1 February 1962), pp. 30-32; and (1 March 1968), p. 42.

|  | *Cyrus S. Eaton* | *William R. Daley* |
|---|---|---|
| Otis & Co. | — | President |
| Chesapeake & Ohio Rwy. | Board Chairman | — |
| Portsmouth Corp. | Board Chairman | President and Treasurer |
| Steep Rock Iron Mines, Ltd. | Board Chairman | Director |
| West Kentucky Coal Co. | Board Chairman | Director |
| Detroit Steel Corp. | Director | Director |
| Cleveland-Cliffs Iron Co. | Director | Director |

Again when Donald H. Carter and the Murchison brothers were reported in June 1960 as big stockholders in Holt, Rinehart & Winston, Inc. (a large publishing company not in the *Fortune* 500, which has since been merged into CBS), no reference was made to the fact that Carter was an agent or ally of the oil-rich Texas financiers, serving as he did at the time on the board of directors of the Murchison-owned Royal Gorge Bridge & Amusement Co. (a very small Colorado concern) and the New York Central RR (in which the Murchisons had a substantial interest).[33]

One final defect in the SEC's "insider" transaction records lies in the fact that the controlling piece of pertinent legislation in this area, the Securities and Exchange Act of 1934, stated that "principal" owners of corporate stock (the third category of persons required to report changes in shareholdings to the SEC) shall be defined as those holding more than 10 percent of any class of a company's stock (which is registered on a national exchange and not specifically exempted from the provisions of this act). Hence, if a person other than an officer or director (or one of his business associates or relatives living at the same home address) owned, say, 9.8 percent of a corporation's common stock, he would not have to report his holdings to the SEC, even though such information might be of prime importance both from the standpoint of regulating "insider" transactions and determining the locus of power in a concern.[34] Yet it is a matter of common

[33]Carter was described as being "an old Murchison friend and associate" in *Fortune* (July 1961), p. 57. There was also apparently another error of omission in this particular June 1960 SEC entry in that the Sun Investment Co. was listed as a seemingly independent concern holding an additional 6.3 percent of the stock of Holt, Rinehart & Winston, although according to the 1960 *Moody's Bank & Finance Manual* (p. 1122), Carter was actually president of this Texas-based securities firm. As a matter of fact, it would appear that the Sun Investment Co. was itself nothing more than an investment arm of the Murchison family, since the vice-president of the company, Holman Jenkins, was referred to in this same *Fortune* article as a Murchison lawyer. All told, Carter and Jenkins made up two of the three officers and directors of the Sun Investment Co.

[34]Until recently, another fairly conspicuous omission of a similar sort lay in the fact that corporations with unlisted securities (those traded "over the counter" rather than through one of the regular exchanges) did not have to report any "insider" transactions (or their equivalent) to the SEC. As of 1955 such concerns represented 99 percent of all outstanding insurance company and bank shares in the country, not to mention those of a number of rather sizable industrial firms. It was not until 1964 that Congress, at the SEC's urging, imposed considerably stricter requirements bringing many unlisted companies under the

knowledge today that, given the widespread dispersion of stock ownership in most large corporations, shareholdings of as little as 5 percent, and in some cases no more than 3 percent, can be of profound importance in the shaping of corporate policy.[35] Indeed it is now generally agreed in most major business circles that working control of any large company can usually be obtained through possession of something like 4 or 5 percent of the voting stock, a state of affairs of which SEC reporting procedures have yet to take effective note.[36]

Thus for a variety of reasons the stock ownership figures found in the SEC *Official Summary* are often very much on the low side, at least insofar as overall family and other entrepreneurial holdings are concerned. And it is for these reasons that the author has chosen—really, it would be more accurate to say, been forced—to rely primarily on another set of data on the subject, namely, the family and other outside holdings in various concerns listed from time to time in such major sources as Standard & Poor's *Corporation Records, Fortune, Forbes,*

scope of the "insider" reporting process (a most commendable move, but one too late to be of much help in this study). Thus, not very surprisingly, only one of New York City's big commercial banks had any of its stock listed on the New York Stock Exchange as of mid-1968, and even in this case, a majority of the bank's shares were still being traded over the counter. See *Forbes* (1 March 1955), p. 17; *Business Week* (16 October 1965), p. 170; and *New York Times* (18 July 1968), p. 49.

[35] As a matter of fact, this is a point made in more general or nonquantitative fashion many years ago by Robert Gordon who stressed, albeit perhaps inadequately, the dual ramifications of the dispersion of stock ownership, nothing that there was, on the one hand, a great mass of small shareholders, each owning but a minute fraction of a company's voting stock, while emphasizing at the same time that there was also a substantial amount of corporate ownership concentrated in the hands of relatively small groups of large stockholders. See Robert A. Gordon, *Business Leadership in the Large Corporation* (Washington, D.C.: The Brookings Institution, 1945), p. 157.

[36] In its March 1, 1967 issue, for example, *Forbes* pointed out (p. 36) that the Harriman (or Brown Bros. Harriman) interests still retained undisputed control over the Union Pacific RR, even though they held barely 3 percent of the outstanding common stock. (Nothing was said in this article, however, about their possible holdings of preferred stock, which also have voting rights.) In fact, Peter Drucker has gone so far as to claim that in some cases absolute control of a large corporation can be obtained through the ownership of less than 1 percent of the voting stock (*The New Society: The Anatomy of the Industrial Order*, Harper & Bros., N.Y., 1950, p. 340). The author, however, is not at all sure that he agrees with this contention and has thus set the "working control" percentage in this study at approximately 4 or 5 percent (although there are certain exceptions to this rule). Also see *New York Times* (7 November 1955), p. 20, and, with reference to the Straus family's effective control (based on but 5 percent of the voting stock) of R.H. Macy & Co., *Time* (4 October 1968), p. 96. The above cut-off point, of course, is not a hard and fast figure, but rather a rough rule of thumb, which is based on the (up to now) generally accepted assumption that nonfamily institutional investors with big stock ownership interest do not, as a rule, represent an active and unified voting force in corporate affairs. In some cases, however, particularly where certain powerful interests are involved, much more than 5 or even 10 percent may be required. For instance, in the mid-1960s Philip J. Levin, a New Jersey real estate magnate (and apparently an economic lone wolf), bought up to 14.3 percent of the stock of MGM, but still failed in his headline-making battle for control because of the existence of other powerful blocs which successfully countered his takeover effort. See *Fortune* (May 1967), p. 150 and *Time* (1 September 1967), p. 59.

*Business Week, New York Times, Time* and *Moody's.*[37] Since such information is not presented regularly in the above publications, the author has, in order to give maximum feasible consistency and thoroughness to his research efforts, searched carefully through the above magazines and newspaper over the following fairly long periods of time:

> *Fortune* (1950 to late 1971)
> *Time*, business section (1955 to late 1971)
> *Business Week* (1955 to late 1971)
> *Forbes* (1955 to late 1971)
> *New York Times*, business and finance section (1960 to late 1971)

Where appropriate, he has made use of the stock ownership data listed (relatively infrequently, unfortunately) at the end of various corporate entries in *Moody's* manuals in, as a rule, the mid-1960s. In addition, the author thumbed through the latest issue (available at the time, 1967-68) of Standard & Poor's *Corporation Records*, but did not utilize this source any more than was absolutely necessary because, from a research standpoint, it has certain serious limitations.[38] Except in one instance, he has also chosen not to rely on corporate proxy statements, which are usually small pamphlets or sheets designed to be discarded after a company's annual meeting or the receipt of a new statement the following year. The author has, however, referred extensively to the 1963 House Select Committee on Small Business report, *Chain Banking*, since this document contains virtually the only substantial mass of information assembled thus far on stock ownership in big commercial banks.[39]

The results of this research and analysis show a marked difference in stock ownership totals as contrasted with those arrived at through an examination of the SEC's "insider" records in particular, as may be seen by a glance at the fol-

---

[37]The author has also read through *Dun's Review* and *Finance* from 1960 to the present, but obtained relatively little pertinent information from these journals. He has not relied on such sources as *Wall Street Journal, Barron's, Newsweek,* or *U.S. News and World Report* because upon examination they did not prove to be very helpful.

[38]Like Standard & Poor's other similar smaller directory, *Standard Listed Stock Reports* (cited only twice in this study), it suffers from a number of serious shortcomings. Neither of these sources, for example, gave any indication, as of about 1967, that such major concerns as Dow Chemical, General Tire & Rubber, West Virginia Pulp & Paper, and W.R. Grace & Co. were controlled by various wealthy families. In addition, they often merely stated that the officers and directors of a company held "X" percent of the stock, without specifying which individuals owned the most sizable blocks, in some cases simply noting that the stock was closely held. Moreover, the loose-leaf-replacement nature of these publications makes it virtually impossible to confirm earlier citations.

[39]Several other Congressional studies also proved to be of some use. These documents were the 1963 House Committee on Banking and Currency report, *Bank Holding Companies: Scope of Operation and Stock Ownership*, the 1962 House Select Committee on Small Business report on *Tax-Exempt Foundations and Charitable Trusts: Their Impact on the Economy*, and the 1955 Senate Committee on Banking and Currency report on *Factors Affecting the Stock Market*. On three occasions, moreover, certain books were cited as providing pertinent evidence of family influence or control.

lowing figures. The first figures generally represent cumulative percentages compiled from data contained in various issues (from 1955 through late 1971) of the SEC *Official Summary;*[40] the second totals are drawn from the magazine and newspaper sources listed above and are incorporated in Table 3-1 of this study:[41]

| Name of Company | Controlling or Dominant Family | Family Stockholding Percentage | |
|---|---|---|---|
| | | Culled from Various Issues of the SEC's "Insider" Records | Taken from Table 3-1 of this Study |
| General Tire & Rubber Co. | O'Neil | 5.3% | 20% |
| Ralston Purina Co. | Danforth | 13.8 | 22 |
| Champion Papers Inc. | Thomson-Robertson | 5.2 | 20 |
| Timken Roller Bearing Co. | Timken | 12.1 | 30 |
| Brunswick Corp. | Bensinger | 5.3 | 40 |
| West Virginia Pulp & Paper Co. | Luke | 5.5 | 30 |
| Upjohn Co. | Upjohn-Light | 13.5 | 60 |

These disparities are obviously of very sizable proportions, and the author is of the firm opinion that the higher figures are the more accurate ones.[42] Therefore, wherever possible, he has chosen to rely largely on the above business journals,

[40]In these and all other SEC computations in this study the author took his total outstanding (voting) stock ownership figures from the appropriate *Moody's* manuals, checking carefully as to stock splits and corporate acquisitions and matching as much as possible the reported SEC holding as of a particular month with the proper outstanding share ownership aggregate. For "insider" data prior to 1955 the author has in a few instances made selective use of comparable statistics (after checking each pertinent entry and computation) compiled by Don Villarejo for his autumn 1961 article in *New University Thought.*

[41]The cumulative totals in the first columns were arrived at by adding the percentage held by one person in, say, 1958, to that recorded as held by one or more other members of the family in subsequent years. It is assumed here (and also with regard to a substantial amount of the SEC data incorporated in Tables 3-1 and 4-1 and Appendix C) that the first figure did not change to any appreciable extent with the passage of time. (The stock ownership percentages in the SEC column are not listed, by the way, in Table 3-1 because in these cases the higher figures are viewed as the more valid ones.)

In the SEC calculations made in this study, the author has added the stock ownership totals of all family members together wherever he has knowledge of such kinship ties, as in the above Upjohn-Light family and Thomson-Robertson family. However, over the years there have undoubtedly been a number of persons listed in the various SEC "insider" transaction records who were related (albeit sometimes distantly) to a company's controlling family, but whom the author has been unable to properly identify. Thus most of the SEC family stock ownership totals incorporated in this study are probably very much on the low side.

[42]For like reason the author has relied in several instances on stock ownership data contained in various magazines rather than that found in the aforementioned House committee report on *Chain Banking.* For example, *Time* stated on two separate occasions in recent

directories, and the Congressional bank study, plus pertinent sections of *New York Times* and *Time*, and has utilized the SEC's *Official Summary* only when no other data were available. In this manner one can arrive at a much more reliable set of findings than have been established by other economic analysts to date.[43]

years (1956 and 1962) that the Rockefeller family interests owned approximately 5 percent of the stock of the Chase Manhattan Bank. Yet according to this Congressional report (which for each bank was based on the officially recorded holdings of just the 20 largest individual, corporate and institutional stockowners, the 10 highest ranking officers, and all members of the board of directors), their 1962 shareholdings amounted to only about 2.4 percent. See *Time* (24 December 1956), p. 57 and (7 September 1962), p. 67, and the U.S. Select Committee on Small Business, House of Representatives, 87th Congress, *Chain Banking* (Washington, D.C.: U.S. Government Printing Office, 1963), p. 129.

[43] Even the carefully compiled TNEC figures do not in many cases reveal the true total family stockholdings in various concerns, for these governmentally amassed data are based on the ownership aggregate of just those members of a family who happen to be an officer, director, or one of the 20 largest stockholders in a company. For more on this point, see Robert A. Gordon, *Business Leadership in the Large Corporation* (Washington, D.C.: The Brookings Institution, 1945), p. 169.

# 3

## Corporate Control Analysis of Major American Industrial Concerns

Using primarily the business and government sources of stock ownership information described in the latter part of Chapter 2, the author has made a company-by-company analysis of the control status of most of America's large corporations (exclusive of public utilities, insurance companies, and certain other miscellaneous enterprises and financial institutions) as of the mid-1960s. These findings are presented in summary form in Table 3-1, which covers the country's top 300 industrials and constitutes an essential section of this chapter, and Table 4-1, which treats the top 50 merchandising firms, top 50 transportation companies, and top 50 commercial banks, and is included as a part of Chapter 4. With but two exceptions (which will be discussed shortly), no concern in this 450-firm study has been classified as probably under family control—a status hereafter signified by the abbreviation PF—unless two conditions were met.[1] One important condition was that approximately 4-5 percent or more of the voting stock was held by a family, group of families, or some affluent individual according to one of the preceding sources[2] or, alternatively, in a few cases a

[1] The author has made no distinction in this monograph between what some might call "management" families (defined here as those which wield control through expertise as well as stock ownership) and those very rich families, representing either old or new wealth, which own a huge block of stock in a concern. To the best of the author's knowledge, comparatively few large companies today are controlled by executives who have risen to power via the stock option route, and he suspects that most families which now dominate corporations through a combination of expertise and shareholdings had, at one time at least, a very substantial stock ownership base of authority.

[2] Actually in some cases, control can be exercised through the ownership of an even smaller amount of stock if a family has such well-established relations and connections that it can marshal additional voting strength in time of crisis or corporate proxy battle. Unfortunately, extended socioeconomic ties of this nature are almost impossible to trace in a thorough and systematic fashion, and this possibly important concept has therefore not been employed in this study. However, see *Forbes* (1 September 1971), p. 29 for one pertinent example involving the Westmoreland Coal Co. and its effective control by the Leisenring clan. This family, although it owns less than 2 percent of the shares of its parent concern, the Penn Virginia Corp., claims it can muster, through an elaborate network of wealthy (albeit sometimes distant) relatives and friends and other companies it controls, up to 40 percent of the voting stock, if necessary.

It should perhaps be emphasized again that both Larner and Sheehan used a stock ownership minimum of 10 percent as their criterion for control (which may account for some of the difference between their findings and those arrived at in this study), but even the second writer admitted that he was being very conservative in this regard. In his more recent works, Adolf Berle, by the way, continued to adhere to his old and probably very much outdated stock ownership standard, strongly implying at one point that control of a corporation could only be attained through the ownership of something like 20 or 25 percent of the voting stock, plus control of the board of directors (although the manner of determining

statement that a certain concern was family controlled was located in one of the aforementioned publications.[3] The second condition was that there has been either inside or outside representation (with, in fact, often both forms of representation) on the part of a family on the board of directors of a company, generally over an extended period of time.[4] In almost every instance in which a corporation was classified as probably under the control of a wealthy individual, family, or group of families (identified by name wherever possible), documentation has been provided in the form of one or more recent citations, which usually contained stock ownership statistics.[5] In addition, other pertinent information has been supplied in the same column (labeled "Evidence or Comments") as to whether the dominant family or individual has been associated with a partic-

---

this latter condition was left, unfortunately, quite unclear). For what is apparently Berle's only published postwar pronouncement of a quantitative nature on this subject, see his *Economic Power and the Free Society* (New York: Fund for the Republic, 1957), a relatively succinct analysis which is reproduced in Andrew Hacker, ed., *The Corporation Takeover* (New York: Harper & Row, 1964), pp. 91-107.

[3] A control statement is simply an assertion in one of the above sources that a particular company was controlled or dominated by a certain family, which the author sometimes accepted (after carefully checking the board of directors over a period of time for signs of marked family influence or control) as sufficient evidence in lieu of stock ownership data. On three separate occasions in recent years, for example, it has been reported that the Lazarus family had effective control over the affairs of the nation's eighth largest merchandising concern, Federated Department Stores, Inc. (see *Forbes*, 1 October 1967, p. 66; *Time*, 19 January 1968, p. 83; and *Forbes*, 15 February 1970, p. 49).

[4] The reason for laying down this latter condition can perhaps best be illustrated by the following example. In 1961, according to *Fortune* (March 1961, p. 151), Cyrus Eaton's Cleveland-Cliffs Iron Co. controlled 4.3 percent of the stock of the Inland Steel Co., 5.1 percent of the stock of the Youngstown Sheet & Tube Co., and 5.2 percent of the stock of the Wheeling Steel Corp., but had no (at least direct) representatives on the boards of the first two companies and only one representative (out of eleven outside directors) on the board of the Wheeling Steel Corp. All this would therefore seem to indicate that Cyrus Eaton had not been able to translate his rather sizable stock ownership into anything like working control of these corporations.

At the same time the author is willing to concede that a company can be controlled without any direct representation on the board of directors, so long as a person or family has at least approximately 4-5 percent of the voting stock and some trusted nonfamily figures serving on the board. However, the latter are usually very difficult to detect. For one such case involving Ametek, Inc. (which was ranked #517 in 1970), see *Forbes*, 15 September 1968, p. 74.

[5] All stock ownership figures included in this study, even those listed for the latter part of the 1950s or the late 1960s, are still assumed to hold, at least approximately, for the mid-1960s. In all cases where the date of the source cited was after 1965, the author checked back to 1965 to see whether the composition of the board of directors appeared to reflect at that time the stock holdings indicated in the post-1965 publication. The author has also examined the 1965 make-up of the board of directors of all concerns with documentary citations prior to that time in order to see whether there seemed to be any change in control status in the intervening years.

Unless otherwise noted, all stock referred to in these tabulations is that designated as voting stock, with appropriate computational adjustments having been made to take into account, where necessary, different classes of stock (usually preferred stock) which may have either no regular voting rights or in some instances disproportionate voting power (such

ular concern through outside representation on the board of directors (a situation indicated by the abbreviation O-BD), the holding of important managerial posts (signified by the abbreviation I-BD), or a combination of the two (abbreviated I & O-BD), ordinarily over a considerable period of time.[6] In those cases where control appeared to rest with a single affluent individual rather than with a family or group of families, this state of affairs has been signalized by the addition of an "I" (for individual) in parenthesis after the PF (probably family) designation. However, it should be cautioned, one should not place too much emphasis on this distinction because of the many knotty problems involved (checking out all family ties, appraising the entrepreneurial or leadership potential of the corporate heirs of either new or old wealth, etc.) in making such determinations.[7] Hence, it was decided in this study that domination of a corpo-

as, say, 8 or 10 votes per share). It should be noted that there were a few cases where rather extraordinary legal circumstances prevailed which rendered certain big blocks of stock inoperative. In 1965, for example, the Corning Glass Works and Owens—Illinois Glass Co. each owned about 31 percent of the stock of the Owens—Corning Fiberglas Corp., but because of a 1949 court ruling were prohibited from voting their shares, with the result that the considerably smaller Boeschenstein family holdings were, on a relative scale, magnified into effective working control of the company. In another case, about 33 percent of the stock of the Consolidated Electronics Industries Corp. was placed under the control of a management dominated trust at the time of World War II (to prevent it from falling into German hands). Thus in the middle and late 1960s, the Philips lamp (family) interests of Holland, which were the ultimate beneficiaries of this trust, did not exercise any appreciable amount of influence over the affairs of this firm.

[6]In this study, the expression "over the years" has been used to show control wielded for approximately a decade or more (that is, from at least the mid-1950s to 1965), the phrase "in recent years" to signify control attained since around 1960. The terms I-BD and O-BD should not be taken to mean that there were one or more family representatives serving in either an inside or outside capacity in every year during the period indicated. There may have been managerial or directorship gaps in this regard, which nevertheless do not render invalid any overall judgments made as to family control status. In like manner, the designation I & O-BD does not necessarily signify that there has always been both inside and outside representation on a firm's board of directors. In some years, it may have been just inside representation, in other years outside, and at still other times both.

It should be stressed again that all corporate control determinations in this study were made as of January 1965, not some time (even a year to two) shortly before or after this date. In the early 1960s, for example, Trans World Airlines, Inc. passed from the hands of Howard Hughes into a form of management control imposed by various major financial (creditor) institutions, and has been so classified in Table 4-1. On the other hand, the Atlantic Refining Co. was most likely, up to recently, a management run firm, but came under the control of New Mexico's Robert O. Anderson as the result of a merger consummated about 1964. Note also that during the early and mid 1960s, the Chrysler Corp. was probably dominated indirectly by the Hanna interests, although this apparently proved to be only a temporary phenomenon as they evidently relinquished control some time in the late 1960s.

[7]Such an individual, for instance, may be just at the point of starting to establish a corporate family dynasty (as in the case apparently of Chicago magnate Henry Crown and the late Clint Murchison of Texas oil fame). In addition, it is often difficult, as indicated earlier, to ascertain all the members of an entrepreneur's family, especially when this individual type of control is of recent origin and the man is a secretive or publicity-shy person.

ration by a single wealthy individual with a great deal of stock in the concern would be treated, for all practical purposes, as a form of family control.[8]

Two fairly clear-cut cases will illustrate the first control classification—probably family (PF)—used in this analysis. For instance, in July 1963 it was reported that the various members of the founding Firestone family owned 29 percent of the stock of the huge Firestone Tire & Rubber Co., at which time they held four out of nine seats on its all-management board of directors (including the top posts of Board Chairman and President).[9] Sometimes family control of a corporation is exercised indirectly too, through the vehicle of another independent stock ownership concern. In 1965, for example, *Moody's Bank & Finance Manual* showed that about 22 percent of the stock of the National Steel Corp. was owned by the M.A. Hanna Co., an investment company which had three representatives on the big steel firm's board of directors (with one of these individuals serving, in fact, as Chairman of its Finance Committee). An article in *Forbes* at about this time indicated, furthermore, that well over half of the stock of the M.A. Hanna Co. was itself most likely owned by different members of the famous Ohio Hanna family (who held one or more of the high managerial positions and, overall, at least five of the twelve seats on its board of directors).[10] Such stock ownership and directorship figures leave little doubt as to the locus of power in these concerns.

The two companies for which the author failed to find any significant share ownership information, but which he still feels fairly sure were family controlled, have been so classified simply on the basis of very marked family representation (both as executives and outsiders) on their boards of directors. One of these concerns is the nation's largest tobacco company, the R.J. Reynolds Tobacco Co., which, judging from the data assembled here, would certainly appear to have been dominated over the years by the Reynolds and Gray families, particularly the latter. Following in the footsteps of William N. Reynolds, Bowman Gray (scion of a prominent North Carolina banking family) served, for instance, as president of this big corporation from 1924 to 1931 and as board chairman from 1931 until his death in 1935. His brother, James A. Gray, served in turn as president of the (R.J.) Reynolds Tobacco Co. from 1934 to 1946, as chairman of the executive committee from 1946 to 1949, and finally as board chairman from 1949 to 1954. At roughly this point in time the Gray family line

[8]Even if one wanted to adhere to this other, more restricted view of the term "family control," and the various corporations controlled by wealthy individuals (rather than families) were eliminated from all subsequent calculations, it would not substantially affect this study's overall findings, which are contained in Tables 3-1 and 4-1 (see Chapter 4 with regard to the latter). A check of the firms classified PF, for example, indicates that about 73 percent of the top (PF-designated) merchandising firms, over 80 percent of the top (PF) transportation companies, and better than 85 percent of the top (PF) commercial banks and industrial concerns were dominated by one or more families.

[9]See entry #32 of Table 3-1 for pertinent citations.

[10]See entry #56 of Table 3-1. These five are Warren Bicknell, Jr. (who married a Hanna), R. Livingston Ireland (whose mother was a Hanna), R. Livingston Ireland III, Gilbert W. Humphrey (who married into the Ireland family), and his father, George M. Humphrey.

was temporarily broken by the appointment of John C. Whitaker (whose aunt had married into the Reynolds family), who served as president of the company from 1948 to 1952 and as board chairman from 1952 to 1959.[11] In 1957, however, the Gray family resumed its reign over corporate affairs, with a second Bowman Gray (the son of the first) serving a short stint as president of the company from 1957 to 1959 before assuming the board chairmanship, a post which he retained through 1965.[12] Moreover, his uncle, Alexander H. Galloway, a former treasurer of the firm, was elected president of the company in 1960, a position he too held through 1965.[13]

In like manner it can be shown, albeit perhaps in a more roundabout way, that the Libbey-Owens-Ford Glass Co. (#258 in Table 3-1) has probably been controlled by the Ford-Knight family of Detroit and Toledo, Ohio. From the mid-1950s to 1965, for example, George P. MacNichol, Jr. (whose mother was a Ford) served as either president or board chairman of this big concern, and a minimum of three (and sometimes four) of the outside representatives on the board of directors were members of this wealthy interrelated set of family interests. Though no pertinent stock ownership totals are apparently readily available concerning this company, *Business Week* did reveal recently that 60 percent of the stock of the Wyandotte Chemicals Corp. (a top 500-ranked firm, the make-up of whose board of directors has been much like that of the Libbey-Owens-Ford Glass Co. over the years) was owned by the some 200 descendants of this chemical concern's founder, John B. Ford (no relation to the automobile Fords).[14] Thus it is probably safe to assume that the Ford-Knight family held a very sizable and most likely controlling block of stock in the Libbey-Owens-Ford Glass Co. up to the middle or late 1960s.

To turn now to the second control category used in this analysis, the designa-

[11] See *Fortune* (December 1957), p. 242, and appropriate issues of *Who's Who in America*. In addition, William R. Lybrook (a nephew of Wm. N. Reynolds) served as vice-president and secretary of the company in the mid-1960s, and Charles H. Babcock (who married a Reynolds) and Gordon Gray (a former high federal official and brother of the second Bowman Gray) served as two of the four outside directors of the firm.

[12] In this study, it is assumed that all families or various individuals identified as probably in control of designated concerns were fairly close-knit groups (as has apparently been true of the Reynolds and Gray families), unless reliable sources indicated the existence of considerable conflict or dissension. While it is certainly true that disputes may arise occasionally within a family or coterie of friendly business associates exercising control over a particular company, such clashes are relatively rare and most likely of little overall consequence as far as this study is concerned, for one side or another usually wins ultimately (rather than some set of independent management forces). For example, with reference to the familial struggle within the Hoover Co. in the early 1950s and the longstanding feud besetting the Moody economic enterprises in Texas, see *Fortune* (June 1964), p. 146 and ibid. (March 1971), pp. 109-12 and 156-58.

[13] All of the above officials, by the way, served in other lesser corporate capacities prior to assuming these high posts. There were also, of course, certain other executives who held these important positions in the various intervening years, but none (other than S. Clay Williams) served for very long.

[14] See *Business Week* (8 November 1969), p. 50 and Stephen Birmingham, *The Right People* (New York: Dell Publishing Co., 1969), pp. 145-46. The above interrelated families include the Fords, Knights, MacNichols, Ballantynes, and Bacons.

tion "possibly family" (abbreviated F?) has been employed to describe those corporations which showed some definite signs of family influence (usually in the form of representation on the board of directors, though occasionally stock ownership statistics, or some combination of the two), but for which there were insufficient available data from which to make a reliable assessment of control status. However, in every case some evidence has been presented (minimally specified, as a rule, in abbreviated board of directorship terms) for placing a concern in this category, and one or more families have been identified as being prominently associated with the company in question. For example, although the 1963 Congressional *Chain Banking* study revealed that the Bimson family apparently owned only about 2 percent of the stock of the Valley National Bank of Phoenix[15] (which was 38th on *Fortune's* top 50 list and was so ranked in the third section of Table 4-1), a look at its upper-managerial echelons over the years would lead one to think that this institution may indeed be under family control, for Walter R. Bimson served as president of the bank from 1933 to 1953 and as board chairman from 1953 through 1965, while his brother Carl held the reins as president from 1953 to 1962, at which time he assumed his present post of vice-chairman. In 1963, furthermore, Earl L. Bimson (Walter's son) was made an executive vice-president of the bank and four years later was elevated to the position of president.[16] Similarly, it would appear that the Ashland Oil & Refining Co. (of Kentucky) may have been a family-dominated firm, since Paul G. Blazer served as president from 1936 to 1944, as board chairman from 1944 to 1957, and finally as chairman of the finance committee from 1957 through 1965, while his nephew Rexford S. Blazer was president of the concern from 1951 to 1957 and its board chairman from 1957 through 1965. In addition, since a 1955 U.S. Senate report showed that a very sizable percentage (close to 21 percent) of the stock of the Ashland Oil & Refining Co. was held by officers, directors, and other associated interests, it is quite possible that a good deal of this stock was owned by the Blazer family.[17] A third business enterprise placed in the possibly family control category is the First National City Bank of New

[15]Since this report was not geared toward ascertaining overall family control totals, but rather just the individual holdings of the leading officers, directors, and 20 largest shareowners of each institution, it was often very hard to tell whether some of these persons (with different last names) were related to one another, and there was no way of knowing whether all of the various members of a particular family had been included on this rather select list.

[16]Some people may feel that, on the basis of the above inside directorship data, this bank should have been classified as probably under family control. This, of course, is a matter of individual or professional judgment, and the author has tried to err on the conservative side in making all determinations as to possible or probable family control. For example, according to a number of reports, the General Dynamics Corp. was most likely controlled by Henry Crown in the first part of 1965, but because of certain evidence which raises some question about this matter (see *Forbes*, 15 March 1970, p. 17) the author decided to place this concern in the possibly family category.

[17]See the U.S. Senate Committee on Banking and Currency staff report, *Factors Affecting the Stock Market* (Washington: U.S. Government Printing Office, 1955), p. 168. This report, which collected data on concentrated shareholdings in 1,043 large corporations, also contained a certain amount of information on sizable shareholdings of various outside forces, some of which were undoubtedly family interests. Where appropriate, such findings have been incorporated into this study as additional (though somewhat dated) supporting evidence as to possible or probable family control.

York City. This was done in part because of the rather marked family flavor of the bank's (regular) board of directors, which included in 1965 board chairman James Stillman Rockefeller and, as important outside representatives on the board, two other kinship-connected persons, Reginald B. Taylor (of the bank's founding Taylor-Pyne family) and J. Peter Grace (whose niece wed Eben W. Pyne). Additional evidence of an even stronger nature may be found in the make-up of the bank's trust board (a rarely constituted corporate body oversee-ing its huge trust department operations), which was headed for a time (1957-61) by the aforementioned Eben W. Pyne and had, as outside members, such other prominent closely-linked figures as Robert Winthrop, Jr. (whose grandmother was the former Katherine Taylor), Hunt T. Dickinson (a grand-nephew of W.H. Tilford, a former Standard Oil Co. official), William R. Coe (son-in-law of H.H. Rogers of Standard Oil and various other economic inter-ests), Samuel Sloan Duryee (who was related to the Auchincloss-Jennings-Rockefeller families), and Henry C. Taylor (who wed the daughter of Walter Jen-nings, a former director and secretary of the Standard Oil Co. who was related, by marriage, to William Rockefeller, brother of the first John D.). While no one company can be regarded as a typical possibly family firm, a considerable num-ber of other concerns were placed in this category for much the same reasons.

The third control classification used in this study—probably management (PM)—includes those concerns which appeared to be management dominated. In all firms so designated, the author found no significant stock ownership data or other evidence, such as representation on boards of directors, which would in-dicate that these companies were under family control. For instance, from 1945 to the latter part of 1964 the Bethlehem Steel Corp. had a completely inside board of directors, with apparently none of the various managerial members being related to one another or holding any sizable blocks of stock in the con-cern.[18] The American Tobacco Co. had an entirely inside board of directors for an even longer period, from 1930 to the latter part of 1964, at which time two professional men (a management consultant and an accountant) were appointed to its board of directors.[19] Since no indicators of family control were uncovered with regard to such corporations, no facts or figures have, as a rule, been pre-sented in Tables 3-1 and 4-1 concerning companies classified as management dominated.

The author's overall industrial findings are summarized in the following table, which contains a company-by-company breakdown (with supporting evidence, where appropriate) of the control status of the 300 largest manufacturing and mining concerns in the United States as of 1965.

---

[18] In October 1964, four outsiders (three prominent businessmen and a college president) were appointed to the board of directors of Bethlehem Steel, but they still constituted only a fairly small percentage of the total body. Actually, many of the firms classified as manage-ment controlled in this study have a majority of their board membership made up of out-siders, but this, in the author's judgment, is not necessarily a decisive factor in the deter-mination of a company's control status.

[19] See *New York Times* (30 September 1964), p. 64 and (23 December 1964), p. 37. The author, by the way, has used the term "appointed," rather than "elected" (to the board of directors) because, while it is not technically correct, it much more accurately reflects the manner in which most directors are, in fact, selected.

**Table 3-1**

**Company-by-Company Corporate Control Analysis of America's 300 Largest Manufacturing and Mining Concerns as of 1965**

Abbreviation and Explanation Key:

PF – Probably Family

F? – Possibly Family

PM – Probably Management

I-BD – significant family representation as inside members of the board of directors

O-BD – significant family representation as outside members of the board of directors

I & O-BD – significant family representation as both inside and outside members of the board of directors (though not necessarily at the same time; in those relatively few instances where significant gaps have occurred, the author has used the designation I or O-BD)

By the phrase "over the years," the author means from at least roughly 1955 to 1965, by the term "in recent years," less than the last five to eight years of this time period (although in both cases, there may be some gaps in certain years)

NYT – New York Times

S&P – Standard & Poor's

SEC OS – SEC's Official Summary of Securities Transactions and Holdings

| 1965 Rank (based on 1964 volume of sales) | Name of Company | Type of Control | Evidence or Comments |
|---|---|---|---|
| 1. | General Motors Corp. | PM | |
| 2. | Standard Oil Co. of N.J. | F? | According to the 1962 House Select Committee on Small Business report on *Tax-Exempt Foundations and Charitable Trusts: Their Impact on the Economy* (p. v), seven Rockefeller-controlled foundations owned about 3.6% of the stock as of the end of 1960—furthermore, as of Dec. 1954, the Rockefeller Foundation itself owned 3.1% of the stock and, according to the 1955 U.S. Senate report on *Factors Affecting the Stock Market* (pp. 178 and 195), certain other large shareholders (the Rockefeller family?) owned another 3.2% of the stock |

| No. | Company | | | Notes |
|---|---|---|---|---|
| 3. | Ford Motor Co. | PF | | As of the mid-1960s, the Ford family controlled 39% of the voting stock (see *Fortune*, 15 June 1967, p. 181); also I-BD over the years |
| 4. | General Electric Co. | | PM | |
| 5. | Socony Mobil Oil Co. | | F? | Rockefeller and other associated families?–see I-BD over the years |
| 6. | Chrysler Corp. | PF (indirectly) | | As of the mid-1960s, the Hanna-controlled Consolidation Coal Co. had 7.8% of the stock (see *NYT*, 5 April 1964, Sect. 3, p. 1, *Forbes*, 15 April 1964, p. 41, and *Forbes*, 1 November 1965, p. 17); also I-BD in recent years |
| 7. | United States Steel Corp. | | PM | |
| 8. | Texaco Inc. | | PM | |
| 9. | Internatl. Business Machines Corp. | PF | | According to *Time* (28 March 1955, p. 84 and 2 July 1956, p. 68), the Watson family had about 6% of the stock as of the mid-1950s–however, according to *Fortune* (September 1956, p. 114), the Watson family had only about 3% of the stock; also I & O-BD over the years |
| 10. | Gulf Oil Corp. | PF | | According to *Forbes* (1 May 1964, p. 22), the Mellon family had about 32% of the stock–a little later, according to *Fortune* (October 1967, pp. 121-22), the Mellon family had about 25% of the stock; also O-BD over the years |
| 11. | Western Electric Co. (actually a subsidiary of A.T.&T.) | | PM | |

**Table 3-1** *(cont.)*

| 1965 Rank | Name of Company | Type of Control | Evidence or Comments |
|---|---|---|---|
| 12. | E.I. du Pont de Nemours & Co. | PF | As of the mid-1960s, the du Pont family owned 30% of the stock of the Christiana Securities Co., which in turn owned 29% of the stock of E.I. du Pont de Nemours & Co. (see *Fortune*, 15 June 1967, p. 181); also I & O-BD over the years |
| 13. | Swift & Co. | F? | Swift family may have had about 7% of the stock as of 1960 or 1961 (see *New University Thought*, Autumn 1961, p. 52)–control may now have passed from the Swift family to Norton Simon who had as of 1965 between 2.9% and 3.8% of the stock (see *Fortune*, June 1965, p. 148 and *Forbes*, 1 December 1964, p. 22); also I & O-BD over the years |
| 14. | Shell Oil Co. | PM (foreign) | |
| 15. | Standard Oil Co. of Indiana | F? | Rockefeller and Blaustein families?–as of the mid-1960s, Jacob Blaustein and family controlled about 3.6% of the stock (see *Forbes*, 15 September 1968, p. 26)–according to the 1962 House Select Committee on Small Business report on *Tax-Exempt Foundations and Charitable Trusts: Their Impact on the Economy* (p. v), five Rockefeller-controlled foundations owned about 3.5% of the stock as of the end of 1960; also (with reference to Blaustein) O-BD over the years |
| 16. | Standard Oil Co. of Calif. | F? | Rockefeller family reportedly owned about 5% of the stock as of the late 1950s (see *Fortune*, November 1958, p. 118) |
| 17. | Westinghouse Electric Corp. | PM | |
| 18. | Bethlehem Steel Corp. | PM | |

| | | | | |
|---|---|---|---|---|
| 19. | International Harvester Co. | | F? | McCormick family?–see I & O-BD over the years |
| 20. | North American Aviation, Inc. | PM | | |
| 21. | Goodyear Tire & Rubber Co. | PM | | |
| 22. | Boeing Co. | PM | | |
| 23. | Natl. Dairy Products Corp. | PM | | |
| 24. | Procter & Gamble Co. | PM | | |
| 25. | Armour & Co. | | PF | As of the mid-1960s, the Prince family trust had about 6% of the stock (see *Forbes*, 15 March 1966, p. 34); also I & O-BD over the years |
| 26. | Union Carbide Corp. | PM | | |
| 27. | Radio Corp. of America | | F? | Sarnoff family?–see I-BD over the years |
| 28. | General Telephone & Electronics Corp. | PM | | |
| 29. | Lockheed Aircraft Corp. | | F? | Gross family?–see I-BD over the years |
| 30. | General Dynamics Corp. | | F? | H. Crown owned between 13% and 16% of the voting stock as of early or mid-1960s (see *NYT*, 9 April 1965, p. 40 and *Forbes*, 15 April 1962, p. 38)—in addition, see *Forbes* (1 March 1967, p. 27 and 15 March 1970, p. 17); also O-BD in recent years |
| 31. | Internatl. Telephone & Telegraph Corp. | PM | | |

**Table 3-1** *(cont.)*

| 1965 Rank | Name of Company | Type of Control | Evidence or Comments |
|---|---|---|---|
| 32. | Firestone Tire & Rubber Co. | PF | As of the mid-1960s, the Firestone family had 29% of the stock (see *Fortune*, July 1963, p. 102); also I & O-BD over the years |
| 33. | Monsanto Chemical Co. | F? | Queeny family? (see *Forbes*, 15 July 1965, p. 19); also I-BD over the years |
| 34. | Phillips Petroleum Co. | PM | |
| 35. | General Foods Corp. | PM | |
| 36. | Borden Co. | PM | |
| 37. | Sperry Rand Corp. | PM | |
| 38. | Republic Steel Corp. | PM | |
| 39. | Continental Oil Co. | PM | |
| 40. | International Paper Co. | PF | Phipps-Grace family and possibly Auchincloss and Hinman families—Phipps-controlled Bessemer Securities Corp. probably owned roughly 4.5% (computed indirectly by the author) of the stock as of 1954 (see *Fortune*, November 1960, p. 163); also O-BD over the years |
| 41. | Eastman Kodak Co. | PM | |
| 42. | United Aircraft Corp. | PM | |
| 43. | American Can Co. | F? | Wm. H. Moore family (of New York City)?—see O-BD over the years |
| 44. | Burlington Industries, Inc. | PM | |

| | | | | | Notes |
|---|---|---|---|---|---|
| 45. | Continental Can Co. | PM | | | |
| 46. | Sinclair Oil Corp. | PM | | | |
| 47. | Cities Service Co. | PM | | | |
| 48. | Caterpillar Tractor Co. | PM | | | |
| 49. | U.S. Rubber Co. | | PF | | As of early and mid-1960s, the du Pont family had 14% of all the presumably voting stock (see *Business Week*, 22 October 1960, p. 101 and *Fortune*, December 1964, p. 122); also I & O-BD over the years |
| 50. | Dow Chemical Co. | | PF | | Dow family had about 12% of the stock as of early and mid-1960s (see *Business Week*, 14 October 1961, p. 138 and *Forbes*, 15 August 1967, p. 25); also I & O-BD over the years |
| | Subtotal: top 50 | 29 (58%) | 11 (22%) | 10 (20%) | |
| 51. | Armco Steel Corp. | | | F? | Verity family? (see *Forbes*, 1 October 1968, p. 33); also I-BD over the years |
| 52. | Allied Chemical Corp. | | PF (foreign?) | | As of the mid-1960s, the Solvay family (of Belgium) had about 8% of the stock (see *NYT*, 16 October 1967, p. 71) – the Loeb (Rhoades) interests and associated families had about 3.6% of the stock (see *Forbes*, 15 February 1967, p. 47) – the (Eugene) Meyer family (of Washington, D.C.) may have a substantial interest too (see *Fortune*, October 1954, pp. 119-23 and 161-71); also O-BD over the years |
| 53. | Aluminum Co. of America | | PF | | Mellon family had about 30% of the stock as of the mid-1960s (see *Forbes*, 1 May 1964, p. 22 and *Fortune*, October 1967, pp. 121-22); also O-BD over the years |

**Table 3-1** *(cont.)*

| 1965 Rank | Name of Company | Type of Control | Evidence or Comments |
|---|---|---|---|
| 54. | General Tire & Rubber Co. | PF | O'Neil family had about 20% of the stock as of the mid-1960s (see *Forbes*, 1 October 1966, p. 32 and *Fortune*, 15 June 1967, p. 181); also I-BD over the years |
| 55. | American Motors Corp. | PM | |
| 56. | National Steel Corp. | PF (indirectly) | M.A. Hanna Co. had about 22% of the stock as of the mid-1960s (see *NYT*, 5 April 1964, Sec. 3, p. 1)—about 75% of the stock of the M.A. Hanna Co. owned by descendants and relatives of the Hanna family (see *Forbes*, 1 November 1965, pp. 16-17); also I & O-BD over the years |
| 57. | Jones & Laughlin Steel Corp. | F? | Possibly controlled by the Jones, Laughlin and Mellon families (the last two being intermarried)—see O-BD over the years |
| 58. | R.J. Reynolds Tobacco Co. | PF | Reynolds, Gray and other families (see *Fortune*, December 1957, p. 242); also I & O-BD over the years |
| 59. | Minnesota Mining & Mfg. Co. | PF | As of 1960-1961, Ordway, McKnight and other families represented on BD owned about 26.7% of the stock (see *Forbes*, 15 March 1960, p. 19, and SEC *OS*, December 1961); also I & O-BD over the years |
| 60. | Singer Co. | PF | As of the mid-1960s, the S.C. Clark family (of New York City) owned at least 11.0% of the stock (see SEC *OS*, January 1964 and September 1965); also O-BD over the years |
| 61. | Anaconda Co. | PM | |
| 62. | Corn Products Co. | PM | |

| No. | Company | PM | PF | F? | Notes |
|---|---|---|---|---|---|
| 63. | Inland Steel Co. | | PF | | As of the late 1950s, the Block and Ryerson families had close to 8% of the stock (see *Fortune*, July 1958, p. 99)—as of the mid-1960s, the Block family probably owned between 4% and 5% of the stock (see *Time*, 3 November 1967, p. 97); also I-BD over the years |
| 64. | B.F. Goodrich Co. | PM | | | |
| 65. | McDonnell Aircraft Corp. | | PF | | As of the mid-1960s, J.S. McDonnell, Jr., owned 13% of the stock (see *Fortune*, 15 June 1967, p. 180); also I & O-BD over the years |
| 66. | Ralston Purina Co. | | PF | | As of the mid-1960s, the Danforth family had 22% of the stock (see *Fortune*, 15 June 1967, p. 181); also I & O-BD over the years |
| 67. | Sun Oil Co. | | PF | | According to *Fortune* (15 June 1967, p. 181), the Pew family had at least 44% of the stock—according to *Forbes* (15 October 1967, p. 28), the Pew family had 56.5% of the stock; also I & O-BD over the years |
| 68. | Coca-Cola Co. | | PF | | Woodruff family in control (see *Time*, 14 February 1955, p. 90 and *Fortune*, February 1966, p. 121)—in the early and mid-1960s, the Woodruff Foundation had 15.2% of the stock of Coca-Cola Internatl. Corp., which in turn controlled 23.6% of the stock of the Coca-Cola Co. (see SEC *OS*, August 1960 and the 1965 *Moody's Industrial Manual*, p. 2524); also I & O-BD over the years |
| 69. | FMC Corp. | | | F? | Crummey-Davies families (of San Jose, Calif.)?—see I-BD over the years |
| 70. | Pittsburgh Plate Glass Co. | | PF | | As of the mid-1960s, the Pitcairn family had 26% of the stock (see *Fortune*, 15 June 1967, p. 181); also I & O-BD over the years |

**Table 3-1** *(cont.)*

| 1965 Rank | Name of Company | Type of Control | Evidence or Comments |
|---|---|---|---|
| 71. | Deere & Co. | PF | As of the mid-1960s, the descendants of Charles H. Deere owned 14% of the stock (see *Forbes*, 15 June 1966, p. 31 and *Fortune*, 15 June 1967, p. 181); also I-BD over the years |
| 72. | Olin Mathieson Chemical Corp. | PF | As of the early 1960s, J.M. and S.T. Olin had 11.6% of the stock (see SEC *OS*, February 1961); also I & O-BD over the years |
| 73. | W.R. Grace & Co. | PF | As of the late 1950s, the Grace and other associated families controlled about 30% of the stock (see *Business Week*, 25 January 1958, p. 107) – as of the mid-1960s, J.H. Phipps, M.G. Phipps and J.P. Grace owned at least 5.9% of the voting stock (see SEC *OS*, February 1964, May 1964, and March 1965) – in addition, see *Business Week* (17 April 1971), p. 114; also I & O-BD over the years |
| 74. | Colgate-Palmolive Co. | F? | Colgate family probably had at least 3.2% of the stock and perhaps as much as 3.9% in recent years (see SEC *OS*, October 1956, January 1964, and August 1966); also I & O-BD over the years |
| 75. | American Cyanamid Co. | F? | Duke family? – see I & O-BD over the years |
| 76. | Martin Marietta Co. | PM | |
| 77. | Wilson & Co. | PM | |
| 78. | Bendix Corp. | PM | |
| 79. | Youngstown Sheet & Tube Co. | PM | |
| 80. | Textron Inc. | PM | |

| No. | Company | | | Notes |
|---|---|---|---|---|
| 81. | Borg-Warner Corp. | F? | | Ingersoll and Johnson families (of Chicago)?—see I & O-BD over the years |
| 82. | Celanese Corp. of America | | PM | |
| 83. | Owens-Illinois Glass Co. | F? | | Levis family? (see *Forbes*, 1 June 1967, p. 28)—according to the 1955 U.S. Senate *Factors Affecting the Stock Market* report (p. 176), certain large outside shareholders (mostly the Levis family?) owned 6.8% of the stock as of December 1954 and various officers, directors and associates (possibly some members of the Levis family?) owned another 6.6% of the stock as of the same point in time; also I & O-BD over the years |
| 84. | American Tobacco Co. | | PM | |
| 85. | Litton Industries, Inc. | PF(I) | | C.B. Thornton had 7.2% of the stock as of the early 1960s (see SEC *OS*, January 1961); also I-BD over the years |
| 86. | J.P. Stevens & Co. | PF | | Stevens family still had 20% of the stock as of 1971 (see *Business Week*, 13 November 1971, p. 64, plus *Fortune*, April 1963, p. 103); also I & O-BD over the years |
| 87. | National Lead Co. | | PM | |
| 88. | Tidewater Oil Co. | PF | | As of the mid-1960s, J. Paul Getty controlled 78.7% of the stock of the Getty Oil Co. which, in turn, controlled directly or indirectly 80.5% of the stock of the Tidewater Oil Co. (see *Fortune*, December 1967, p. 111); also I-BD over the years |
| 89. | Minneapolis-Honeywell Regulator Co. | PF | | Honeywell and Sweatt families had about 3% of the stock as of 1959 (see *Fortune*, May 1959, p. 118); also I & O-BD over the years |
| 90. | National Cash Register Co. | | PM | |

**Table 3-1** *(cont.)*

| 1965 Rank | Name of Company | Type of Control | Evidence or Comments |
|---|---|---|---|
| 91. | Crown Zellerbach Corp. | F? | Zellerbach family?—see I & O-BD over the years |
| 92. | Weyerhaeuser Co. | PF | As of the middle or late 1960s, the Weyerhaeuser and other founding families still owned about 40% of the stock (see *Forbes*, 1 April 1966, p. 30, and, for some specific evidence, SEC *OS*, June 1969); also I & O-BD over the years |
| 93. | Campbell Soup Co. | PF | As of the mid-1960s, the Dorrance family had at least 51% of the stock (see *Fortune*, 15 June 1967, p. 179); also I & O-BD over the years |
| 94. | John Morrell & Co. | PF | Probably controlled by the Morrell-Foster family—as of 1965 the Morrell-Foster family had at least 5.3% of the stock (see SEC *OS*, March 1965); also I & O-BD over the years |
| 95. | Douglas Aircraft Co. | F? | Douglas family? (see *Forbes*, 15 December 1966, p. 36 and Osborn Elliott's *Men at the Top*, New York: Harper & Bros., 1959, p. 73); also I-BD over the years |
| 96. | Atlantic Refining Co. | PF(I) | As of 1965, Board Chairman and Chief Executive Officer Robt. Anderson had about 5% of the stock (see *Business Week*, 29 May 1965, p. 36, *Dun's Review*, September 1965, p. 40, and *Business Week*, 18 April 1970, p. 62); also I-BD in recent years |
| 97. | Allis-Chalmers Co. | PM | |
| 98. | Reynolds Metals Co. | PF | Reynolds family of Virginia (an arm of the Reynolds Tobacco family of N.C.) owned all the voting stock of the U.S. Foil Co. which, in turn, owned 50.7% of the stock of the Reynolds Metals Co. as of 1960 (see *Forbes*, 1 May 1960, p. 23); also I-BD over the years |

| No. | Company | PM | | PF | Notes |
|---|---|---|---|---|---|
| 99. | St. Regis Paper Co. | | | PF(I) | As of about 1960, R.K. Ferguson had 28.8% of the stock of the Eastern States Corp. which, in turn, owned 9.0% of the stock of the St. Regis Paper Co. (see SEC *OS*, September 1959 and the 1960 *Moody's Bank and Finance Manual*, p. 639); also I & O-BD over the years |
| 100. | Standard Brands, Inc. | PM | 20 (20%) | 36 (36%) | |
| | Subtotal—top 100 | 44 (44%) | | | |
| 101. | American Smelting & Refining Co. | PM | | | |
| 102. | National Biscuit Co. | | F? | | Wm. H. Moore family (of New York City)?– see O-BD over the years |
| 103. | Beatrice Foods Co. | PM | | | |
| 104. | Pure Oil Co. | PM | | | |
| 105. | Signal Oil & Gas Co. | | | PF | As of the mid-1960s, the Mosher family owned at least 39.6% of the stock (see SEC *OS*, May 1963 and April 1967)–also see *Fortune* (November 1958, p. 69); also I-BD over the years |
| 106. | Grumman Aircraft Eng'rg. Corp. | | | PF(I) | L.R. Grumman had 5.8% of the stock as of 1961 (see SEC *OS*, January 1961); also I-BD over the years |
| 107. | Whirlpool Corp. | PM | | | Up to recently controlling blocks of stocks most likely held by RCA and Sears, Roebuck & Co.—now probably independent |
| 108. | Genesco Inc. | | | PF | W.M. Jarman had about 5.0% of the stock as of 1962 (see SEC *OS*, March 1962); also I & O-BD over the years |
| 109. | American Home Products Corp. | PM | | | |

**Table 3-1** *(cont.)*

| 1965 Rank | Name of Company | Type of Control | Evidence or Comments |
|---|---|---|---|
| 110. | Union Oil Co. of Calif. | PM | |
| 111. | Eaton Mfg. Co. | PM | |
| 112. | American Radiator & Standard Sanitary Corp. | PM | |
| 113. | Kimberly-Clark Corp. | PF | In recent years, the Kimberly, Schweitzer and Sensenbrenner families have had at least 7.3% of the stock (see SEC *OS*, November 1955, February 1965, and October 1966); also **I & O-BD** over the years |
| 114. | Thompson Ramo Wooldridge Inc. | PM | |
| 115. | White Motor Co. | PM | |
| 116. | Kennecott Copper Corp. | F? | Guggenheim family?—see O-BD over the years |
| 117. | General Mills, Inc. | PF | Probably controlled by the Bell family of Minn. (see *Forbes*, 1 October 1963, pp. 20-24); also **I & O-BD** over the years |
| 118. | Hercules Powder Co. | PM | |
| 119. | Standard Oil Co. of Ohio | PM | |
| 120. | United Merchants & Mfrs., Inc. | PF | According to 1967 proxy statement, the Schwab family owned about 4.4% of the stock—in addition, see *Forbes* (1 July 1959), p. 31; also **I-BD** over the years |

| | | | | |
|---|---|---|---|---|
| 121. | Kaiser Aluminum & Chemical Corp. | | PF | In recent years, the Kaiser family (of Calif.) has owned at least 63.6% of the stock of Kaiser Industries (see SEC OS, January 1959 and February 1959) which, together with the wholly-owned Henry J. Kaiser Co., owned 42% of the stock of the Kaiser Aluminum & Chemical Corp. (see Fortune, April 1963, p. 91); also see I & O-BD over the years |
| 122. | Mead Corp. | | PF | Mead Investment Co. and G.H. Mead (of Ohio) owned 12.3% of the stock as of 1951 (see SEC OS, January 1951 and February 1951)—according to 1957 Moody's Industrial Manual (p. 1670), the Mead Investment Co. owned 9.4% of the stock as of February 1957; also I & O-BD over the years |
| 123. | Natl. Distillers & Chemical Corp. | | F? | As of late 1951, W.G. Maguire owned at least 15.2% of the common stock (which elects 4 out of 7 directors) of the Missouri-Kansas Pipe Line Co. and at least 31.0% of the Class B stock which elects the other 3 directors (see SEC OS, November 1951)—as of 1965, the Missouri-Kansas Pipe Line Co. owned 9.6% of the stock of the Panhandle Eastern Pipe Line Co. which, in turn, owned 12% of the stock of Natl. Distillers (see the 1965 Moody's Public Utility Manual, p. 1613); also O-BD over the years—perhaps also Bierwirth family? |
| 124. | Pullman Inc. | | F? | Carry-Osborne family or Mellon and Casey families? (see Forbes, 15 September 1970, p. 72 and NYT, 9 March 1966, p. 51 and 21 February 1971, Sect. 3, p. 5); also I & O-BD over the years |
| 125. | Marathon Oil Co. | | PF | Dominated by the Donnell family of Ohio (see Time, 13 August 1965, p. 66); also I-BD over the years |
| 126. | Continental Baking Co. | PM | | |
| 127. | H.J. Heinz Co. | | PF | As of 1965, H.J. Heinz II owned 7.8% of the stock and had right to vote another 28.7% (see 1965 Moody's Industrial Manual, p. 809)—in addition, see Forbes (1 March 1971), p. 32; also I & O-BD over the years |

**Table 3-1** *(cont.)*

| 1965 Rank | Name of Company | Type of Control | Evidence or Comments |
|---|---|---|---|
| 128. | Ogden Corp. | PF | According to *Forbes* (1 October 1963, p. 35), the Allen family or Allen & Co. of New York City had 30% of the stock—according to the 1965 *Moody's Industrial Manual* (p. 2141), Allen & Co. had 25.9% of the stock; also I & O-BD over the years |
| 129. | Georgia-Pacific Corp. | F? | Cheatham family?–see I-BD over the years |
| 130. | Chas. Pfizer & Co. | PM | |
| 131. | Carnation Co. | PF | As of the mid-1960s, the E.H. Stuart family (of Los Angeles) had 51% of the stock (see *Fortune*, 15 June 1967, p. 181); also I-BD over the years |
| 132. | Sunray DX Oil Co. | PM | |
| 133. | Johns-Manville Corp. | PM | |
| 134. | Hygrade Food Products Corp. | PF | Up to the latter part of 1968, the Slotkin family had about 23 per cent of the voting stock (see *Forbes*, 15 September 1970, p. 37); also I-BD over the years |
| 135. | Raytheon Co. | PM | |
| 136. | Pillsbury Co. | PF | Pillsbury family had at least 3.4% of the stock in the 1960s (see SEC *OS*, July 1965 and February 1966)—in addition, see Osborn Elliott, *Men at the Top* (pp. 67-68); also I & O-BD over the years |
| 137. | American Metal Climax, Inc. | F? | Hochschild family had 5.2% of the stock as of 1958 (see SEC *OS*, January 1958)—in addition, the British-based Selection Trust Ltd. owned 11.3% of American Metal Climax (according to the 1965 *Moody's Industrial Manual*, p. 2899); also I & O-BD over the years |

| | | | | | |
|---|---|---|---|---|---|
| 138. | Lever Brothers Co. | PM (foreign) | | | |
| 139. | Avco Corp. | PM | | | |
| 140. | Babcock & Wilcox Co. | PM | | | |
| 141. | McGraw-Edison Co. | | F? | | In recent years, the McGraw and Edison families have had about 5.6% of the stock (see SEC *OS*, October 1956, July 1960 and September 1964); also I & O-BD over the years |
| 142. | Philip Morris, Inc. | | | PF | Cullman family had at least 7.5% of the stock as of the mid-1950s (see SEC *OS*, February 1955 and November 1956)—in addition, see *NYT*, 22 January 1961, Sect. 3, p. 3 and *Forbes*, 15 August 1965, p. 30; also I & O-BD over the years |
| 143. | Motorola, Inc. | | | PF | As of 1965, R.W. Galvin, family and associates had 17.9% of the stock (see 1965 *Moody's Industrial Manual*, p. 1178); also I-BD over the years |
| 144. | Foremost Dairies, Inc. | | F? | | In recent years, P.E. Reinhold had over 3.0% of the stock (see SEC *OS*, January 1956 and October 1961); also I & O-BD over the years |
| 145. | American Sugar Co. | | F? | | M.J. Ossorio (of Philippines and U.S.A.) had 4.2% of the stock as of 1958 (see SEC *OS*, January 1958); also O-BD over the years |
| 146. | Time Inc. | | | PF | As of the mid-1960s, the Luce interests owned 16% of the stock (see *NYT*, 11 March 1967, p. 10); also I & O-BD over the years |

**Table 3-1** *(cont.)*

| 1965 Rank | Name of Company | Type of Control | Evidence or Comments |
|---|---|---|---|
| 147. | Geo. A. Hormel & Co. | PF | As of the mid-1960s, the Hormel Foundation had 58% of the stock (see SEC *OS*, August 1966)—*Fortune* claims family had over half of the voting stock (see *Fortune*, 15 June 1967, p. 181); also I & O-BD over the years |
| 148. | California Packing Corp. | PM | |
| 149. | Hunt Foods & Industries, Inc. | PF | As of 1965, the (Norton) Simon family had 27% of the stock (see *Fortune*, June 1965, p. 147); also I & O-BD over the years |
| 150. | American Machine & Foundry Co. | PM | |
| 151. | Central Soya Co. | PF | McMillen family had at least 4.8% of the stock as of the mid-1960s (see SEC *OS*, December 1967); also I & O-BD over the years |
| 152. | Ashland Oil & Refining Co. | F? | Blazer family?—according to the appendix of the 1955 U.S. Senate report on *Factors Affecting the Stock Market* (p. 168), officers, directors and associates of this firm (perhaps largely reflecting Blazer family holdings) owned 20.9% of the stock as of December 1954—see I-BD over the years |
| 153. | Container Corp. of America | PM | |
| 154. | Burroughs Corp. | PM | |
| 155. | Kaiser Industries Corp. | PF | Kaiser family (of Calif.) owned 63.6% of the stock as of 1959 (see SEC *OS*, January and February 1959); also I-BD over the years |
| 156. | Phelps Dodge Corp. | F? | Dodge and other closely linked families?—see I & O-BD over the years |

|  |  | | | |
|-----|---------|---|---|---|
| 157. | Champion Papers Inc. | | PF | As of the mid-1960s, the Thomson-Robertson family had about 20% of the stock (see *Forbes*, 15 March 1967, p. 47); also I & O-BD over the years |
| 158. | Scott Paper Co. | PM | | |
| 159. | Johnson & Johnson | | PF | As of 1965, the Johnson family (of New Jersey) had at least 34.2% of the stock (see 1965 *Moody's Industrial Manual*, p. 493); also I & O-BD over the years |
| 160. | Quaker Oats Co. | | PF | In recent years, the Stuart family (of Chicago) probably has had at least 3.9% of the stock (see SEC *OS*, November 1952, July 1966 and October 1966)—in addition, see *Fortune*, September 1957, p. 80 and *Forbes* (15 October 1969), p. 66; also I & O-BD over the years |
| 161. | U.S. Plywood Corp. | F? | | Ottinger family?—Ottinger family had at least 9.0% of the stock as of the mid or late 1950s (see SEC *OS*, November 1954 and September 1959); also I & O-BD over the years |
| 162. | International Packers, Ltd. | PM | | |
| 163. | Anheuser-Busch, Inc. | | PF | Anheuser and Busch families owned about 65% of the stock as of 1955 (see *Time*, 11 July 1955, p. 85)—in more recent years, according to *Business Week* (13 July 1968, p. 104), these two families still owned over 40% of the stock; also I & O-BD over the years |
| 164. | Budd Co. | PM | | |
| 165. | Dana Corp. | | PF(I) | As of 1965, C.A. Dana owned 26% of the stock (see *Forbes*, 15 December 1965, p. 33); also I-BD over the years |

**Table 3-1** *(cont.)*

| 1965 Rank | Name of Company | Type of Control | | Evidence or Comments |
|---|---|---|---|---|
| 166. | Zenith Radio Corp. | PM | | |
| 167. | Rockwell-Standard Corp. | | PF | As of the mid-1960s, the Rockwell and Timken families (of Pittsburgh and Canton, Ohio) owned about 8% of the stock (see *Fortune*, June 1967, p. 101); also I & O-BD over the years |
| 168. | Boise Cascade Corp. | F? | | Weyerhaeuser and associated family interests? (see *Forbes*, 1 April 1966, p. 30); also I & O-BD over the years |
| 169. | Armstrong Cork Co. | PM | | |
| 170. | Ingersoll-Rand Co. | | PF | As of the mid-1960s, the Phipps-Grace family probably controlled at least 4.6% of the stock (see SEC *OS*, September 1963 and November 1968); also I & O-BD over the years |
| 171. | Crane Co. | | PF(I) | As of the mid-1960s, Thomas Mellon Evans (of Pittsburgh) owned 18% of the stock (see *Fortune*, 15 June 1967, p. 182); also I-BD in recent years |
| 172. | Kellogg Co. | PM (indirectly) | | As of 1965, 50.4% of the stock was owned by the apparently management-dominated W.K. Kellogg Foundation (see the 1965 *Moody's Industrial Manual*, p. 380) |
| 173. | Clark Equipment Co. | PM | | |
| 174. | International Shoe Co. | | PF | Probably controlled by the Rand-Johnson family (of St. Louis) (see *Forbes*, 15 July 1964, p. 32 and 15 January 1968, p. 40)—in recent years, the Rand-Johnson family interests probably controlled at least 6.5% of the stock (see SEC *OS*, March 1961, February 1962, and September 1968); also I-BD over the years |
| 175. | Air Reduction Co. | PM | | |

| # | Company | | | Notes |
|---|---|---|---|---|
| 176. | Hess Oil & Chemical Corp. | | PF | As of 1965, Leon Hess owned, directly or indirectly, 58% of the stock (see 1965 *Moody's Industrial Manual*, p. 2260); also I & O-BD over the years |
| 177. | Warner-Lambert Pharm. Co. | PM | | |
| 178. | Koppers Co. | | PF | As of the mid-1960s, the Mellon family had at least 20% of the stock (see *Fortune*, October 1967, pp. 121-22); also O-BD over the years |
| 179. | Agway, Inc. | PM | | (Actually an agricultural cooperative) |
| 180. | Timken Roller Bearing Co. | | PF | As of the mid-1960s, the Timken family (of Canton, Ohio) owned 30% of the stock (see *Forbes*, 1 May 1963, p. 26); also I & O-BD over the years |
| 181. | Cudahy Packing Co. | | PF | As of 1963, the Cudahy family had 23% of the common stock (see *Fortune*, February 1963, p. 53)—as of 3 October 1962, according to the 1965 *Moody's Industrial Manual* (p. 484), the family had 21.4% of the stock; also I & O-BD over the years |
| 182. | Joseph E. Seagram & Sons, Inc. | | PF (foreign?) | As of the mid-1960s, a subsidiary of Distillers Corp.—Seagram Ltd., 32% of whose stock has been controlled by the Bronfman family of Canada and New York City (see *Fortune*, November 1966, p. 146); also I & O-BD over the years |
| 183. | Corning Glass Works | | PF | As of the mid-1960s, Houghton family had at least 30% of the stock (see *Fortune*, February 1966, p. 125)—according to the 1965 *Moody's Industrial Manual* (p. 1747), the family had 32.8% of the stock; also I & O-BD over the years |
| 184. | Texas Instruments Inc. | | PF | J.E. Jonsson and E. McDermott had 17.0% of the stock as of 1960 (see SEC *OS*, April 1960); also I-BD over the years |
| 185. | Carrier Corp. | PM | | |

**Table 3-1** *(cont.)*

| 1965 Rank | Name of Company | Type of Control | Evidence or Comments |
|---|---|---|---|
| 186. | Ling-Temco-Vought, Inc. | PF | As of the mid-1960s, J.J. Ling had 16.6% of the stock (see *Time*, 17 March 1967, p. 94); also I-BD over the years |
| 187. | General American Transportation Corp. | PM | |
| 188. | International Milling Co. | PF | As of about 1964, roughly 75% of the stock was held or controlled by the Bean family (see *Dun's Review*, September 1969, p. 74)—in addition, see *Time* (31 January 1955, p. 80); also I-BD over the years |
| 189. | Rohm & Haas Co. | PF | Haas family and associates owned 52% of the stock as of 1960 (see *Forbes*, 15 March 1960, p. 30); also see I-BD over the years |
| 190. | Worthington Corp. | PM | |
| 191. | U.S. Gypsum Co. | PM | |
| 192. | Sherwin-Williams Co. | PM | |
| 193. | Fruehauf Corp. | PM | |
| 194. | Cerro Corp. | F? | Burden family?—see O-BD over the years |
| 195. | Combustion Engineering, Inc. | F? | Santry family?—see I & O-BD over the years |
| 196. | Brunswick Corp. | PF | Bensinger family had about 40% of the stock as of late 1959 (see *Fortune*, November 1959, p. 159); also I & O-BD over the years |
| 197. | West Virginia Pulp & Paper Co. | PF | Luke family had about 30% of the stock as of late 1962 (see *Forbes*, 15 December 1962, p. 29); also I & O-BD over the years |
| 198. | Northrop Corp. | PM | |

| | | | | | | |
|---|---|---|---|---|---|---|
| 199. | Richfield Oil Corp. | PM | | | | 30% of stock owned by Cities Service Co. and 29% owned by the Sinclair Oil Corp. (both probably management firms) |
| 200. | Mack Trucks, Inc. | | | | PF(I) | Up to at least 1964, C.A. Johnson (of New York City) owned 28.7% of the Central Securities Corp., which owned 26.7% of the Northeast Capital Corp., which in turn owned 29% of Mack Trucks (see *Forbes*, 15 October 1959, p. 52 and 1 December 1965, p. 46); also O-BD over the years |
| | Subtotal Top 200 | 86 (43.0%) | 35 (17.5%) | | 79 (39.5%) | |
| 201. | A.O. Smith Corp. | | | | PF | As of the mid-1960s, the Smith family (of Milwaukee) controlled over half of the voting stock (see *Fortune*, 15 June 1967, p. 178)—according to the 1965 *Moody's Industrial Manual* (p. 1076), the Smith Investment Co. had 53.1% of the stock; also I & O-BD over the years |
| 202. | Owens-Corning Fiber-glas Corp. | | | | PF | As of the mid-1960s, the Boeschenstein family had close to 5% of the outstanding stock, which (because Owens-Illinois Glass Co. and the Corning Glass Works are not permitted to vote their respective 31% shares) has amounted to an effective voting interest of about 13-14% (see *Business Week*, 4 March 1967, p. 122); also I-BD over the years |
| 203. | Avon Products, Inc. | | | | PF | As of the mid-1960s through early 1970s, the (Van Alan) Clark family of New York City had 14% of the stock and the Henderson family had another 3.6% (see SEC *OS*, August 1966 and *NYT*, 28 November 1971, Sect. 3, p. 7); also O-BD over the years |
| 204. | Gillette Co. | PM | | | | |
| 205. | Diamond Internatl. Corp. | | F? | | | Walters family?—see I-BD in recent years |

**Table 3-1** *(cont.)*

| 1965 Rank | Name of Company | Type of Control | Evidence or Comments |
|---|---|---|---|
| 206. | Republic Aviation Corp. | F? | Up to May 1960, the Wm. H. Moore estate (of New York City) owned about 14.6% of the stock (see SEC *OS*, June 1960); also O-BD over the years |
| 207. | Consolidation Coal Co. | PF (indirectly) | As of 1964, the family-controlled M.A. Hanna Co. owned 19% of the stock (see *NYT*, 5 April 1964, Sec. 3, p. 1); also I & O-BD over the years |
| 208. | Oscar Mayer & Co. | PF | As of the middle or late 1960s, the Mayer family owned about 79-80% of the stock (see *Time*, 12 April 1968, p. 95 and *Fortune*, February 1969, p. 136); also I-BD over the years |
| 209. | Liggett & Myers Tobacco Co. | PM | |
| 210. | Alleghany Ludlum Steel Corp. | PM | |
| 211. | Archer Daniels Midland Co. | PF | J.H. and T.L. Daniels had 4.9% of the stock as of 1956 (see SEC *OS*, May 1956)—as of 1968, *Forbes* (1 September 1968, p. 20) reported that 17% of the stock was in "friendly" hands; also I & O-BD over the years |
| 212. | Pet Milk Co. | PF | As of the mid-1960s, the Latzer, Mayer and Kaeser families (of St. Louis) controlled about 45% of the stock (see *Dun's Review*, March 1965, p. 91)—in addition, see *Forbes*, 1 July 1963, p. 34; also I-BD over the years |
| 213. | Libby, McNeill & Libby | F? (foreign) | As of the mid-1960s, M. Sindona (of Italy) had at least 9.5% of the stock (see *NYT*, 16 August 1964, Sec. 3, p. 1); also O-BD in recent years |

| No. | Company | | | Notes |
|---|---|---|---|---|
| 214. | Merck & Co. | PF | | Merck family had at least 10.2% of the stock as of the late 1950s (see SEC *OS*, August 1957 and December 1959); also I & O-BD over the years |
| 215. | Rexall Drug & Chemical Co. | | PM | |
| 216. | Crucible Steel Co. | | PM | |
| 217. | Kaiser Steel Corp. | PF | | As of the mid-1960s, the Kaiser family-controlled Kaiser Industries and Henry J. Kaiser Co. owned about 79% of the stock (see *Fortune*, April 1963: p. 91); also I & O-BD over the years |
| 218. | Collins Radio Co. | PF | | As of the mid-1960s, the Collins family had 19.8% of the stock (see *S&P Corporation Records*, Vol. C-E, December 1966-January 1967, p. 7750)—as of 1970 A.A. Collins had 18% of the stock (see *Business Week*, 7 March 1970, p. 20); also I-BD over the years |
| 219. | Stauffer Chemical Co. | PF | | As of the mid-1960s, the Stauffer and de Guigne families had over 20% of the stock (see *Forbes*, 1 September 1968, p. 19); also I & O-BD over the years |
| 220. | Flintkote Co. | | PM | |
| 221. | ACF Industries, Inc. | | PM | |
| 222. | Ethyl Corp. | PF | | As of the mid-1960s, the Gottwald family had at least 14.3% of the stock (see SEC *OS*, May, June & July 1966)—according to *Forbes* (1 October 1968, p. 68), the Gottwald family had about 20% of the stock; also I-BD in recent years |
| 223. | M. Lowenstein & Sons, Inc. | PF(I) | | L. Lowenstein had at least 40% of the stock as of 1962 (see *Forbes*, 1 June 1962, p. 15)—as of 1967 L. Lowenstein and estate had 33.9% of the stock (see *Finance*, December 1967, p. 29); also I-BD over the years |

**Table 3-1** *(cont.)*

| 1965 Rank | Name of Company | Type of Control | Evidence or Comments |
|---|---|---|---|
| 224. | P. Lorillard & Co. | PM | |
| 225. | Cannon Mills Co. | PF | As of 1965, the Cannon family had at least 15.7% of the stock (see the 1965 *Moody's Industrial Manual*, p. 737); also I-BD over the years |
| 226. | Sterling Drug Inc. | PM | |
| 227. | Xerox Corp. | PM | |
| 228. | Rath Packing Co. | PF | As of the mid-1960s, the Rath and Donnell families (of Iowa) had 14.8% of the stock (see *S&P Corporation Records*, Vol. P-S, December 1966-January 1967, p. 6996)—in addition, see *Fortune* (February 1969, p. 136); also I & O-BD over the years |
| 229. | Bristol-Myers Co. | F? | Bristol family?—see I-BD over the years |
| 230. | Eli Lilly & Co. | PF | As of the mid-1960s, E. Lilly owned 6.4% of the stock (see SEC *OS*, June 1966), and family-controlled foundation probably owned much more—according to *Forbes* (15 April 1971, p. 34), the Lilly family owns about 25% of the stock and the family-controlled Lilly Foundation has another approximately 22.5% of the stock; also I-BD over the years |
| 231. | Revere Copper & Brass, Inc. | PM | 34.6% of the voting stock owned by American Smelting & Refining Co. (see 1965 *Moody's Industrial Manual*, p. 2589) |
| 232. | H.K. Porter Co. | PF(I) | As of the mid-1960s, Thomas Mellon Evans (of Pittsburgh) owned 62% of the stock (see *Fortune*, 15 June 1967, p. 182); also I-BD over the years |
| 233. | Studebaker Corp. | PM | |

| | | | |
|---|---|---|---|
| 234. | Interlake Steel Corp. | | PF(I) | As of the mid-1960s, John Sherwin controlled (through ownership of about 9.7% of the stock of Pickands, Mather & Co.) 9% of the stock of the Interlake Steel Corp. (see SEC *OS*, November 1967 and the 1968 *Moody's Industrial Manual*, p. 1181)—in addition, see SEC *OS*, December 1956; also O-BD over the years |
| 235. | Dresser Industries, Inc. | PM | | |
| 236. | Newport News Shipbuilding & Dry Dock Co. | PM | | 6.9% of the stock held by the Tri-Continental Corp. and associated concerns (see 1965 *Moody's Bank & Finance Manual*), which may be controlled by J. & W. Seligman & Co. (a now management concern?); also I & O-BD over the years |
| 237. | Wheeling Steel Corp. | | PF | Norton Simon had about 10% of the stock as of about 1965 (see *NYT*, 22 November 1966, p. 55); also I & O-BD in 1965 |
| 238. | Union Bag-Camp Paper Corp. | | PF | As of around 1956, Camp family probably owned over 15% of the stock (see *Forbes*, 15 November 1965, p. 44)—Calder family also involved; also I & O-BD over the years |
| 239. | Glidden Co. | | F? | Joyce family? (see *Business Week*, 30 March 1963, pp. 60-61, and *Fortune*, March 1957, pp. 132-33); also see I-BD over the years |
| 240. | National Gypsum Co. | PM | | |
| 241. | Skelly Oil Co. | | PF (indirectly) | As of the mid-1960s, the Getty-controlled Getty Oil Co. owned 64.8% of the Mission Corp. which, in turn, controlled 71% of the stock of the Skelly Oil Co. (see *Fortune*, December 1967, p. 111); also O-BD over the years |
| 242. | General Cable Corp. | PM | | 36.3% of the stock owned by the American Smelting & Refining Co. (see 1965 *Moody's Industrial Manual*, p. 2595) |
| 243. | American Bakeries Co. | | F? | Cushman family? (see *Forbes*, 1 December 1969, p. 23 and SEC *OS*, December 1963); also see I or O-BD over the years |

**Table 3-1** *(cont.)*

| 1965 Rank | Name of Company | Type of Control | Evidence or Comments |
|---|---|---|---|
| 244. | Grinnell Corp. | PM | |
| 245. | Pepsi-Cola Co. | PM | |
| 246. | Eltra Corp. | PF | As of 1969, G. Wattles still had 35% of the stock of the American Mfg. Co., which in turn owned 25% of the stock of the Eltra Corp. (see *Forbes*, 1 May 1969, p. 23); also I & O-BD over the years |
| 247. | Norton Co. | PF | As of the mid-1960s, the Norton family had over 50% of the stock (see *Forbes*, 1 December 1967, p. 44); also I-BD over the years |
| 248. | Kerr-McGee Oil Industries, Inc. | PF | Kerr family had 22% of the stock as of 1959 (see *Fortune*, March 1959, p. 184); also I & O-BD over the years |
| 249. | Hoover Co. | PF | As of the mid-1960s, the Hoover family had about 70% of the voting stock (see *Fortune*, June 1964, p. 143); also I & O-BD over the years |
| 250. | Essex Wire Corp. | PF(I) | As of the mid-1960s, W.F. Probst owned about 15.5% of the stock (see SEC *OS*, June 1967); also I-BD in recent years |
| 251. | Brown Shoe Co. | PM | |
| 252. | Springs Cotton Mills | PF | As of the mid and late 1960s, the Close-Springs family had about 60% of the stock (see S&P *Corporation Records*, Vol. P-S, October-November 1967, p. 5690 and *Forbes*, 1 March 1969, p. 62)—in addition, see *Forbes*, 15 March 1967, p. 42; also I & O-BD over the years |
| 253. | Addressograph-Multigraph Corp. | PF(I) | F.H. Woods owned 6% of the stock as of 1960 (see SEC *OS*, February 1960); also I & O-BD over the years |
| 254. | Land O'Lakes Creameries | PM | |

| No. | Company | | Notes |
|---|---|---|---|
| 255. | Westinghouse Air Brake Co. | F? | Mellon family or interests? (see *Time*, 19 March 1949, p. 14, *Business Week*, 1 June 1963, p. 108, *NYT*, 9 March 1966, p. 51, and *Forbes*, 15 August 1969, p. 44)—see O-BD over the years |
| 256. | American Brake Shoe Co. | PM | |
| 257. | McLouth Steel Corp. | PF | As of the mid-1960s, the Cudlip family had 4.1% of the stock (see SEC *OS*, November 1963 and Feburary 1965); also I & O-BD over the years |
| 258. | Libbey-Owens-Ford Glass Co. | PF | Probably controlled by the Ford-Knight family (of Detroit and Toledo)—according to the 1955 U.S. Senate report on *Factors Affecting the Stock Market* (p. 174), certain large, presumably outside shareholders (possibly the Ford-Knight family) owned 3.3% of the stock as of December 1954 and the officers, directors and associates (a number of whom may be members of the Ford-Knight family) owned another 2.2% of the stock at this same point in time—see I & O-BD over the years |
| 259. | Joseph Schlitz Brewing Co. | PF | As of the mid-1960s, the Uihlein family and close kin owned 92% of the stock (see *Fortune*, 15 June 1967, p. 182); also I-BD over the years |
| 260. | Cone Mills Corp. | PF | As of the mid-1960s, the Cone family interests owned 42% of the stock (see *Finance*, September 1967, p. 7)—in addition, see *Fortune*, 15 June 1967, p. 182); also I & O-BD over the years |
| 261. | Pacific Car & Foundry Co. | PF | Probably controlled by the Pigott family, along with perhaps Reed family—as of the late 1960s, Mrs. Pigott (now Mrs. J.A. McCone) and her son, C.M. Pigott, had at least 10% of the stock (see SEC *OS*, February 1966 and February 1971); also I or O-BD over the years |
| 262. | Consumers Cooperative Assoc. | PM | (Actually an agricultural cooperative) |

**Table 3-1** *(cont.)*

| 1965 Rank | Name of Company | Type of Control | Evidence or Comments |
|---|---|---|---|
| 263. | Campbell Taggart Assoc'd. Bakeries | F? | Taggart family?–see I & O-BD over the years |
| 264. | Tecumseh Products Co. | PF | As of 1955, R.W. Herrick had 53% of the stock (see *Fortune*, July 1955, p. 99)–as of 1970, the Herrick family had 51% of the stock (see *Forbes*, 15 July 1970, p. 58); also I & O-BD over the years |
| 265. | Otis Elevator Co. | PM | |
| 266. | Cluett, Peabody & Co. | PM | |
| 267. | Magnavox Co. | PF(I) | As of 1965, F. Freimann had about 7.1% of the stock (see SEC *OS*, November 1965); also see I-BD over the years |
| 268. | International Minerals & Chemical Corp. | PM | |
| 269. | Consolidated Electronics Industries Corp. | PM | |
| 270. | Philadelphia & Reading Corp. | PF | Probably controlled by the Newman and Hyland interests (see *Business Week*, 20 April 1957, pp. 99-106, *Fortune*, August 1959, pp. 84-88, *Forbes*, 1 December 1970, p. 58 and *Finance*, December 1970, p. 49); also I & O-BD over the years |
| 271. | Cummins Engine Co. | PF | As of the mid-1960s, J.I. Miller and kin (of Indiana) owned 62% of the stock (see *Fortune*, 15 June 1967, p. 180); also I & O-BD over the years |
| 272. | Admiral Corp. | PF | As of the mid-1960s, the Siragusa family owned 39% of the stock (see *Forbes*, 1 February 1966, p. 20)–according to the 1965 *Moody's Industrial Manual* (p. 1120), R.D. and I.O. Siragusa had 28.6% of the stock; also I-BD over the years |

| | | | | |
|---|---|---|---|---|
| 273. | Kelsey-Hayes Co. | PM | | |
| 274. | General Precision Equipment Corp. | PM | | |
| 275. | Emerson Electric Mfg. Co. | PM | | |
| 276. | Smith, Kline & French Lab's. | | PF | Smith, Kline and Boyer families (of Philadelphia) owned at least 16.0% of the stock as of about 1960 (see SEC OS, June 1959 and April 1961); also I-BD over the years |
| 277. | Crown Cork & Seal Co. | | PF(I) | J.F. Connelly owned 19.2% of the stock as of late 1962 (see *Fortune*, October 1962, p. 118)—according to the 1965 *Moody's Industrial Manual* (p. 1760), Connelly had 12.1% of the stock; also I-BD in recent years |
| 278. | J.I. Case Co. | PM | | |
| 279. | Kayser-Roth Corp. | | PF | As of the mid-1960s, 36.9% of the stock owned by the Harrison Factors Corp., which was controlled in turn by C.H. Roth and associates of New York City (see S&P *Corporation Records*, Vol. F-K, February-March 1968, p. 5760)—in addition, see *NYT*, 12 March 1968, p. 57; also I-BD over the years |
| 280. | Abbott Laboratories | PM | | |
| 281. | R.R. Donnelley & Sons Co. | | PF | As of 1965, descendants of R.R. Donnelley owned about 52% of the stock (see 1965 *Moody's Industrial Manual*, p. 358); also I-BD over the years |
| 282. | Midland-Ross Corp. | PM | | |

**Table 3-1** *(cont.)*

| 1965 Rank | Name of Company | Type of Control | Evidence or Comments |
|---|---|---|---|
| 283. | Hooker Chemical Corp. | F? | As of at least 1961, Hooker family had 6.2% of the stock (see 1961 *Moody's Industrial Manual*, p. 564); also I & O-BD over the years |
| 284. | Upjohn Co. | PF | About 60% of the stock owned by descendants and kin of W.E. Upjohn (see *Fortune*, July 1959, p. 108); also I & O-BD over the years |
| 285. | Colorado Fuel & Iron Corp. | PF | Probably controlled by Allen family or Allen & Co. of New York City (see *Fortune*, May 1954, pp. 125 and 170-72, plus *Forbes*, 15 November 1960, p. 27); also I & O-BD over the years |
| 286. | Thiokol Chemical Corp. | PM | |
| 287. | United Shoe Machinery Corp. | F? | Brown family of Boston? (see *NYT*, 28 April 1968, Sec. 3, p. 3); also I-BD over the years |
| 288. | Hershey Chocolate Corp. | PM | |
| 289. | Stokely-Van Camp, Inc. | PF | As of the mid-1960s, the Stokely family owned at least 19.6% of the stock (see SEC *OS*, October 1965 and October 1967); also I-BD over the years |
| 290. | Parke, Davis & Co. | F? | Buhl and Whitney families controlled at least 20% of the stock as of 1953 (see *Fortune*, September 1953, p. 110); also O-BD over the years |
| 291. | Sunshine Biscuits, Inc. | PM | |
| 292. | Engelhard Industries, Inc. | PF | As of 1965, 72% of the stock owned by Engelhard Hanovia, Inc., a family-controlled holding company (see *Forbes*, 1 August 1965, p. 20); also I-BD over the years |

| No. | Company | | | | Comments |
|---|---|---|---|---|---|
| 293. | Revlon, Inc. | | | PF(I) | As of 1965, C.H. Revson owned 18.7% of the stock (see SEC OS, August 1965); also I-BD over the years |
| 294. | Link-Belt Co. | PM | | | |
| 295. | Scovill Mfg. Co. | | F? | | Sperry and Goss families?—see I & O-BD over the years |
| 296. | Sunbeam Corp. | | F? | | Gwinn family?—see I-BD over the years |
| 297. | Times Mirror Co. | | | PF | As of the mid-1960s roughly half of the stock was owned by the Chandler family (see Forbes, 15 June 1964, p. 30); also I & O-BD over the years |
| 298. | McGraw-Hill, Inc. | | | PF | McGraw family owned at least 25.5% of the stock as of the middle or late 1950's (see SEC OS, March 1955 and November 1958)—as of 1968, D.C. McGraw, related trusts, and the D.C. McGraw Foundation had 27.8% of the stock (see S&P Corporation Records, Vol. L-O, June-July 1968, p. 7193); also I & O-BD over the years |
| 299. | Emhart Mfg. Co. | PM | | | |
| 300. | General Aniline and Film Corp. | PM | | | Up to March 1965 under federal government control |
| | Total Top 300 | 124 (41.3%) | 48 (16.0%) | 128 (42.7%) | |

Notes: For the above ranking of the first 300 industrial concerns, see "The Fortune Directory," Fortune (July 1965), pp. 149-59.

All divisional computations based on SEC Official Summary data were done by slide rule, which it was felt was sufficiently accurate for purposes of this study. In many instances a number of monthly SEC stock ownership citations are listed in the "Evidence or Comments" column, none of which may refer to the holdings of the family or families identified as controlling a particular concern. In such cases there is, as a rule, only one large stock ownership figure listed in each of the company's monthly entries, and the reader can usually assume that the person holding these shares is related to the firm's economically dominant family, a fact which can frequently be corroborated through the use of Who's Who in America or some other reliable source of biographical information.

A statistical summary of the above family versus management control totals, computed on the basis of the top 50, 100, 200 and 300 manufacturing and mining firms, is as follows:[20]

**Corporate Control Summary of Table 3-1 Findings for the First 300** *Fortune-*
**Ranked Publicly Owned Industrial Concerns as of 1965**

| Business Category | Probably Management Control | Possibly Family Control | Probably Family Control |
|---|---|---|---|
| Industrial concerns | | | |
| top 50 | 58.0% | 22.0% | 20.0% |
| top 100 | 44.0 | 20.0 | 36.0 |
| top 200 | 43.0 | 17.5 | 39.5 |
| top 300 | 41.3 | 16.0 | 42.7 |

Thus, aside apparently from the first 50 industrials in the *Fortune* ranking, most of which were judged to be dominated by management or fell into the uncertain intermediate category described as possibly family (which some might prefer to call possibly management), the other major concerns in the above tabulation were characterized by a substantial amount of family control.[21] These (PF) findings obviously conflict very markedly with those arrived at by both Larner (in either his 1966 article or 1970 book) and Sheehan, as may be seen by a look at the following figures (taken from Chapter 1 and Appendix B):[22]

[20] From the standpoint of corporate control, there were three somewhat unusual concerns in the top 300 industrials. Two of these firms—Agway, Inc. and the Consumers Cooperative Association—were essentially cooperative enterprises (farm co-ops), without the normal form of economic control based on widely held stock ownership (Agway's securities are, for example, sold only to its members), and were thus unlikely to be family dominated. The third concern was the General Aniline & Film Corp., which, as a result of the federal government's takeover of this former arm of the German I.G. Farben complex during World War II, was under the control of either the Alien Property Custodian or the U.S. Attorney General from February 1942 to March 1965, when it was turned back to private interests.

[21] Unfortunately, the author has not been able, for want of further adequate information, to reduce the number of concerns assigned to the "possibly family" category, and he is reluctant to even make an estimate as to what proportion of these firms might ultimately prove, upon the presentation of additional evidence, to be either family or management controlled corporations. A number of companies placed in this indeterminate category could, of course, simply be passing through a major organizational transition from one form of control to another.

[22] The author came up with a total of 20 percent for the first 100 industrial firms listed in Appendix A of Larner's 1970 book by including both the National Steel Corp. (which Larner had, upon the discovery of additional data, reclassified) and the Coca-Cola Co. (which Larner claimed here was minority controlled, although on page 11 he asserted it was management dominated). The author did not consider the Shell Oil Co. and Minnesota Mining & Mfg. Co. as concerns controlled by family or entrepreneurial interests for the reasons given in Appendix B. The 22 percent figure was arrived at by treating the Ethyl Corp. as a probably family controlled firm (albeit according to Larner, indirectly, through the legal mechanism of a voting trust) and by excluding Lever Bros. as a most likely manage-

**Summary of Sheehan and Larner Family Control Findings**

| Business Category | 1967 *Fortune* Article by Robert Sheehan | 1966 *American Economic Review* Article by Robert Larner | 1970 Book, *Management Control and the Large Corporation,* by Robert Larner |
|---|---|---|---|
| Industrial concerns (publicly owned) | | | |
| top 100 | 11.0% | 18.0% | 20.0% |
| top 200 | 17.0 | | 22.0 |
| top 300 (or rough approximation thereof) | 24.3 | | 26.6 (of top 290) |

Quite clearly, then, these sources considerably understate the amount of family control in the largest manufacturing and mining concerns in the United States. Indeed, according to the author's corporate control data and calculations, Larner and Sheehan failed to identify anywhere from close to 40 to 60 percent, and in one case almost 70 percent, (depending on the writer's work and the numerical ranking) of the big family-controlled firms in the mid-sixties.

It should also be pointed out that Table 3-1 and the above statistical control summary did not take into account any of the various privately owned companies referred to earlier (see the first part of Chapter 2, especially Table 2-1). Since many of these concerns are engaged in some sort of manufacturing activity (the making of roads and buildings, the provision of news and information, etc.), a number of these often overlooked enterprises should be included in any final set of calculations concerning the magnitude of family control in America's large industrial corporations. If all such specially classified companies with sales or revenues in excess of those of the above *Fortune*-ranked firms were incorporated in these overall tabulations, it would increase certain family-control totals listed in Table 3-1, as seen by a glance at the following recomputed corporate control figures:[23]

ment dominated company and American Metal Climax, Inc. because of its uncertain control status. The 26.6 percent total was established by counting two corporations for which Larner had no stock ownership information (Potlatch Forests, Inc. and the Boise Cascade Corp.) as probably family dominated firms, while viewing three other companies—the Certain-teed Products Corp., Texas Instruments Inc., and Libby, McNeill & Libby—as management controlled concerns because no evidence was presented to indicate that the outside interests Larner cited in this regard were, in fact, family forces.

[23] The revised top 200 control status figures, which represent a shift of 1 percent in the PM and PF findings contained in Table 3-1, were arrived at by adding five huge industrial concerns—Deering Milliken, Inc., the Hearst Corporation, Hughes Aircraft Co., Hughes Tool Co., and the Tribune Co. (of Chicago)—to the first 200 ranking (thereby pushing out two management dominated companies and three family controlled firms previously in this select category). The revised top 300 control status figures, which represent a shift of (+) 2.0 percent in PF findings, (-) 1.3 percent in PM totals, and (-) 0.7 percent in F? findings, were arrived at by adding 10 big privately owned manufacturing concerns—the above five enterprises, plus the Bechtel Corp., Gates Rubber Co., Mars Inc., Dubuque Packing Co., and Field Enterprises, Inc.—to the top 300 list (thereby pushing out the last 10 companies in

**Revised Corporate Control Summary for the First 300 Publicly and Privately Owned Industrial Concerns as of 1965**

| Business Category | Probably Management Control | Possibly Family Control | Probably Family Control |
|---|---|---|---|
| Industrial concerns | | | |
| top 50 | 58.0% | 22.0% | 20.0% |
| top 100 | 44.0 | 20.0 | 36.0 |
| top 200 | 42.0 | 17.5 | 40.5 |
| top 300 | 40.0 | 15.3 | 44.7 |

Thus with the addition of the large privately owned mining and manufacturing concerns, the statistical picture has been altered somewhat, so that a brief look at the above figures now reveals that family controlled firms actually outnumber those dominated by management at some point shortly after the count reaches the top 200 industrial ranking.

What is more, if one were to pursue this line of economic control analysis even further, it would in all probability show a constantly increasing trend toward family control. The author has, for example, made a less intensive study of the various big industrial enterprises ranked from 301 to 500 by *Fortune* in 1965. Of the 200 companies found in this rather select business category, the author is reasonably certain that a little over half could be classified as probably family controlled corporations (see Appendix C, which contains a company-by-company control analysis of these frequently lesser known firms).[24] If then, to make the proper adjustment for the previously included 10 privately owned industrial concerns, the 102 probably family-controlled firms ranked from 301 through 490 on *Fortune's* 1965 list, together with the 4 companies so classified in the 291-300 range (but not counted in the above revised top 300 tabulation),

---

this category, four of which were management dominated concerns, four were probably family controlled firms, and two were considered to be under possible family control). The author did not include the Columbia Broadcasting System, Inc. and American Broadcasting Companies, Inc. in this revised set of corporate control calculations because he was not sure how these companies should be classifed (they have traditionally been treated as public utilities, although their work is similar to that of newspaper publishing companies). He also did not count the probably management controlled Halliburton Co. in these computations, but this omission was most likely offset by the exclusion of the Pittston Co., Reader's Digest Assn., Inc., and the E.W. Scripps Co. (all family controlled firms), which the author could conceivably have added to the above list, but did not do so because he chose to err on the side of safety.

[24] If these 108 probably family firms were added to the 128 such concerns listed in Table 3-1, it would raise the probably family control total from 42.7 percent to 47.2 percent. This is a little less than the relative increase which Sheehan found in his survey, which showed that 24.3 percent of the top 300 manufacturing and mining companies and 29.6 percent of the 500 largest industrial enterprises were dominated by various wealthy families (see Sheehan, *Fortune*, 15 June 1967, pp. 179-80). The author, however, decided not to utilize these particular corporate control findings because of his inclusion of a number of privately owned industrial concerns in the final calculations.

were added to the 134 publicly and privately owned corporations already described as probably family controlled, this would bring the top 500 corporate
control figure up to a total of 48.0 percent. However, this figure (like the 42.7
percent finding for the first 300 manufacturing and mining firms) is somewhat
misleading, since it does not take into account a fairly substantial number of
privately owned industrial concerns which would appear to be of sufficient size
to be ranked in the top 301-to-500 category. If all these concerns, which com-
prise a total of 17 privately owned companies and one largely unincorporated
business enterprise (the Newhouse publishing and communications operation),
plus two manufacturing firms which were inadvertently omitted from the 1965
*Fortune* 500 ranking (Publicker Industries, Inc. and Heublein, Inc.), were added
into this final top 500 tabulation (thereby pushing out 20 corporations ranked
from 471 through 490, eleven of which were probably family dominated), it
would increase the top 500 family control figure to 49.8 percent.[25] On the basis
of these data, it seems fair to conclude that about 45 percent of the top 300
industrial concerns and approximately 50 percent of the 500 largest manufacturing and mining firms were dominated by various family or entrepreneurial interests in the mid-sixties.[26] These, furthermore, are conservative figures and, in the
author's opinion, they represent the most reliable findings that can be assembled
on this difficult and important subject without resort to governmental subpoena
and investigatory powers.

Now some might argue that because of the gigantic size of the first 50 indus-

[25]These 17 privately owned companies, all of which had estimated revenues well above the
volume of sales registered by the 471st largest firm in the mid- and late sixties (in 1964, for
instance, it was $105,000,000), are: P. Ballantine & Sons; C.F. Braun & Co. (a southern
California contractor); California & Hawaiian Sugar Refining Corp., Ltd.; the Daniel Con-
struction Co. (of South Carolina); Encyclopaedia Britannica, Inc.; Great Lakes Carbon
Corp.; Hallmark Cards, Inc.; Theo. Hamm Brewing Co.; S.C. Johnson & Son, Inc.; J.A. Jones
Construction Co. (of North Carolina); Peter Kiewit Sons Inc. (a big Nebraska contractor);
Reader's Digest Assn., Inc.; Rock Island Oil & Refining Co. (now known as Koch Industries,
Inc.); F. & M. Schaefer Brewing Co.; E.W. Scripps Co. (the Scripps-Howard newspapers);
Simpson Timber Co.; and Triangle Publications, Inc. (For more information on the dominant families in these concerns, see the second part of Appendix C, and for fairly reliable
estimates of their annual sales, see *Forbes* (1 February 1965), pp. 33-35; *Fortune* (February
1965), p. 54; *Fortune* (15 July 1966), pp. 224-25, and 327-48; *Forbes* (1 August 1968), p.
41; and *Forbes* (15 May 1969), pp. 186-92.) Publicker Industries, Inc. and Heublein, Inc.
are discussed in footnote 8 of Chapter 2. With regard to the Newhouse publications and
communications network, which was valued at $200,000,000 back in 1962, although it was
run in rather unorthodox fashion from a desk in the owner's Manhattan apartment, see *Fortune* (July 1962), p. 58.

Again, the author was somewhat conservative in his selection of privately owned concerns deemed large enough to warrant top 500 (really 470) ranking, and did not list several
firms which could conceivably have been incorporated in this tabulation, such as the Adolph
Coors Co., Abney Mills, and Ball Bros. Co. Inc. The author also did not include any companies from *Fortune's* recently compiled miscellaneous ranking, because cursory examination indicated that it contained roughly the same number of management controlled industrial concerns as family dominated firms of top 500 size (as of 1965). If anything, there
would appear to have been more of the latter (like the Morrison-Knudson Co. and United
Artists Corp.), which could therefore push the above finding up over the 50 percent mark.

[26]Actually, if the author eliminated all de facto corporate subsidiaries (such as Revere Copper & Brass, General Cable, McCall's, Thos. J. Lipton, Inc., Pacolet Industries, and Warwick
Electronics, Inc.) from these tabulations, thereby adding a few more lesser-ranked com-

trial firms (which accounted for almost 50 percent of the total volume of sales registered by the *Fortune* 500 in 1964), the predominantly management control findings for this category were much more significant than the percentages arrived at for, say, the 200, 300 or 500 largest industrial concerns. However, the 58 percent probably management versus 20 percent probably family control totals for the top 50 industrials (see Table 3-1) are in some respects rather misleading, for this particular set of figures happens to be very much the product of *Fortune's* mode of industrial ranking, which was based on volume of sales. If, for example, the top 50 industrials were listed according to assets, the above differential would largely disappear, since this would result in a shift in the ranking of 15 large manufacturing and mining firms and the tabulation of a substantially revised set of percentages, which is as follows:[27]

> Top 50 industrial concerns:    38% probably family controlled
> (ranked on basis of 1964 assets)    20% possibly family
> 42% probably management controlled

Thus the use of assets as a means of establishing the first 50 industrial corporations leads to the computation of control totals which are fairly close to those arrived at for the top 100 or 200 manufacturing and mining firms, grouped on the basis of sales. From the standpoint of overall assets, therefore, it may be said that there are almost as many family controlled concerns as management dominated firms for even the first 50 category.

A discerning look at Table 3-1 also reveals that there are certain interesting patterns of industrial control based on such factors as line of economic activity (product) and region. Most of the big electrical companies in the United States,

---

panies to the overall computational process, it would push the above totals up over the 45 and 50 percent marks for the first 300 and 500 industrials respectively. It should also be borne in mind that about 15 percent of the top 300 industrial concerns and a somewhat lesser percentage of the 500 largest manufacturing and mining corporations also fell into the possibly family control category, so that if, as is likely, a number of these companies were found upon more careful and intensive investigation to be family controlled firms, the above percentage totals would climb a little higher. Moreover, if the author had taken the time to extend his research efforts even further—to, say, the top 1,000 industrial concerns (a listing of which was presented for the first time in the May and June 1970 issues of *Fortune*)—chances are the analysis would reveal an ever-increasing trend toward family control, since this phenomenon is, generally speaking, a characteristic of smaller companies.

[27]The 15 corporations added to the top 50 list (compiled on the basis of assets) were Alcoa, Allied Chemical Corp., Anaconda Co., Armco Steel Corp., Atlantic Refining Co., Celanese Corp. of America, Inland Steel Co., Jones & Laughlin Steel Corp., Kaiser Aluminum & Chemical Corp., National Steel Corp., Olin Mathieson Chemical Corp., Reynolds Metals Co., R.J. Reynolds Tobacco Co., Sun Oil Co., and Tidewater Oil Co. The 15 corporations that were at the same time, of necessity, deleted from the top 50 category were Armour & Co., Boeing Co., Borden Co., Burlington Industries, Inc., Caterpillar Tractor Co., Continental Can Co., General Dynamics Corp., General Foods Corp., Lockheed Aircraft Corp., North American Aviation, Inc., National Dairy Products Corp., Sperry Rand Corp., Swift & Co., United Aircraft Corp., and U.S. Rubber Co.

for instance, appear to be management dominated.[28] A very sizable percentage of the nation's major aircraft and other primarily government defense contract concerns are under management control too, as are a majority of the heavy machinery manufacturers. In many spheres of economic activity, of course, the control picture can best be summarized as consisting of a more or less equal division between management dominated companies and family controlled firms, as in the case of oil, steel and other metals.[29] Yet in a number of other important areas family controlled corporations clearly outnumber those dominated by management. Family controlled firms have, for example, a very strong hold in the textile-and-apparel and food-and-beverage lines, as Sheehan himself pointed out in *Fortune*.[30] And they predominate in such diverse fields as chemicals, lumber and paper, publishing, and the manufacture of glass.[31]

As indicated earlier, there are also some very definite regional patterns of corporate control. The vast majority of the big industrial concerns with their main offices located in New England and upper New York State are, for instance, under management control, with close to 80 percent (11 out of 14) of such companies, whose control status has been fairly clearly established, being classified as probably management firms.[32] Roughly 60 percent (51 out of 84)

---

[28]There are, to be sure, considerable problems involved in deciding whether certain concerns fall into one or another manufacturing category. Since many corporations today are of an extremely diversified character, the author could only be guided by what appeared to be a company's primary line (or lines) of business, as this could best be determined from the pertinent business and product entries in *Poor's Register of Corporations, Directors and Executives*. Some firms have such extensive operations that they should really be described as conglomerates, although there is as yet no precisely conceived and widely accepted definition of that now common term. A number of firms, furthermore, have markedly transformed the principal nature of their business over the years, W.R. Grace & Co., for instance, shifting very largely from shipping and other activity to the production of chemicals in the post-World War II period. Thus this corporation has been classified as a chemical company, though it has been engaged in such work for only a comparatively short time. The author, by the way, also deviated somewhat from the standard (Bureau of the Census) industrial classification procedure in that he did not place drugs, soaps and personal products in the chemicals category, and treated aircraft and other heavily defense-oriented concerns as a special separate group of companies.

[29]With regard to petroleum, however, it should be pointed out that the management dominated firms were on the whole considerably larger than the family controlled concerns, in addition to which there were four huge oil companies placed in the "possibly family" category. If these latter corporations were reclassified on the basis of additional evidence, they could tip the scales either way.

[30]See Robert Sheehan, "Proprietors in the World of Big Business," *Fortune* (15 June 1967), p. 182.

[31]Actually, the number of companies included in many of these categories is, from a statistical standpoint, fairly small, but this is an unavoidable result of dealing with just the top 300 concerns. There are, for example, only four companies listed in the publishing category. Nevertheless, when one considers the number of privately owned firms in this field, the above description of the publishing industry as family dominated seems fully justified.

[32]Two other major industrial concerns in this general area—the Scovill Mfg. Co. and United Shoe Machinery Corp.—fell into the "possibly family" category. However, the author felt it best to exclude all such designated companies from any of the regional calculations made in this part of the study.

of the large New York metropolitan area-based corporations (whose control status has been clearly established) are most likely management controlled firms too.[33] But in many other sections of the country the situation is quite different. In Michigan, Illinois and Ohio, for example, there are just about as many family controlled companies as management dominated ones.[34] In Pennsylvania, thanks to a rather unusual set of circumstances, 60 percent (15 out of 25) of the major industrial corporations in the state are probably family controlled firms.[35] As one might expect, this pattern of industrial control is even more pronounced in the less urbanized states of the Midwest. Almost 80 percent (15 out of 19) of this area's big industrial concerns, most of which are located in Minnesota and Missouri, are family controlled companies—a not altogether surprising finding since many are food or beverage firms.[36] Similarly, in the South the great majority of the large corporations are family dominated enterprises (although it is true that the statistical margin is much closer in the big oil-producing states of Texas and Oklahoma). On the Pacific Coast family controlled firms also appear to exceed the number of management dominated concerns, but this dif-

[33] A few of the firms based in New York City are, in point of fact, controlled by foreign economic interests, as in the case of Lever Bros. and the Shell Oil Co., two apparently management dominated corporations. Joseph E. Seagram & Son, Inc. is a subsidiary of a Canadian concern under the effective control of the Bronfman family, which has strong business and marriage ties to certain New York City banking circles, and may thus be considered to some extent an American clan. The Allied Chemical Corp. is also family dominated, but the author is not sure whether control rests with the Solvay forces of Belgium or various American family interests.

[34] In the case of Illinois, four of the eleven firms classified as family controlled are big food concerns, which are as a rule family dominated affairs. However, there are also, by way of counterbalance, a rather large number of Illinois corporations in the "possibly family" category, some of which may actually be family controlled.

[35] This particular state's family control figure would climb to about 70 percent if these computations were made on the basis of the Philadelphia and Pittsburgh metropolitan areas only, for this would eliminate three interior Pennsylvania concerns (the Bethlehem Steel Corp., Armstrong Cork Co., and Hershey Chocolate Corp.) which, like most such companies in upper New York State and New England, are management dominated. One of the reasons for the unusually high family control total in Pennsylvania is that three of the big industrial concerns in Pittsburgh (Alcoa, Gulf Oil Corp., and Koppers Co.) are dominated by the Mellon family. Moreover, two other Pittsburgh-based firms—the Consolidation Coal Co. and National Steel Corp.—are controlled by the Hanna interests of Ohio (though they apparently work fairly closely with the Mellon forces). And, as noted before, the Atlantic Refining Co. of Philadelphia has since 1964-65 been controlled by a wealthy New Mexico oilman and rancher (Robert O. Anderson). The Campbell Soup Co. (of Camden, N.J.) has been included in these Pennsylvania computations because it is actually an integral part of the Philadelphia metropolitan area. There were also, it should be observed, two other Pennsylvania companies which were placed in the possibly family control category.

[36] In this particular case, there would appear to be a very definite relationship between region and primary line of activity, for 10 of the 18 food and drink companies classified as management dominated have their main offices located in and around New York City, whereas only 2 of the 25 food and beverage concerns under family control are headquartered there. In this midwestern region, which the author defined as including Minnesota, Iowa, Missouri, Kansas, Nebraska, and the Dakotas, there was one company classified as possibly under family control. In Indiana and Wisconsin, which the author treated separately, the pattern was again one of predominantly family controlled concerns.

ferential (11 to 7) is largely the product of the three Kaiser companies located in the San Francisco Bay area.[37]

These figures notwithstanding, many people may quite understandably assume that the primary factor in determining whether a large industrial corporation is either family or management controlled is not so much a matter of region or line of business as it is a natural, almost inevitable, product of time. Most companies were originally formed, of course, by some family or able and enterprising individual who often, after many years of toil and effort, turned the reins of corporate power over to ambitious offspring or other trusted relatives. However, with the passage of time, the growing complexity of industry and technology, and frequently the loss of family entrepreneurial interest, many companies, it is argued, have passed rather logically into management hands. Thus, according to this line of reasoning, the older the company the more likely it is to be under firm management control. Yet actual investigation of the facts reveals that there is apparently relatively little truth to this contention. The author, for instance, compared the dates of establishment of over 150 of the top 300 industrial concerns and found that, with reference to those started prior to World War I, there was only a comparatively slight difference in the proportion of firms now classified as either family or management controlled.[38] All told, two-thirds of the family controlled firms examined were started back in the pre-World War I era, while close to 75 percent of the management dominated companies were established in this early industrial period.[39] Other evidence that time alone is not the principal determinant of a company's control status may be seen in the fact that most of the big aircraft and defense contract concerns, which grew to giant proportions during World War II and subsequent years of international tension and conflict, are management dominated. Thus, judging by these data, it would certainly seem that region and line of economic activity are more important factors than age of company. However, in conclusion, it should also be emphasized that these particular findings are only of a preliminary nature and that obviously much more research needs to be done in this area.

[37]If, for purposes of statistical analysis, the three big Kaiser concerns were simply counted as one huge company, this would bring the probably family controlled total down to nine, only two more than the number of management dominated corporations. There were also eight other firms in this area which, for lack of additional pertinent data, were placed in the possibly family control category.

[38]The two major categories of companies excluded from these computations are those placed in the indeterminate "possibly family" group and those engaged in the manufacture of food and beverages, an unusual number of which are family controlled firms concentrated in the Midwest. The above figures, it should be borne in mind, are simply overall findings. In some areas of economic activity, time has apparently played a fairly decisive role in determining the character of corporate control.

[39]As one might gather from this statement, the great majority of the fortunes generated by these large corporate enterprises date back many years. In only a comparatively small number of cases can the individuals and families listed in this study be said to represent new wealth. Some of the most conspicuous such figures are the late Henry J. Kaiser (primary metals and defense); Henry Crown (contracting, defense, and other investments); J. Paul Getty (oil); and Norton Simon (food and other interests).

# 4

## Corporate Control Analysis of Major American Merchandising, Transportation, and Commercial Banking Concerns

Utilizing basically the same approach as employed in the preceding chapter, the author, as indicated earlier, has made a similar control status study of the 50 largest merchandising firms, 50 biggest transportation companies, and top 50 commercial banks in the country as of the mid-1960s (using the rankings found in the August 1965 issue of *Fortune* magazine). That is to say, the author classified the above-listed concerns as probably family controlled (PF) only if two important conditions were met. One was that at least about 4 or 5 percent of the voting stock be held by one or more families or wealthy persons according to some authoritative business or professional source or government publication (such as *Forbes, Fortune* or the SEC *Official Summary*) or, alternatively and less frequently, a statement that a particular corporation was family dominated in one of these news articles. The second condition was that there must have been either inside or outside representation (with, as a matter of fact, often both forms of representation) on the part of a family on the board of directors of the company, generally over an extended period of time (10 years or more). In almost every instance of such control identified in this section of the study, documentation has once again been provided in the form of one or more specific citations, which usually contained recent stock ownership statistics. In addition, as in Table 3-1, other pertinent information has been supplied in the same column (labeled "Evidence or Comments") as to whether the dominant family or individual has been associated with a company through outside representation on the board of directors (O-BD), the holding of important managerial posts (I-BD), or some combination of the two (I & O-BD), ordinarily over a fairly long period of time. In those cases where control seemed to rest with a single affluent individual or entrepreneur rather than with a family or group of families, this state of affairs has been signified by the insertion of an "I" in parenthesis after the abbreviation PF (probably family).

The second control category used in this analysis, the designation "possibly family" (F?) which is discussed in more detail in Chapter 3, has been employed to describe those firms which showed some definite signs of family influence (usually in the form of representation on the board of directors), but for which there were insufficient data available to make a reliable assessment of corporate control status. However, in every instance some evidence has been presented (minimally specified in abbreviated board of directorship terms) for placing a concern in this category, and one or more families have been identified as being prominently associated with the company in question.

**Table 4-1**
**Company-by-Company Corporate Control Analysis of America's Top 50 Merchandising Firms, Top 50 Transportation Companies, and Top 50 Commercial Banks as of 1965**

Abbreviation Key: Same as Table 3-1, except for U.S. Select Committee on Small Business, House of Representatives, 87th Congress, *Chain Banking* (Washington, D.C.: Government Printing Office, 1963)—hereafter referred to as the 1963 *Chain Banking* report

## MERCHANDISING FIRMS

| 1965 Rank (based on 1964 volume of sales) | Name of Company | Type of Control | Evidence or Comments |
|---|---|---|---|
| 1. | Sears, Roebuck & Co. | PM | |
| 2. | Great Atlantic & Pacific Tea Co. | F? | As of 1963, nearly one-third of stock held by the Hartford family heirs and approximately one-third by the management-dominated John A. Hartford Foundation (see *Fortune*, March 1963, p. 106, and 1 September 1968, p. 144); only indirect (outside) family representation on board of directors in recent years |
| 3. | Safeway Stores, Inc. | F? | May be controlled by Merrill (Lynch) interests—as of 1955 Merrill family interests owned over 5.7% of the stock (see *Forbes*, 15 September 1955, p. 36)—in addition, see *Fortune*, October 1958, p. 116 and *Business Week*, 13 April 1957, p. 64; also I & O-BD over the years. |
| 4. | Kroger Co. | PM | |
| 5. | J.C. Penney Co. | PM | |
| 6. | Montgomery Ward & Co. | PM | |
| 7. | F.W. Woolworth Co. | F? | As of 1960 founders' heirs controlled about 5% of the stock, A.P. Kirby's total being about 3.7% (see *Fortune*, January 1960, p. 216); also O-BD over the years |

|  |  | | | |
|---|---|---|---|---|
| 8. | Federated Dept. Stores, Inc. | | PF | Controlled by the Lazarus family (see *Time*, 19 January 1968, p. 83 and *Forbes*, 1 October 1967, p. 66 and 15 February 1970, p. 49); also I-BD over the years |
| 9. | Acme Markets, Inc. | | PF | As of the late 1950s through the mid-1960s, the Robinson and Park families had at least 3.8% of the stock (see SEC *OS*, February 1958, January 1961, June 1963, and March 1965); also I-BD over the years |
| 10. | National Tea Co. | | PF(I) (foreign) | As of the mid-1960s, 57% of the stock controlled (through a series of other concerns) by W.G. Weston of Canada (see *Fortune*, 1 June 1967, pp. 118-19); also I & O-BD over the years |
| 11. | Food Fair Stores, Inc. | | PF | As of the mid-1960s, 30% of the stock owned by the Friedland family (see *Forbes*, 1 August 1965, p. 14); also I & O-BD over the years |
| 12. | Allied Stores Corp. | PM | | |
| 13. | Winn-Dixie Stores, Inc. | | PF | As of the mid-1960s, 28% of the stock owned by the Davis family (see *Forbes*, 15 May 1964, p. 38); also I-BD over the years |
| 14. | McKesson & Robbins, Inc. | PM | | |
| 15. | Jewel Tea Co. | PM | | |
| 16. | May Dept. Stores Co. | | PF | As of the mid-1960s, the May family had a minimum of 3.9% of the stock (see SEC *OS*, January 1965, and January, July and October 1966); also I-BD over the years |
| 17. | W.T. Grant Co. | | PF(I) | As of the early 1960s, 16.6% of the stock owned by W.T. Grant (see SEC *OS*, June 1961); also I-BD over the years |

**Table 4-1** *(cont.)*

| 1965 Rank | Name of Company | Type of Control | Evidence or Comments |
|---|---|---|---|
| 18. | Grand Union Co. | PM | |
| 19. | First National Stores, Inc. | PF | Probably controlled by the O'Keeffe family (see *Forbes*, 1 October 1967, p. 26); also I & O-BD over the years |
| 20. | S.S. Kresge Co. | PF | As of the mid-1960s about 29.4% of the stock owned by the Kresge Foundation (see 1965 *Moody's Industrial Manual*, p. 587), which is probably family controlled; also I-BD over the years |
| 21. | Consolidated Foods Corp. | PF | As of 1965 7.8% of the stock owned by Nathan Cummings (see SEC *OS*, September 1965); also I & O-BD over the years |
| 22. | R.H. Macy & Co. | PF | As of 1965 the Straus family had about 7% of all the presumably voting stock (see *Time*, 8 January 1965, p. 60); also I & O-BD over the years |
| 23. | McCrory Corp. | PF(I) | As of the early 1960s M. Riklis and associates had over 40% of the stock of the Rapid-American Corp., which in turn controlled 38% of the stock of the McCrory Corp. (see *Fortune*, February 1962, p. 123 and *Forbes*, 15 January 1969, p. 43); also I-BD in recent years |
| 24. | Graybar Electric Co. | PM | |
| 25. | Gimbel Bros., Inc. | PF | As of 1965 B.F. Gimbel and associates had 14.1% of the stock (see 1965 *Moody's Industrial Manual*, p. 260); also I & O-BD over the years |
| 26. | Anderson, Clayton & Co. | PF | Clayton family owned about 40% of the stock as of both 1959 and 1969 (see *Time*, 17 August 1959, p. 86 and *Forbes* 15 September 1969, p. 74); also I & O-BD over the years |

| No. | Company | Code | Notes |
|---|---|---|---|
| 27. | Gamble-Skogmo, Inc. | PF | In recent years the Gamble family probably owned most of the stock of Founders, Inc., which in turn controlled 37.7% of the stock of Gamble-Skogmo (see 1965 *Moody's Industrial Manual*, p. 1367, *Fortune*, October 1960, p. 223 and *Forbes*, 1 April 1962, p. 33)—according to the *SEC OS* (December 1963), B.C. Gamble owned indirectly (largely through Founders, Inc.) about 31.7% of the stock as of the mid-1960s; also I-BD over the years |
| 28. | E.J. Korvette, Inc. | PF(I) | E. Ferkauf owned 28% of the stock as of 1962 (see *Time*, 6 July 1962, p. 61); also I-BD in recent years |
| 29. | Colonial Stores, Inc. | PF(I) | As of the mid-1960s R.B. Stearns controlled 25% of the stock of the Nat'l. Food Products Corp. which, in turn, owned 33.7% of the stock of Colonial Stores (see *S&P Corporation Records*, Vol. L-O, June-July 1967, p. 7218); also I-BD over the years |
| 30. | Super Valu Stores, Inc. | F? | Newell family*—see I & O-BD over the years |
| 31. | Arden-Mayfair, Inc. | PM | |
| 32. | Associated Dry Goods Corp. | PM | |
| 33. | Minerals & Chemical Philip Corp. | PF | As of 1965 20% of the stock owned by Engelhard Hanovia, Inc., a family-controlled holding company (see *Forbes*, 1 August 1965, p. 20); also I-BD in recent years |
| 34. | Allied Supermarkets, Inc. | PF(I) | As of the early 1960s 5.5% of the stock owned by C. Allen, Jr. and associates of New York City (see SEC *OS*, September 1960 and July 1961); also O-BD over the years |
| 35. | City Products Corp. | F? | H. Crown and Sinek interests? (see *Fortune*, October 1955, p. 125 and also August 1956, p. 122); also I & O-BD over the years |

**Table 4-1** *(cont.)*

| 1965 Rank | Name of Company | Type of Control | Evidence or Comments |
|---|---|---|---|
| 36. | Stop & Shop, Inc. | PF | As of 1965 26% of the stock owned by the Rabb family (see *Fortune*, December 1965, p. 84); also **I-BD** over the years |
| 37. | Walgreen Co. | PF | As of the mid-1960s the Walgreen family owned at least 4.8% of the stock (see SEC *OS*, January 1964); also **I**-BD over the years |
| 38. | Interstate Dept. Stores, Inc. | PM | |
| 39. | Western Auto Supply Co. | PM | Controlled by the Beneficial Finance Co. (most likely a management firm) |
| 40. | J.J. Newberry Co. | PF | In recent years approximately 30% of the stock owned by the Newberry family (see SEC *OS*, July 1959, October 1964, and June 1965); also **I** & O-BD over the years |
| 41. | City Stores Co. | PF | Controlled by the Bankers Securities Corp. (see the 1965 *Moody's Bank & Finance Manual*, p. 1210) which was controlled in turn by A.M. Greenfield who had, directly or indirectly, about 59% of the stock (see SEC *OS*, January 1958); also **I** & O-BD over the years |
| 42. | Fleming Co. | PF | As of 1965, the Fleming family had 13.8% of the stock (see the 1966 *Moody's Industrial Manual*, p. 380); also **I**-BD over the years |
| 43. | Lucky Stores, Inc. | PM | |
| 44. | Food Giant Markets, Inc. | PF(I) | As of 1965 H.L. Fierman had 8.4% of the stock and T.E. Cummings had 17.1% (see SEC *OS*, November 1965); also **I**-BD in recent years |

| | Name of Company | Type of Control | Evidence or Comments |
|---|---|---|---|
| 45. | Red Owl Stores, Inc. | PF | As of the mid-1960s the Ford Bell family (of Minn.) owned 17% of the stock (see 1967 *Moody's Industrial Manual*, p. 1986); also I-BD over the years |
| 46. | Spiegel, Inc. | PF | Spiegel family had 20% of the stock as of 1961 (see *Fortune*, June 1961, p. 152); also I-BD over the years |
| 47. | G.C. Murphy Co. | F? | Shaw and Paxton families?—see I-BD over the years |
| 48. | Marshall Field & Co. | F? | Field family?—see O-BD over the years |
| 49. | Southland Corp. | PF | As of the mid-1960s the Thompson family had 16.7% of the stock (see SEC *OS*, March 1967); also I-BD over the years |
| 50. | Automatic Canteen Co. of America | PF(I) or syndicate | As of the early 1960s N. Leverone had about 6.0% of the stock (see SEC *OS*, January 1961); with regard to the Lannan interests, see *Time*, 25 July 1955, p. 81; also I or O-BD over the years |
| Total | | 14 (28%) | 7 (14%)     29 (58%) |

## TRANSPORTATION COMPANIES

| 1965 Rank (based on 1964 operating revenues) | Name of Company | Type of Control | Evidence or Comments |
|---|---|---|---|
| 1. | Southern Pacific Co. | PM | |
| 2. | Pennsylvania RR | F? | A little over 10% of the stock was controlled in the mid-1960s by Howard Butcher III (see *Forbes*, 1 May 1962, p. 34 and 15 December 1965, p. 26); also O-BD in recent years—perhaps a number of "old Philadelphia" families involved too |

**Table 4-1** (*cont.*)

| 1965 Rank | Name of Company | Type of Control | Evidence or Comments |
|---|---|---|---|
| 3. | New York Central RR | PF | In 1964-65 about 15% of the stock was owned by the Alleghany Corp., 60% of whose stock in turn was controlled by the Kirby family associated with F.W. Woolworth Co. (see the 1966 *Moody's Transportation Manual*, p. 1201 and *NYT*, 15 September 1967, p. 69); also I & O-BD in recent years |
| 4. | Atchison, Topeka & Sante Fe RR | PM | |
| 5. | United Air Lines, Inc. | PM | |
| 6. | Pan American World Airways, Inc. | PM | |
| 7. | Trans World Airlines, Inc. | PM | |
| 8. | Union Pacific RR | PF | Controlled by the Harriman family, although it had only about 3% of the common stock as of the mid-1960s (see *Forbes*, 1 March 1967, p. 36); also I & O-BD over the years |
| 9. | Norfolk & Western Rwy. | F? (indirectly) | According to the 1966 *Moody's Transportation Manual*, (p. 1234), about 56% of the stock owned (through a subsidiary) by the PRR, which might be considered a family firm in recent years; also O-BD over the years |
| 10. | American Airlines, Inc. | PM | |
| 11. | Greyhound Corp. | PM | |

| No. | Company | PM | F? | PF | Notes |
|---|---|---|---|---|---|
| 12. | Eastern Air Lines, Inc. | | F? | | L. Rockefeller has owned about 3.2% of the stock in recent years (see SEC OS, May 1959 and Time, 26 November 1963, p. 94); also O-BD over the years |
| 13. | Missouri-Pacific RR | PM | | | |
| 14. | Baltimore & Ohio RR | | | PF (indirectly) | Controlled by the Chesapeake & Ohio Rwy. in recent years (see the 1966 Moody's Transportation Manual, p. 1302); also O-BD in recent years |
| 15. | Chesapeake & Ohio Rwy. | | | PF | Probably controlled by Cyrus Eaton—as of the mid or late 1950s, Eaton and kin had at least 3.3% of the stock (see Forbes, 1 May 1956, p. 17, Time, 19 January 1959, p. 80, and SEC OS, July 1955 and June 1957); also I & O-BD over the years |
| 16. | Southern Rwy. | | F? | | Milbank and Leisenring families? (with regard to the latter, see Forbes, 1 September 1971, p. 29); also O-BD over the years |
| 17. | Illinois Central RR | | | PF (indirectly) | Through the mid-1950s and 1960s the Harriman-dominated Union Pacific RR probably exercised control through the ownership of about 24% of the stock (see SEC OS, February 1955, Forbes, 1 June 1966, p. 22, and NYT, 2 September 1971, p. 47); also O-BD over the years |
| 18. | Chicago, Burlington & Quincy RR | PM | | | Great Northern Rwy. and Northern Pacific Rwy. each owned about 48.6% of the stock (see the 1966 Moody's Transportation Manual, p. 543). |
| 19. | Louisville & Nashville RR | | F? (indirectly) | | May be controlled indirectly (through Mercantile Safe Deposit & Trust Co. of Baltimore) by Thomas Baldwin Butler (see NYT, 21 November 1969, p. 77) |
| 20. | Great Northern Rwy. | PM | | | |

**Table 4-1** *(cont.)*

| 1965 Rank | Name of Company | Type of Control | Evidence or Comments |
|---|---|---|---|
| 21. | Delta Air Lines, Inc. | F? | Woolman and perhaps one other family?–C.E. Woolman has at least 3.1% of the stock (see SEC *OS*, July 1966, *Business Week*, 25 November 1961, p. 63 and *NYT*, 25 April 1964, p. 32); also I-BD over the years |
| 22. | Chicago, Milwaukee, St. Paul & Pacific RR | PF(I) | As of 1956 about 13% of the voting stock controlled by J.P. Lannan and A.M. Wirtz or a syndicate headed by them (see *Fortune*, August 1956, p. 190)–in addition, see *Forbes*, 15 November 1959, p. 21; also I & O-BD over the years |
| 23. | Northern Pacific Rwy. | PM | |
| 24. | Chicago & North Western Rwy. | PM | |
| 25. | Erie-Lackawanna RR | PM | |
| 26. | Northwest Airlines, Inc. | PM | |
| 27. | Consolidated Freightways, Inc. | PM | |
| 28. | Chicago, Rock Island & Pacific RR | PF | As of 1961 12% of the stock controlled by the H. Crown and Norris families (see *Fortune*, January 1961, p. 144)–according to *Forbes* (15 October 1967) p. 25, the Crown family owned 5-6% of the stock–Crown family listed as having 8.6% as of mid-1968 (see *Forbes*, 15 July 1968, p. 32)–in addition, see *Forbes*, 15 January 1966, p. 42; also O-BD over the years |
| 29. | Atlantic Coast Line RR | F? | May be controlled indirectly (through the Mercantile Safe Deposit & Trust Co. of Baltimore) by Thomas Baldwin Butler (see *NYT*, 21 November 1969, p. 77); also I-BD in recent years |

| | | | | |
|---|---|---|---|---|
| 30. | Seaboard Air Line RR | PM | | |
| 31. | U.S. Lines Co. | | F? | As of 1956 Vincent Astor had about 4.9% of the stock (see SEC *OS*, July 1956; also O-BD over the years)—Franklin family may also be involved (see I-BD over the years) |
| 32. | St. Louis—San Francisco Rwy. | PM | | |
| 33. | McLean Industries, Inc. | | PF | As of the mid-1960s the McLean family had at least 40.3% of the stock (see SEC *OS*, February and May 1967); also I-BD over the years |
| 34. | National Airlines, Inc. | | PF(I) | 14.5% of the stock held by L.B. Maytag, Jr. (a member of the Maytag Co. family) and D. Swim in recent years (see *NYT*, 12 April 1962, p. 49 and 12 July 1962, p. 36, as well as *Forbes*, 1 June 1967, p. 51); also I-BD in recent years |
| 35. | Pacific Intermountain Express Co. | PM | | |
| 36. | New York, New Haven & Hartford RR | PM | | |
| 37. | Western Air Lines, Inc. | PM | | |
| 38. | American Export Isbrandtsen Lines | | PF (foreign) | Controlled by Holland's Isbrandtsen family, which has had about 26% of the stock in recent years (see *Forbes*, 1 August 1962, p. 32); also I-BD in recent years |
| 39. | Matson Navigation Co. | | PF | As of mid-1960s 93.7% of the stock owned by Alexander & Baldwin, Inc., 20.3% of whose stock was in turn owned by Baldwin family of Hawaii (see S&P *Corporation Records*, Vol. L-O, June-July 1967, p. 8369 and Vol. A-B, June-July 1967, p. 6582); also O-BD in recent years |

Table 4-1 (cont.)

| 1965 Rank | Name of Company | Type of Control | Evidence or Comments |
|---|---|---|---|
| 40. | Braniff Airways, Inc. | PF(I) | 58% of the stock owned by the Greatamerica Corp., 40% of whose voting stock was in turn owned by T.V. Post (see the 1965 *Moody's Bank & Finance Manual*, p. 1668 and *Fortune*, January 1965, p. 184); also I-BD in recent years |
| 41. | Roadway Express, Inc. | PF | As of mid-1960s the Roush family had at least 11.3% of the stock and possibly as much as 44% of the stock (see SEC *OS*, July 1967 and September 1971); also I-BD over the years |
| 42. | Leaseway Transportation Corp. | PF | As of the mid-1960s the O'Neill family had at least 36.9% of the stock (see SEC *OS*, April 1967 and August 1968); also I-BD in recent years |
| 43. | Reading Co. | PF (indirectly) | Chesapeake & Ohio Rwy. had in 1965 (indirectly—through the B&O RR) about 38.3% of the stock (see the 1966 *Moody's Transportation Manual*, p. 183); also O-BD in recent years |
| 44. | American President Lines, Ltd. | PF | As of 1965, 52% of the stock owned by the Natomas Co. (see the 1965 *Moody's Industrial Manual*, pp. 1814-15), 29.4% of whose stock was owned by R.K. Davies of San Francisco (see SEC *OS*, January 1965); also I & O-BD over the years |
| 45. | Moore-McCormack Lines, Inc. | PF | As of 1955 the (Wm. T.) Moore and McCormack families (of New York City) held about 16.4% of the stock (see SEC *OS*, January 1955)—Moore family interests still have about 5% of the stock (see S&P *Standard Listed Stock Reports*, 19 July 1968, p. 1550); also I & O-BD over the years |
| 46. | Continental Air Lines, Inc. | PM | |

| No. | Name of Company | Type of Control | | | Evidence or Comments |
|---|---|---|---|---|---|
| 47. | Soo Line RR | PM | | | |
| 48. | Associated Transport, Inc. | | PF | | Probably controlled by the Horton and perhaps Seymour families—as of the mid-1960s the Horton family (of Charlotte, N.C.) had about 14% of the stock (see *S&P Corporation Records*, Vol. A-B, October-November 1967, p. 6171); also I & O-BD over the years |
| 49. | Denver & Rio Grande Western RR | PM | | F? | (John) Evans family (of Denver)?—see I-BD over the years |
| 50. | Gulf, Mobile & Ohio RR | PM | | | |
| | Total | 23 (46%) | 9 (18%) | 18 (36%) | |

## COMMERCIAL BANKS

| 1965 Rank (based on 1964 assets or resources) | Name of Company | Type of Control | | | Evidence or Comments |
|---|---|---|---|---|---|
| 1. | Bank of America (SF) | PM | | | |
| 2. | Chase Manhattan Bank (NYC) | | PF | | Rockefeller family and associated interests have had about 5% of the stock in recent years (see *Time*, 24 December 1956, p. 57 and 7 September 1962, p. 67; plus Jules Abels, *The Rockefeller Billions*, The Macmillan Co., New York, 1965, p. 358); also I & O-BD over the years |
| 3. | First National City Bank (NYC) | | | F? | Possibly controlled by the Taylor-Pyne, Stillman-Rockefeller and perhaps other Standard Oil families (see, for example, *Fortune*, September 1965, p. 138); also I & O-BD over the years |

**Table 4-1** *(cont.)*

| 1965 Rank | Name of Company | Type of Control | Evidence or Comments |
|---|---|---|---|
| 4. | Manufacturers Hanover Trust Co. (NYC) | PM | |
| 5. | Chemical Bank New York Trust Co. (NYC) | PM | |
| 6. | Morgan Guaranty Trust Co. (NYC) | PM | |
| 7. | Continental Illinois National Bank & Trust Co. (Chicago) | PM | |
| 8. | Security First Natl. Bank (LA) | PM | |
| 9. | Bankers Trust Co. (NYC) | PM | |
| 10. | 1st Natl. Bank of Chicago | PM | |
| 11. | Wells Fargo Bank (SF) | F? | Hellman family?–see I & O-BD over the years |
| 12. | Crocker-Citizens Natl. Bank (SF) | PF | As of 1963 the Crocker family had about 3.5% of the stock and its Provident Securities Co. had another 5.3% (see 1963 *Chain Banking* report, p. 280 and *NYT*, 5 September 1969, p. 53); also I & O-BD over the years |
| 13. | Mellon Natl. Bank & Trust Co. (Pittsburgh) | PF | According to the 1963 *Chain Banking* report (p. 175), the Mellon family had at least 29.4% of the stock–according to *Forbes* (1 May 1964) p. 22 and *Fortune* (October 1967), p. 122, the Mellon family owned around 40% of the stock; also I & O-BD over the years |
| 14. | Irving Trust Co. (NYC) | PM | |

| # | Bank | | | | Notes |
|---|------|---|---|---|-------|
| 15. | United Calif. Bank (LA) | PM | | | Subsidiary of the Western Bancorporation (most likely a management firm) |
| 16. | Natl. Bank of Detroit | | | PF | Probably controlled by certain GM families—as of 1963 E.E. Fisher and Fisher & Co. owned 4.4% of the stock and C.S. Mott had another 0.9% (see 1963 *Chain Banking* report, pp. 227 and 416); also I & O-BD over the years |
| 17. | 1st Natl. Bank of Boston | PM | | | |
| 18. | Cleveland Trust Co. | | | PF(I) | According to *Forbes* (15 April 1967), p. 26, George Gund owned more than 10% of the stock; also I-BD over the years |
| 19. | 1st Penna. Banking & Trust Co. (Phila.) | PM | | | |
| 20. | Franklin Natl. Bank (Mineola, N.Y.) | | F? | | As of 1963 the Roth family (of Mineola, N.Y.) owned at least 2.8% of the stock (see 1963 *Chain Banking* report, p. 126); also I-BD over the years |
| 21. | Republic Natl. Bank of Dallas | | | PF(I) | As of 1963 K. Hoblitzelle owned 1.9% of the stock, the Hoblitzelle Foundation 1.3% of the stock, and the Hoblitzelle Profit Sharing Trust another 3.0% (see 1963 *Chain Banking* report, p. 260); also I-BD over the years |
| 22. | Harris Trust & Savings Bank (Chicago) | | | PF | As of 1963 the Harris family owned 30.6% of the stock (see 1963 *Chain Banking* report, p. 215); also I & O-BD over the years |
| 23. | 1st Natl. Bank of Dallas | PM | | | |
| 24. | Manufacturers Natl. Bank of Detroit | | | PF | As of 1963 the Ford family (of the Detroit automobile industry) owned at least 3.7% of the stock (see 1963 *Chain Banking* report, p. 225); also O-BD over the years |

**Table 4-1** (*cont.*)

| 1965 Rank | Name of Company | Type of Control | Evidence or Comments |
|---|---|---|---|
| 25. | Philadelphia Natl. Bank | PM | |
| 26. | Detroit Bank & Trust Co. | F? | As of 1962 the Couzens family owned at least 4.4% of the stock (see the 1963 *Chain Banking* report, p. 224); also O-BD over the years |
| 27. | Seattle-First Natl. Bank | PM | |
| 28. | Pittsburgh Natl. Bank | PF | Controlled by the Hillman family of Pittsburgh—as of 1963 the J.H. Hillman & Sons Co. owned 8.7% of the stock and the Hillman Foundation had another 1.0% (see 1963 *Chain Banking* report, p. 176)—as of 1969 the Hillman family had 5.9% of the stock (see *Forbes*, 15 September 1969, p. 54); also O-BD over the years |
| 29. | Union Bank (LA) | F? | Possibly controlled by the Volk family (see *NYT*, 18 July 1971, Sect. 3, p. 5); also I-BD in recent years |
| 30. | 1st Natl. Bank of Oregon (Portland) | PM | Affiliate or subsidiary of the Western Bancorporation (most likely a management firm) |
| 31. | U.S. Natl. Bank of Portland | PM | |
| 32. | Bank of California (SF) | PM | |
| 33. | Marine Trust Co. of Western N.Y. (Buffalo) | F? (indirectly) | Subsidiary of the Marine Midland Corp. which may be controlled by the Schoellkopf and other families (see *NYT*, 24 April 1966, Sec. 3, p. 1 and 14 November 1967, p. 63); also O-BD over the years and I-BD starting in 1966 |

| No. | Bank | PM | F? | PF | Notes |
|---|---|---|---|---|---|
| 34. | Northern Trust Co. (Chicago) | | | PF | As of 1963 the Smith family (of Chicago) had 34.1% of the stock (see 1963 *Chain Banking* report, pp. 218 and 408); also I & O-BD over the years |
| 35. | Marine Midland Trust Co. of NYC | | F? (indirectly) | | Subsidiary of the Marine Midland Corp. which may be controlled by the Schoellkopf and other families (see *NYT*, 24 April 1966, Sec. 3, p. 1 and 14 November 1967, p. 63); also O-BD over the years and I-BD starting in 1966 |
| 36. | Natl. City Bank of Cleveland | | F? | | As of 1963 3.3% of the stock controlled by the M.A. Hanna Co. (see 1963 *Chain Banking* report, p. 165), which was in turn controlled by the Hanna family (see *Forbes*, 1 November 1955, p. 16); also O-BD over the years |
| 37. | Wachovia Bank & Trust Co. (N.C.) | | F? | | Hanes and certain other N.C. textile and tobacco families? (see *Business Week*, 24 September 1960, pp. 122-32); and also I & O-BD over the years |
| 38. | Valley Natl. Bank (Phoenix) | | F? | | Binson family?—see I-BD over the years |
| 39. | Girard Trust Bank (Phila.) | PM | | | |
| 40. | 1st City Natl. Bank of Houston | | | PF | Probably controlled by Elkins and also perhaps the Anderson families—as of 1963 4.0% of the stock owned by the Elkins family, 1.0% by the Elkins, Weems . . . law firm, and 2.0% by W.I. Weems (see 1963 *Chain Banking* report, p. 264); also see *Business Week*, 31 July 1965, p. 89; also I & O-BD over the years |
| 41. | Mercantile Trust Co. (St. Louis) | PM | | | |
| 42. | Central Natl. Bank (Cleveland) | PM | | | |

**Table 4-1** (*cont.*)

| 1965 Rank | Name of Company | Type of Control | Evidence or Comments |
|---|---|---|---|
| 43. | First Wisconsin Natl. Bank (Milwaukee) | PF (indirectly) | Subsidiary of the First Wisconsin Bankshares Corp., which has probably been controlled by the Uihlein family which had at least 6.7% of the stock and very likely as much as 7.7% as of 1963 (see U.S. House of Representatives, Committee on Currency and Banking, *Bank Holding Companies: Scope of Operations and Stock Ownership*, 88th Congress, U.S. Government Printing Office, Washington, D.C., 1963, p. 82); according to the SEC, the Uihlein family owned at least 12.2% of the stock of the First Wisconsin Bankshares Corp. as of 1961 (see SEC *OS*, January and February 1961); also O-BD over the years |
| 44. | Texas Natl. Bank of Commerce (Houston) | PF | As of 1963 23.3% of the stock owned by the Houston Endowment and another 22.4% by the Commerce Co. (see 1963 *Chain Banking* report, p. 265), both of which have been controlled by the (Jesse) Jones family (see *NYT*, 28 July 1956, p. 17 and 4 September 1965, p. 18)—according to *Business Week* (26 December 1964), p. 46, 53% of stock owned by the Jones family interests; also I & O-BD over the years |
| 45. | Meadow Brook Natl. Bank (Jamaica, N.Y.) | F? (indirectly) | Since early 1965 a subsidiary of the C.I.T. Financial Corp., a concern which may be controlled by S.M. Shoenberg (of May Dept. Stores) and certain other family interests (see, for example, SEC *OS*, July 1966 and January 1968); also I & OD (of C.I.T. Financial Corp.) over the years |
| 46. | Michigan Natl. Bank (Lansing) | PF | As of 1963 the Stoddard family had at least 6.8% of the stock (see 1963 *Chain Banking* report, p. 419); also I & O-BD over the years |

| | |  | | |
|---|---|---|---|---|
| 47. | Fidelity-Phila. Trust Co. | PM | | |
| 48. | 1st Natl. Bank of St. Louis | PM | | |
| 49. | Citizens & Southern Natl. Bank (Georgia) | | PF | Probably controlled by the Lane family (see *Fortune*, November 1969, p. 135 and *Business Week*, 25 July 1970, p. 34)—I & O-BD over the years |
| 50. | Bank of New York | PM | | |
| | Total | 24 (48%) | 11 (22%) | 15 (30%) |

Notes: For the above ranking of the top 50 merchandising firms, top 50 transportation companies, and top 50 commercial banks, see "The Fortune Directory," *Fortune* (August 1965), pp. 174-80.

All divisional computations based on SEC *Official Summary* data were done by slide rule, which it was felt was sufficiently accurate for purposes of this study. In some instances a number of monthly SEC stock ownership citations are listed in the "Evidence or Comments" column, none of which may refer to the holdings of the family or families identified as controlling a particular concern. In such cases there is, as a rule, only one large stock ownership figure listed in each of the company's monthly entries, and the reader can usually assume that the person holding these shares is related to the firm's economically dominant family, a fact which can frequently be corroborated through the use of *Who's Who in America* or some other reliable source of biographical information.

The third control classification utilized in this study, probably management (PM), includes those concerns which appeared to be management dominated. In all firms so designated, the author found no significant stock ownership data or other evidence, such as representation on boards of directors, which would indicate that these companies were under family control. Consequently, except in certain special cases, no facts or figures have been presented in Table 4-1 concerning corporations considered management controlled.

The data sources used in this nonindustrial phase of the corporate control survey are essentially the same as those relied on in the preceding chapter, except that more frequent reference has been made, in the absence of other pertinent stock ownership information, in the third part of this analysis to the 1963 House Select Committee on Small Business report, *Chain Banking*.

The author's overall findings are presented in Table 4-1, which contains a company-by-company breakdown of the control status of the aforementioned *Fortune* top 50 merchandising, top 50 transportation, and top 50 commercial banking concerns, grouped by general economic category (with, in each case of probably family control, considerable supporting data).

The pertinent statistical totals, culled from the above threefold set of data, are as follows:

**Corporate Control Summary of Table 4-1 Findings for the First 50** *Fortune-***Ranked Publicly Owned Merchandising Firms, Transportation Companies, and Commercial Banks as of 1965**

| Business Category | Probably Management Control | Possibly Family Control | Probably Family Control |
|---|---|---|---|
| Merchandising firms—top 50 | 28.0% | 14.0% | 58.0% |
| Transportation companies—top 50 | 46.0 | 18.0 | 36.0 |
| Commercial banks—top 50 | 48.0 | 22.0 | 30.0 |

Thus it is plain to see that the big merchandising concerns in the United States are, more often than not, probably family firms, with 58 percent of the top 50 corporations placed in this control category. However, this figure is somewhat deceiving, for, as pointed out before (with reference to the major industrial concerns), it excludes a number of very large privately owned companies which should have been incorporated in these computations. As a look at the first part of Chapter 2 (especially Table 2-1) readily reveals, at least three big essentially privately owned enterprises—Cargill, Inc., the Continental Grain Co., and the Sperry & Hutchinson Co.—and one large wholesale trading concern—the probably management dominated United Fruit Co.—were omitted from the *Fortune* ranking; all four of these were of sufficient size to be included in the top 50 merchandising category.[1] If these corporations were added into these tabulations (thereby pushing out four other companies previously in this select first 50 ranking, two of which were possibly family firms and two probably management controlled), it would alter the above findings to the point where 60 percent of these concerns would be considered probably family controlled and 30 percent probably management dominated (with the other 10 percent falling in the more indeterminate possibly family category). Thus, on the basis of these data, it may be said that, with regard to the field of merchandising, there were twice as many probably family-controlled firms as managerially-dominated companies in the United States as of the mid-1960s.

Similarly, it should be noted that the above transportation control findings should not be viewed as final, totally accurate figures either, for they too do not reflect certain huge privately owned operations which loom very large in the overall national transportation picture. As pointed out in the first part of Chapter 2, there are three giant transportation complexes in particular–Daniel K. Ludwig's billion dollar (oil tanker) shipping empire, the family dominated States Marine Lines (dry cargo), and the big family controlled truck hauling and rental firm, Ryder System, Inc.–which should really be included in the top 50 transportation list. If therefore these three large business enterprises were added to the first 50 *Fortune* ranking (thereby pushing out one probably management company, one probably family concern, and one possibly family firm), it would bring the above probably family control finding up to a total of 40 percent, four points higher than the family control figure originally arrived at.[2]

Now with regard to the nation's top 50 commercial banks, there are, to the best of the author's knowledge, no big privately owned concerns which *Fortune* failed to take into account in the compilation of its first 50 ranking. However, this does not mean that the above statistical summary finding of 48 percent probably management and 30 percent probably family is absolutely correct. The one relatively minor error in this particular set of computations stems instead from the fact that this list was assembled on the basis of the assets (or resources) of the 50 largest individual banks in the country and ignores (except indirectly

---

[1] The author might also have added the Louis Dreyfus Corp. to this list, but did not do so because there was some question as to whether this big trading concern was large enough to warrant top 50 ranking in 1965. *Forbes* estimated that this company had 1964 sales of over $250 million (without specifying how much more), so that one does not really know if the Louis Dreyfus Corp. exceeded the $266 million sales total of the 50th-ranked merchandising firm on *Fortune's* 1965 list. See *Forbes* (1 February 1965), p. 34.

[2] If all, in effect, subsidiary transportation companies were eliminated from these computations–thereby making room for the three above concerns, plus the family dominated Lykes Steamship Co., the probably management controlled U.S. Freight Co., and Chalk family dominated Trans Caribbean Airways, Inc.–the net result would still be an overall 40 percent family control finding and a 46 percent probably management total for the top 50 transportation companies in the United States.

through a few huge affiliated or subsidiary units which actually appear on this top 50 ranking) the various big bank holding companies in the United States, a number of which represent very sizable interstate or intrastate operations. All told, there were a total of six giant bank holding companies—the Western Bancorporation (which controlled 24 different banks in 11 western states), the Marine Midland Corp. (of New York), the Northwest Bancorporation (which controlled 77 different banks in 7 northern plains states), the First Bank Stock Corp. (which controlled 87 different banks in 5 midwestern states), the First Wisconsin Bankshares Corp., and the BancOhio Corp.—which were of sufficient size as of 1965 to be included in the top 50 banking category. Three of these corporations (the Western Bancorporation, Marine Midland Corp., and First Wisconsin Bankshares Corp.) were already represented indirectly in this ranking through their control of five of the big individual commercial banking units found on *Fortune's* top 50 list. If the other three large bank holding companies were incorporated in this tabulation, it would result in the addition of two probably management dominated bank holding companies, the Northwest Bancorporation and First Bank Stock Corp. (which would, it so happens, merely take the place of two of the aforementioned subsidiary units) and one probably family controlled bank holding company, the BancOhio Corp. (which would push the probably management dominated Bank of New York out of the first 50 ranking).[3] Thus, as may be seen by a glance at the following final set of summary figures for the three economic categories analyzed in this chapter, close to one-third of the nation's top 50 commercial banking concerns were probably dominated by various wealthy families as of 1965:[4]

### Revised Final Corporate Control Summary Findings for the First 50 Publicly and Privately Owned Merchandising Firms, Transportation Companies and Commercial Banks as of 1965

| Business Category | Probably Management Control | Possibly Family Control | Probably Family Control |
|---|---|---|---|
| Merchandising firms—top 50 | 30.0% | 10.0% | 60.0% |
| Transportation companies—top 50 | 46.0 | 14.0 | 40.0 |
| Commercial banks—top 50 | 48.0 | 20.0 | 32.0 |

[3] According to a recent Congressional study of bank holding companies, the Wolfe family interests owned at least 5.1 percent of the stock of the BancOhio Corp. as of 1962 (also see I & O-BD over the years), but there was no evidence presented in this publication to indicate the existence of any significant signs of concentrated stock ownership as regards the First Bank Stock Corp. and Northwest Bancorporation. See the U.S. House Committee on Banking and Currency, *Bank Holding Companies: Scope of Operations and Stock Ownership* (Washington, D.C.: U.S. Government Printing Office, 1963), pp. 79-83.

[4] What is more, if the concept of extended, interlocking family circles were accepted and applied to a number of the old established banks in such socially close-knit cities as Boston and Philadelphia, the percentage of family dominated big banks might well climb to an even higher figure (see, for instance, Nathaniel Burt's *The Perennial Philadelphians*, pp. 165 and 596).

Within two of these three top corporate categories, there are also some interesting economic or regional patterns worth noting in the differential control status of various concerns.[5] For instance, proportionately more large airlines are under management control than are American railroads. According to the data presented in Table 4-1, 60 percent of the major airways are most likely management dominated, whereas less than 50 percent of the nation's most important railroads are so controlled. This, it could be argued, is a rather significant finding lending considerable support to the contention that the age of a company is not the principal determinant of its control status, for most of these (27) railroads date back to the latter part of the nineteenth century, while the ten airlines were formed in the late 1920s or 1930s.[6] The big commercial banks of the United States are all, of course, of the same general operational nature, but an analysis of their control status does reveal certain geographic patterns. In the South and the Midwest, for example, the bulk of the large banks are under family control. The majority of the big banks in both the Northeast and the Far West, however, are management dominated, even though those in the latter region are of more recent origin. In at least this major respect, then, there is some similarity between the corporate control pattern of the top 50 commercial banks and that of the 300 largest industrial concerns in the country.

---

[5]According to the author's data contained in Table 4-1, there were no significant economic or operational differences in the area of merchandising. Roughly the same percentage of big retail food stores were found to be under family control as department and chain stores in the country.

[6]The majority of the country's big shipping lines and trucking concerns were found, on the other hand, to be probably family controlled—a fact which, since a sizable percentage of the shipping companies are fairly old and most of trucking firms relatively new, would again indicate that time itself is not one of the most critical factors affecting a company's control status. The number of trucking, shipping, and airline companies involved in these tabulations is, from a statistical point of view, quite small. But, as indicated earlier, since this analysis has been confined to only the very large (most economically dominant) transportation companies, there does not seem to be any way around this problem.

# 5 Summary Findings and Some Unresolved Issues

Obviously, a number of important conclusions can be drawn from this study. For one thing, contrary to what many might think, the rather pervasive family control exercised over a substantial number of the total 450 industrial, merchandising, transportation, and commercial banking concerns included in this analysis is, for the most part, of a very direct and enduring nature. That is to say, not only is this control exercised through significant stock ownership and outside representation on the board of directors, but also, in a great many cases, through a considerable amount of family managerial direction of these major corporate enterprises.[1] As a rule, moreover, a very sizable percentage of these families have wielded this formidable economic power over a fairly long period of time. Evidence for these assertions can be found in the following set of figures, derived from the data presented in Tables 3-1 and 4-1.[2]

**Summary Findings Concerning Family Corporate Leadership Role in Publicly Owned Major American Family-Dominated Business Concerns**

| Business Category | | Percentage of Family Firms in which Family has Served in Various Major Executive Capacities | Percentage of Family Firms Controlled by Such Interests for Roughly a Decade or More |
|---|---|---|---|
| Industrial concerns | top 50 | 80.0% | 90.0% |
| | top 100 | 86.1 | 94.4 |
| | top 200 | 91.1 | 96.2 |
| | top 300 | 93.0 | 95.3 |
| Merchandising firms | top 50 | 96.5 | 82.8 |
| Transportation companies | top 50 | 76.5 | 55.6 |
| Commercial banks | top 50 | 80.0 | 100.0 |

[1] One very revealing, though perhaps atypical, example of how family influence can play an apparently decisive role in the rise and fall of a person's economic fortunes may be seen in the career of William B. Rand, who joined the United States Lines the year he married Emily Sloane Franklin, the daughter of the company's Board Chairman, John M. Franklin (whose father was also at one time a top corporate executive in this big shipping concern). Mr. Rand thereupon rose rather rapidly to become president of the firm, but resigned (or was dropped) from this important post in 1966, the year he and his wife severed their marital ties. See *New York Times* (16 November 1966), p. 94.

[2] The above set of figures for probably family controlled firms in which various members of the family have been actively engaged in a company's managerial affairs was arrived at by counting all those concerns with marked family representation in the upper executive ranks (vice-president or some higher post), as indicated by the designations I-BD and I & O-BD. The percentage of family firms classified as having been controlled by such interests over a considerable period of time was computed in similar fashion, using the phrase "over the years" (specified as about a decade or more) as the principal means of identification.

In short, with the relatively minor exception of the top 50 transportation companies, something on the order of 80 to 95 percent of the family controlled firms identified in this study have been dominated by families which have taken an active part in their management over the years.[3]

The import of all these facts and figures would thus seem to be quite clear. From the data assembled here and elsewhere (such as in the aforementioned TNEC study), it would certainly appear that while there has been a definite trend toward managerial control of big business over the years, the magnitude of this shift in economic authority has generally been overstated. In fact, as Tables 3-1 and 4-1 plainly show (and they slightly understate the situation because of certain omissions in the *Fortune* rankings), there was just about as much family as management control of large corporations in the mid-1960s. All told, according to the author's calculations, a little over 42 percent of the 450 firms carefully examined in this study have been classified as probably under family control, roughly 41 percent as probably under management control, with about 16.7 percent placed tentatively in the more indeterminate "possibly family" category.[4] Actually, the family controlled figure would go up to almost 44.5

[3]In a number of cases this control is of rather recent origin. While some might argue that such companies do not represent a real tradition of family control, the author can only observe that it is control nonetheless, and no one really knows how long it will last. Likewise the fact that, according to *Fortune* (see the 15 June 1967 issue, p. 182), only about 14 percent of the top 500 industrial firms are still controlled by the original founding family is of little or no concern in this regard, for it does not matter very much, in the author's opinion, whether this control be wielded for 15, 20, or even 50 years; it is still control of a fairly firm and enduring nature. Furthermore, a glance at the TNEC data summarized in the latter part of Appendix A reveals that the great majority of families listed in the late 1930s as in working (at least substantial minority) control of the more than 60 industrial and merchandising firms placed by the author in the probably family category either still dominate (if classified PF in Table 3-1 and 4-1 of this study) or are associated with (if classified F?) these same concerns as of the mid-1960s. As one might gather from these conditions, most of the great corporate wealth in the country continues to be held by white Anglo-Saxon Protestant families. Only a fairly small number of large corporations are controlled by ethnic minority families, the most successful such group being Jewish entrepreneurs who have done well in many of the newer or high risk fields, such as merchandising and clothing. It is relatively rare to find a family with a name like Siragusa (the Admiral Corp.) in the upper ranks of American big business.

[4]While *Fortune's* traditional sixfold classification of corporations (industrials, merchandising firms, transportation companies, public utilities, commercial banks, and life insurance companies) has made much rough sense up to recent times, these categories have begun to break down in the last few years and may soon become relatively meaningless, if the current rapidly accelerating trend toward diversification continues. For instance, since just 1965 Montgomery Ward & Co. merged with the Container Corp. of America; the Tennessee Gas Transmission Co. (which was #4 on *Fortune's* 1965 top 50 utility list) took over both the J.I. Case Co. and the Newport News Shipbuilding & Dry Dock Co.; McLean Industries, Inc. (#29 on the 1969 *Fortune* transportation list) was absorbed into the R.J. Reynolds Tobacco Co.; the Greyhound Corp. bought out Armour & Co.; World Airways, Inc. (which was #50 on the 1970 *Fortune* transportation list) secured control over Los Angeles' big First Western Bank & Trust Co.; and the sizable Paul Revere Life Insurance Co. was merged into the Avco Corp. Not only that, a number of the nation's financially hard-pressed major railroads have begun to branch out into various other areas, such as the manufacture of machinery and clothing, with the result that the Illinois Central RR has been transformed in name and

percent (and the probably management total down to approximately 40.2 percent) if the aforementioned big privately owned firms were added into these computations, as they logically should be. If, on the other hand, at the same time the top 50 public utilities and top 50 life insurance companies were included in the interest of obtaining a more truly overall national picture, this would bring the family control figure down to about 37 or 39 percent (depending on whether or not one counted the above-mentioned privately owned concerns).[5] But this, most people would agree, is still a very sizable total.

The basic question therefore is whether or not this particular corporate state of affairs deserves to be described as a "managerial revolution." And the answer depends partly on one's point of view or frame of reference. Evidence gathered from various business and academic sources, for instance, would indicate that, compared to most other highly industrialized countries, the United States has indeed undergone what might be called a revolution in this regard, for big companies elsewhere in the world are much more likely to be dominated by family interests.[6] However, if by the term "revolution" one means an absolute numerical standard on the order, say, of 85 or 90 percent overall corporate (managerial) control—and this is the general sense in which most writers and economists have used the term to date—then America's managerial revolution is still obviously far from complete.

operation into Illinois Central Industries; the Chicago & North Western Rwy. was made via the merger process into Northwest Industries; while the Atchison, Topeka & Sante Fe RR is now known as Sante Fe Industries. Indeed, in large part because of the sharply accelerated merger trend in recent years, a sizable number of the firms ranked on one or another of *Fortune's* lists in 1965 no longer exist as such company units, but have either been renamed or been merged into other often bigger concerns and thus lost their corporate identity altogether (although they can be traced by checking through the various issues of *Moody's* manuals since 1965).

[5] Since, as pointed out in footnote 4 of Chapter 2, this study does not include any data on service companies, miscellaneous industrial concerns, property and casualty insurance companies, investment banking firms, big savings and loan associations, mutual funds and other financial institutions (a sizable number of which are probably family dominated), the author is not sure what the final overall family control totals would be if these concerns were incorporated into these tabulations. The reader should therefore view the above figures as approximate.

[6] In Sweden, for example, it was recently found that a mere 15 families (some of which were related to one another) controlled about one-third of all industrial production in the country, and that one family in particular, the Wallenbergs, controlled four of the five Swedish companies found on *Fortune's* list of the top 200 foreign industrials, as well as one of the top commercial banks (see *Fortune*, 15 September 1968, p. 202). Moreover, even in economically underdeveloped Pakistan, it was authoritatively reported that 22 families controlled approximately 66 percent of the nation's industrial assets, roughly 79 percent of the total insurance funds, and about 80 percent of the country's overall banking assets (see *New York Times*, 23 February 1970, p. 2). Also with reference to India, see *New York Times*, 28 February 1971, p. 2. Other studies of managerial versus family or outside control of large foreign industrial corporations (about which works the author has some serious reservations regarding definitions and procedures) include P. Sargant Florence, *Ownership, Control and Success of Large Companies: An Analysis of English Industrial Structure and Policy, 1936-1951* (London: Sweet & Maxwell Ltd., 1961) and E.L. Wheelwright and J. Miskelly, *Anatomy of Australian Manufacturing Industry: The Ownership and Control of 300 of the Largest Manufacturing Companies in Australia* (Sydney: Halstead Press, 1967).

As a matter of fact, the rate at which the nation's major industrial corporations have been moving in the direction of managerial control in recent decades can at best be described as moderate, if not actually rather slow. Using the TNEC's fairly reliable set of stock ownership data as a basis for comparison, the author has calculated, for example, that there were as of the late 1930s a minimum of 48 and very possibly as many as 53 of the 108 manufacturing and mining firms (ranked by assets in this detailed federal report) which could or should be classified as being under family control—a total of either about 44 or 49 percent.[7] According to the author's 1965 control status determinations, on the other hand, approximately 36 percent of the top 108 industrial companies (ranked anew on the basis of assets to provide comparability) were probably family controlled.[8] Since there were, overall, 27 years between these two sets of corporate control figures, this means that America's big industrial corporations have been shifting toward a professional form of managerial control at a rate of from roughly 3 to 5 percent per decade, which many would argue is fairly slow.

Additional evidence that the industrial segment of the economy is not moving at a very rapid pace toward the much-heralded goal of managerial supremacy may be seen by looking at the control trend of recent years. A cursory examination of the make-up of the boards of directors of the nation's largest industrial concerns in 1970, for instance, indicates that about 35 percent of the top 100 industrials and about 38 percent of the top 200 are probably family dominated (a slight drop from the 1965 totals of 36 and 39.5 percent respectively).[9] From

[7]Because the author was somewhat uncertain as to just what amount of stock ownership was required to achieve working control of a corporation back in the late 1930s, he compiled two industrial control totals based on slightly different criteria. The first figure of 48 was arrived at by adding up all manufacturing and mining concerns included in the majority ownership, predominant minority ownership, and substantial minority ownership categories (plus any other firm in which at least 10 percent of the voting shares were held, directly or indirectly, by one or more families, which also had a considerable amount of representation on the board of directors). The second figure of 53 reflects the addition of five other corporations—the American Can Co., Crown Zellerbach Corp., National Biscuit Co., Republic Steel Corp., and Swift & Co.—which also show significant signs (such as 7 or 8 percent stock ownership or marked family representation on the board of directors) of being family controlled. The total of 108 manufacturing and mining firms was obtained by subtracting the 17 companies listed in the merchandising, service (amusement), agricultural, and urban transit categories from the overall TNEC aggregate of 120 industrial concerns and adding 5 corporations (the Cities Service Co., General American Transportation Corp., General Telephone Corp., I.T. & T., and Koppers Co.) which were classified as industrial enterprises by *Fortune* in 1965. This special tabulation was made, as indicated above, to ensure that the 1965 and TNEC rankings were really comparable. See pages 350-54 of TNEC Monograph No. 29 for more detail on this matter.

[8]While both sets were computed on the basis of assets, it should be pointed out that there are considerable differences in the make-up of these two separate rankings of the top 108 industrial concerns compiled as of the late 1930s and 1965. In all, about 70 percent of the top 108 firms listed in the TNEC study were still in this select numerical category in 1965. These companies are designated by an asterisk in Table A-2 found in the latter part of Appendix A.

[9]All told, about 42 percent of the 300 largest industrial firms were judged to be family controlled in 1970, which is roughly the same percentage found for the year 1965. However, this should not be taken to mean that there has been no trend toward managerial

these data, it would appear that the trend toward managerial control has not been accelerating in recent years and is, in fact, still only moving at a rate of about 2 or 3 percent per decade.[10] Thus, obviously, not only is the managerial revolution still far from complete, but, if present trends continue, it will not be close to complete until some time well after the turn of the century.

Given then this state of control affairs, certain questions ought to be asked about the economic operation or performance of managerially dominated versus family controlled firms. Is there really any significant difference in the behavior of one or the other type of big business concern? Do managerially dominated companies, for instance, have a higher rate of return (all other things being equal) than family controlled corporations, or are the latter more profitable? Do management controlled concerns pay higher dividends than family firms under similar circumstances? Do family or entrepreneurially dominated enterprises, on the other hand, channel a greater proportion of their income into product research or corporate expansion? Are family controlled companies more active or aggressive than management run firms with regard to corporate acquisition and merger activity? Do managerially dominated concerns have a better history of labor relations over the years? These are but a few of the areas of major economic inquiry that could be examined by interested and competent researchers.[11]

Unfortunately, however, very little research of a reliable nature has been done to date concerning these important matters. This is due chiefly to the fact that while there have been several studies completed in recent years, using the latest <u>tools of statistical</u> analysis, not one has been built on a really solid base of per-control at this particular level on the corporate scale, for the author feels fairly sure that this statistical quirk was probably due to the effects of increasing economic concentration and merger activity, which has led to more somewhat smaller family controlled firms moving up into the *Fortune* 300 ranking. As indicated above, the author's analysis of the control status of these top 300 concerns in 1970 was made largely on the basis of the make-up of their boards of directors, with relatively little reliance placed on systematically compiled pertinent stock ownership data. No attempt has been made, by the way, to examine any possible 1965-to-1970 trends for the top merchandising, transportation, and commercial banking concerns in the country because of the very short period of time involved and the comparatively small number of companies contained in each PM or PF category.

[10] As a result of the increase in the number of professional administrators and executives in the post-World War II period in particular, the rate at which many long-established firms may be moving in the direction of managerial control may actually be greater than that indicated above. But there is also apparently a reverse trend at work due to the various corporate takeovers and mergers in recent years. In just the 5-year period between 1965 and 1970, for instance, the family dominated Lykes Bros. Steamship Co. took over the previously management controlled Youngstown Sheet & Tube Co.; the (PF) McDonnell Aircraft Corp. bought out the (previously F?) Douglas Aircraft Co.; the (PF) Sun Oil Co. secured control of the (previously PM) Sunray DX Oil Co.; the (PF) Tisch-dominated Loew's, Inc. absorbed the (previously PM) P. Lorillard & Co.; and the (PF) Atlantic Refining Co. took over both the (previously PM) Richfield Oil Corp. and the (previously PM) Sinclair Oil Corp. (although it thereupon sold most of the latter's service station outlets to the British Petroleum Corp.).

[11] The author, however, would prefer to leave the analysis of the economic implications of this study's substantive findings to others better qualified to investigate such matters. For a more extended and general treatment of this topic, see Shorey Peterson, "Corporate Control and Capitalism," *Quarterly Journal of Economics* (February 1965), pp. 1-24.

tinent factual information as to the operation of the different types of control categories of business concerns. In large measure these critical data deficiencies were the direct and unavoidable result of the very considerable (and heretofore unresolved) problems involved in identifying which big companies in the country were management dominated and which were family or entrepreneurially controlled. For example, Robert Larner made a fairly elaborate analysis of the overall (1956-62) profitability and (1962-63) rate of executive compensation of a rather sizable number of firms classified in his book, *Management Control and the Large Corporation*, as either managerially dominated or owner controlled, and came to the conclusion that there was relatively little difference between the two types of big business concerns. But Larner's findings are of questionable value because of a substantial number of errors made in the selection of his sample firms designated as under management control. All told, according to the author's (Table 3-1) calculations, of the 128 companies classified by Larner as management controlled (see his Appendix C), 22 (approximately 17 percent) were actually probably family dominated enterprises, while another 25 (nearly 20 percent) showed sufficient signs of such influence to be placed in the possibly family category.[12] With these kinds of faulty data mixed into his analysis, it could be argued that only limited credence should be put in Larner's findings.

Another recent investigation of the economic consequences of the separation of ownership from control was undertaken by Brian Hindley and published in the April 1970 issue of the *Journal of Law and Economics*.[13] In this analysis, for want of more reliable available evidence, Hindley used as his primary means of identifying owner controlled corporations all stockholder efforts made to intervene in corporate affairs or upset established management forces (proxy battles), as reported in the *Wall Street Journal* between 1958 and 1963. In this manner he came up with a total of about 50 manufacturing firms whose operations he then examined in considerable detail. However, this was not a very adequate procedure, as Hindley himself freely admitted, readily acknowledging that proxy fights were not synonymous with attempts made to secure working control.[14]

[12] There were only about four or five errors involved in Larner's selection of his sample of 59 owner controlled firms. However, it should also be pointed out that Larner apparently failed to take into account certain other factors which could have had an important effect on his findings. Larner's owner controlled concerns were, for instance, somewhat smaller than his management dominated corporations (46 percent of the former falling into the lesser 301-500 category, whereas only about 24 percent of the latter did so). In addition, Larner's management-control sample was partially skewed by the presence of a disproportionate number of oil companies and aircraft and defense firms, not to mention various other enterprises. Also in this regard, see David R. Kamerschen, "The Influence of Ownership and Control on Profit Rates," *American Economic Review* (June 1968), pp. 432-47.

[13] See Brian V. Hindley, "Separation of Ownership and Control in the Modern Corporation," *Journal of Law and Economics* (April 1970), pp. 185-221.

[14] See Hindley, p. 189. From the standpoint of appraising the control status of the nation's biggest manufacturing and mining firms, this study is also lacking, since only 9 of the 50-odd presumably owner controlled concerns identified in this manner were in the top 300 *Fortune* ranking in 1962, and only 12 were in the first 500 industrial category. Hindley, moreover, made a separate secondary analysis of the 1930-50 performance of 16 oil com-

Thus this study once again points up the pressing need for more sound stock ownership data and a better mechanism for ascertaining the locus of control in a large corporation.[15]

Finally there is the question as to what, if any, differences exist between management dominated and family controlled firms with reference to their participation in political and civic affairs. Are management concerns, for instance, more uniformly Republican in their orientation, with certain entrepreneurial or family run enterprises, particularly those of a maverick nature (such as those controlled by Chicago magnate J. Patrick Lannan), more closely affiliated with the Democratic party, outside of the South? Are family dominated companies more likely to encourage or compel their middle and upper echelon executives to run for important political office (or serve in some major governmental capacity)? Or are they more influential behind the scenes, relying on big campaign contributions or other subtler forms of pressure to achieve their policy ends indirectly? Do family firms usually play more prominent roles in state and local politics than at the national level of government? And finally in the realm of civic and community affairs, are family controlled corporations more active and economically supportive of worthy projects than management concerns, which may, quite understandably, feel more restrained in this area? In this age of increasing awareness, is one or the other type of company more receptive to outside entreaties to broaden the scope of its social concern or responsibility? These are the kinds of questions which interested and qualified researchers may wish to investigate in greater depth and detail.

They can do so, of course, only on the basis of up-to-date, reliable evidence. This study has attempted to provide such corporate control data for the vast majority of America's large business concerns. In so doing, it has refuted in considerable measure most commonly held notions about the magnitude of the managerial revolution, for it has been shown here that this much-heralded development is, at best, little more than a half-truth.

---

panies and 9 steel corporations under various types of control (managerial, intermediate, and closely held), but because these were classified on the basis of the old outdated TNEC data, the author is not inclined to put much stock in these particular findings.

[15]In another fairly recent article three economists found that 36 selected big owner controlled firms actually outperformed a similar sample of large management dominated concerns (all of which were drawn from *Fortune's* 1964 top 500 industrial list) between 1952 and 1963. However, the author cannot tell from the information presented whether all of the companies classified as either management or owner controlled (none of which were named, of course) were, in fact, dominated by such interests. He also has some rather serious reservations about the manner in which the management and ownership control terms were employed in this corporate analysis. See R.J. Monsen, J.S. Chiu, and D.E. Cooley, "The Effect of Separation of Ownership and Control on the Performance of the Large Firm," *Quarterly Journal of Economics* (August 1968), pp. 435-51.

# Appendixes

# Appendix A

Analysis and Listing of the Top 200
Nonfinancial Concerns Classified
under Various Types of Control in
Berle and Means' *The Modern Corpo-
ration and Private Property* and the
U.S. Temporary National Economic
Committee's Monograph No. 29, *The
Distribution of Ownership in the 200
Largest Nonfinancial Corporations*

# Appendix A

*Berle and Means*

Berle and Means' *The Modern Corporation and Private Property* was, as indicated earlier, a landmark study in many respects. Nevertheless, unfortunately, this book has certain serious flaws.[1] For instance, in the author's estimation, the time period used by Berle and Means for data collection purposes (basically 1928-29 to 1930-31) was much too brief to be very reliable. But an even graver deficiency probably stemmed from the fact that there were simply not enough other sources of information available at this time to make any kind of authoritative judgment as to the control status of many of the top 200 nonfinancial concerns (which were ranked by gross assets as of about January 1, 1930). Perhaps partly as a result, a number of companies were described as being under private or majority ownership, although no real evidence was provided to back up such assertions. As to the National Steel Corp., for example, the authors simply said that its stock "appears to be closely held" (presumably by non-management interests). With regard to such similarly classified concerns as the Crane Co., Singer Mfg. Co., and Deere & Co., the only evidence offered was a terse statement that the bulk of the stock was "believed to be closely held" (pp. 86-87).[2]

What is more, there were 73 other companies (out of the 200 total) for which no data of any kind were presented, 29 of these firms being classified (on the basis of "street knowledge," which some would describe as nothing more than "guesstimates") as presumably under minority interest control, with the remain-

[1] See Adolf A. Berle and Gardiner C. Means, *The Modern Corporation and Private Property* (New York: The Macmillan Co., 1932). For some inexplicable reason, very few writers have ever challenged Berle and Means' stock ownership and control findings. One recent attack, however, was made by Clive S. Beed in an article entitled "The Separation of Ownership from Control," which is contained in the Summer 1966 issue of the *Journal of Economic Studies*. Unlike this study, Beed's argument with Berle and Means does not revolve around the stock ownership issue (since he felt they did not show how concentrated shareholdings were translated into active economic and policy-making power), but concerns the role and influence of corporate directors. Back in 1945 Robert A. Gordon also criticized the mechanical or static criteria employed by Berle and Means in their analysis of the control status of the top 200 nonfinancial firms (see his *Business Leadership in the Large Corporation*, Washington, D.C.: The Brookings Institution, 1945, p. 166). But neither Beed nor Gordon provided very convincing data (Gordon, for instance, using the case study method, examined only 65 unidentified large corporations and was able to obtain personal interviews with major executives in less than half of these companies) concerning the actions and influence of corporate directors, and it would require a truly vast amount of time, effort, and cooperation on the part of big business to compile such information. Hence the approach adopted in this book.

[2] Judging from the make-up of the board of directors of these four companies, the author would be inclined to agree that a substantial percentage of the stock was probably held by family or outside interests, but the point is that Berle and Means presented no evidence to support their claims.

113

ing 44 corporations being designated in much the same fashion as presumably under management control. Yet even a cursory glance at the boards of directors of these 73 concerns indicates that a number were undoubtedly misclassified by Berle and Means. For example, the Firestone Tire & Rubber Co. was placed in the "presumably management" category, although subsequent studies and evidence have shown that it has always been a family controlled corporation. Likewise, it is difficult to see how Swift & Co. could have been portrayed as anything other than a family firm in light of the fact that in 1930 all of its top managerial officials and six of its overall total of nine directors were members of the Swift family.

Furthermore, it should be pointed out that some of the companies classified as controlled by a legal device (that is, some sort of special legal or financial arrangement) were actually dominated by certain outside interests, even though Berle and Means did not happen to take note of this fact. Thus, although the Splawn report clearly revealed that the Van Sweringen brothers were the dominant interests in the Alleghany Corp. (which also controlled, by the way, three other firms ranked in the top 200), Berle and Means chose, despite a great deal of data to the contrary, merely to list this concern as under the control of some pyramiding corporate device.[3]

A complete listing of the different companies classified under various types of control by Berle and Means—together with the author's own evaluation when different (such as when viewed from the standpoint of the ultimate locus of control) is contained in Table A-1.[4]

All told, the author estimates that at least 73 (or 36.5 percent) and perhaps as many as 89 (or 44.5 percent) of the top 200 concerns on Berle and Means' list were controlled by one or more American families. Similarly, he found that no less than 50 (or a little over 47 percent) and possibly as many as 63 (or roughly 59 percent) of their largest 106 industrial firms were actually under the control of various family interests.[5] Shifting over to another important area of economic

---

[3] See U.S. House Report No. 2789, *Regulation of Stock Ownership in Railroads* (Washington, D.C.: U.S. Government Printing Office, 1931), p. 999. The author is not fully satisfied as to the accuracy of all parts of the Splawn report. (Has not, for example, the Union Pacific RR been controlled by the Harriman interests since at least the turn of the century?)

[4] See Berle and Means, *The Modern Corporation and Private Property*, pp. 86-107. The author's evaluations of the corporate control determinations arrived at by Berle and Means are based on a brief check of the make-up of the board of directors of each of these 200 concerns, and are thus of a tentative nature. Since the author was not primarily interested in making a meticulous assessment of Berle and Means' work, he did not attempt to make an exhaustive analysis of their individual company findings. His evaluations, furthermore, do not attempt to appraise the extent to which control may have been exercised by various outside (unrelated) interests, although there undoubtedly were a number of concerns which could be considered in this category, such as the U.S. Steel Corp. (see *Fortune*, March 1936, p. 63).

[5] The more tentative higher totals in the above three summary statements were arrived at by adding all companies described by the author as possibly under family control in Table A-1 to all corporations classified there as probably under family control. These 106 industrials, by the way, include nine merchandising concerns, six amusement companies (including in this category RCA and the Eastman Kodak Co.), a real estate firm, and at least one transportation company, the International Mercantile Marine Co. (the other company placed in this category, Pullman, Inc., actually being a railroad equipment manufacturer).

activity, the author has calculated that a minimum of about 29 percent (and perhaps as many as 36 percent) of the 42 railroads on Berle and Means' list were probably controlled by family forces. And finally, with reference to the public utility category, the author has in like manner determined that a total of about 25 percent of the 52 public utilities on Berle and Means' top 200 list most likely should have been classified as under family control.

Berle and Means' list of the top 200 nonfinancial corporations also appears to have been compiled in somewhat faulty fashion, there being certain errors or omissions in this very important tabulation. These discrepancies stem largely from the fact that in a number of cases Berle and Means used estimated asset figures instead of those found in the various 1930 *Moody's* manuals (their general source of such information for corporate ranking purposes). The International Mercantile Marine Co. was, for instance, listed by Berle and Means as having estimated gross assets of $100 million on or about January 1, 1930, although according to the 1930 *Moody's Industrial Manual* (p. 117), it actually had assets of only about $78 million. Similarly, R.H. Macy & Co. was recorded by Berle and Means as having estimated assets of $97 million as of the above date, although again according to the 1930 *Moody's Industrial Manual* (p. 497), it had, in fact, gross assets of about $77 million. Both of these official *Moody's* figures were considerably less than the lowest corporate asset total listed for Berle and Means' top 200th nonfinancial concern (this being $90.3 million for the Minnesota & Ontario Paper Co.). Thus, to give just two very obvious examples, it would seem that the Sun Oil Co. and Lehigh Valley Coal Corp. (both of which had assets of approximately $88 million as of this point in time) should have been included in Berle and Means' list instead of the International Mercantile Marine Co. and R.H. Macy & Co. It should also be observed that the decision to count a number of subsidiaries or affiliates separately (that is, as individual, at least quasi-autonomous companies rather than as economic arms of other often larger enterprises) undoubtedly had a considerable effect on the composition of Berle and Means' list of the top 200 firms. According to the author's calculations, there were about 30 such concerns in this particular tabulation.

**Table A-1**

**Company-by-Company Listing and Analysis of the Top 200 Nonfinancial Concerns Classified, as of about 1930, under Various Types of Control by Berle and Means, together with Author's Evaluation**

| Control Category, according to Berle and Means | Family Identification and Other Pertinent Information, according to Berle and Means | Ultimate Type of Control, according to Berle and Means | Author's Evaluation When Different |
|---|---|---|---|
| *Private Ownership and Control:* | | | |
| Aluminum Co. of America | Mellon interests | | |
| Ford Motor Co. | Ford family | | |
| Great Atlantic & Pacific Tea Co. | Closely held | | Probably controlled by the Hartford family |
| Gulf Oil Corp. | Mellon interests | | |
| Jones & Laughlin Steel Corp. | Jones and Laughlin families and associates | | |
| Koppers Co. | Mellon interests | | |
| Minnesota & Ontario Paper Co. | Mr. Backus and associates | | |
| National Steel Corp. | Appears to be closely held | | Probably controlled by the Hanna interests |
| Florida East Coast Rwy. Co. | Estate of Mary (Flagler) Bingham | | |
| Virginian Rwy. Co. | Estate of H. H. Rogers | | |
| New England Gas & Elec. Assn. | Assoc'd. Gas & Elec. Co. officials | | Possibly Management |
| Railway & Bus Associates | Assoc'd. Gas & Elec. Co. interests | | Possibly Management |
| *Majority Ownership:* | | | |
| R. H. Macy & Co. | Bulk believed to be closely held | | Probably controlled by the Straus family |

| Company | Ownership | Control Classification | Control Notes |
|---|---|---|---|
| Marshall Field & Co. | Bulk believed to be closely held | | Probably controlled by the Field family interests |
| Phelps Dodge Corp. | Bulk held by Dodge family and associates | | |
| Singer Mfg. Co. | Bulk believed to be closely held | | Probably controlled by the Clark family interests |
| Crane Co. | Bulk believed to be closely held | | Probably controlled by the Crane family |
| Deere & Co. | Bulk believed to be closely held | | Probably controlled by the Deere family |
| Seaboard Air Line Rwy. Co. | Underwriting syndicate headed by Dillon, Read & Co. | | Possibly Management |
| Duke Power Co. | Duke trusts and associates | | |
| Eastern Gas & Fuel Associates | Koppers (Mellon) interests | | |
| Lone Star Gas Corp. | Crawford interests | | |

*Minority Stock Ownership Control:*

| Company | Ownership | Control Classification | Control Notes |
|---|---|---|---|
| Atlantic Refining Co. | Blair & Co. and associates | Minority | Possibly Management |
| Consolidation Coal Co. | Rockefeller family | Minority | |
| E. I. du Pont de Nemours & Co. | du Pont family | Minority | |
| General Motors Corp. | E. I. du Pont de Nemours & Co. (and subsidiaries) | Pyramiding | du Pont family (indirectly) |
| Goodyear Tire & Rubber Co. | Cyrus S. Eaton and associates | Pyramiding | Possibly Management |
| Inland Steel Co. | Cyrus S. Eaton and associates | Minority | Probably controlled by the Block family interests |
| Loew's Inc. | General Theatre (indirectly) | Pyramiding | Possibly family |
| Prairie Oil & Gas Co. | Petroleum Corp. of America | Pyramiding | Possibly Management |

**Table A-1** *(cont.)*

| Control Category, according to Berle and Means | Family Identification and Other Pertinent Information, according to Berle and Means | Ultimate Type of Control, according to Berle and Means | Author's Evaluation When Different |
|---|---|---|---|
| Standard Oil Co. of Indiana | Rockefeller interests | Minority | |
| Standard Oil Co. of N.J. | Rockefeller interests | Minority | |
| Standard Oil Co. of N.Y. | Rockefeller interests | Minority | |
| Tide Water Assoc'd Oil Co. | Holding company executives | Minority | Possibly Management |
| U.S. Rubber Co. | du Pont family | Minority | |
| Vacuum Oil Co. | Rockefeller interests | Minority | |
| Atlantic Coast Line RR Co. | Atlantic Coast Line Co. interests | Pyramiding | |
| Chicago & Eastern Illinois Rwy. Co. | Estate of Thomas F. Ryan | Minority | Possibly Family |
| Chicago Great Western RR Co. | Patrick H. Joyce | Minority | |
| Delaware, Lackawanna & Western RR Co. | Baker and Vanderbilt families | Minority | |
| Erie RR Co. | Alleghany Corp. (and sub.) | Pyramiding | Possibly Management |
| Illinois Central RR Co. | Union Pacific RR (and sub.) | Management | Probably controlled (indirectly) by the Harriman interests |
| Kansas City Southern Rwy. Co. | Alleghany Corp. | Pyramiding | Possibly Management |
| N.Y., Chicago & St. Louis RR Co. | Alleghany Corp. | Pyramiding | Probably controlled by the Van Sweringen interests |
| Norfolk & Western Rwy. Co. | Pennsylvania RR (and sub.) | Management | |
| St. Louis Southwestern Rwy. Co. | N.Y. Investors, Inc. and associates | Pyramiding | Possibly Management |
| Wabash Rwy. Co. | Pennsylvania RR (and sub.) | Management | |
| Western Maryland Rwy. Co. | B & O RR | Management | |
| Western Pacific RR Corp. | Arthur Curtiss James (indirectly) | Minority | |
| Amer. Gas & Electric Co. | Elec. Bond & Share Co. | Management | |

| Company | Control Method | Controlling Interest | Notes |
|---|---|---|---|
| Amer. Power & Light Co. | Management | Elec. Bond & Share Co. | |
| Brooklyn Union Gas Co. | Minority | Koppers-Mellon interests | |
| Columbia Gas & Elec. Corp. | Management | United Corp. | |
| Commonwealth & Southern Corp. | Management | United Corp. and American Superpower Corp. | |
| Commonwealth Edison Co. | Pyramiding | Insull Utility Invest., Inc. and other concerns | Probably controlled by the Insull interests |
| Detroit Edison Co. | Pyramiding | North American Co. | Possibly Management |
| Elec. Power & Light Corp. | Management | Elec. Bond & Share Co. | |
| Middle West Utilities Co. | Pyramiding | Insull Utility Invest., Inc. | Probably controlled by the Insull interests |
| Niagara Hudson Power Corp. | Management | United Corp. | |
| Natl. Power & Light Co. | Management | Elec. Bond & Share Co. | |
| North American Co. | Pyramiding | Central States Elec. Corp. and sub's. or affil's. | Possibly Management |
| Pacific Gas & Elec. Co. | Pyramiding | North American Co. | Possibly Management |
| Pacific Lighting Corp. | Minority | (left blank) | |
| Peoples Gas Light & Coke Co. | Pyramiding | Insull Utility Invest., Inc. and other concerns | Probably controlled by the Insull interests |
| Public Service Co. of Northern Illinois | Pyramiding | Insull Utility Invest., Inc. and other concerns | Probably controlled by the Insull interests |
| United Gas Improvement Co. | Management | United Corp. | |

*Presumably Minority Interest Control:*

| Company | | | Notes |
|---|---|---|---|
| Allied Chemical & Dye Corp. | None | | |
| American Rolling Mill Co. | None | | |
| American Smelting & Refining Co. | None | | |
| Continental Oil Co. | None | | |
| Corn Products Refining Co. | None | | Possibly Management |

**Table A-1** *(cont.)*

| Control Category, according to Berle and Means | Family Identification and Other Pertinent Information, according to Berle and Means | Ultimate Type of Control, according to Berle and Means | Author's Evaluation When Different |
|---|---|---|---|
| Crucible Steel Co. of America | None | | Possibly Management |
| Cuban Cane Products Co. | None | | Possibly Management |
| Glen Alden Coal Co. | None | | Possibly Management |
| Internatl. Mercantile Marine Co. | None | | |
| International Shoe Co. | None | | |
| S.S. Kresge Co. | None | | |
| Long-Bell Lumber Corp. | None | | |
| National Lead Co. | None | | |
| Ohio Oil Co. | None | | |
| Paramount Publix Co. | None | | |
| Phillips Petroleum Co. | None | | |
| Pittsburgh Coal Co. | None | | |
| Pittsburgh Plate Glass Co. | None | | |
| Procter & Gamble Co. | None | | |
| Republic Iron and Steel Corp. | None | | |
| Standard Oil Co. of Calif. | None | | |
| U.S. Realty & Improvement Co. | None | | Possibly Management |
| Warner Bros. Pictures, Inc. | None | | |
| Wheeling Steel Corp. | None | | |
| Associated Telephone Util. Co. | None | | Possibly Management |
| Hudson & Manhattan RR Co. | None | | Possibly Management |
| Stone & Webster, Inc. | None | | |
| Third Ave. Rwy. Co. | None | | Possibly Management |

| Company | Controlling Interest | Type of Control | Remarks |
|---|---|---|---|
| United Rwys. & Elec. Co. of Baltimore | None | | Possibly Management |

*Joint Control by Other Interests* (a pyramiding arrangement):

| Company | Controlling Interest | Type of Control | Remarks |
|---|---|---|---|
| Prairie Pipe Line Co. | Petroleum Corp. of America | Management and Pyramiding | |
| Radio Corp. of America | GE and Westinghouse Elec. & Mfg. Corp. | Management | |
| Sinclair Crude Oil Purchasing Co. | Sinclair Consol'd. Oil Corp. and Standard Oil Co. of Ind. | Management and Minority | Probably controlled by the Sinclair interests |
| Boston & Maine RR Co. | N.Y., New Haven & Hartford RR (indirectly) and Pennroad Corp. | Management | |
| Chicago, Burlington & Quincy RR Co. | Great Northern Rwy. and Northern Pacific Rwy. | Management | |
| Chicago, Rock Island & Pacific Rwy. Co. | St. Louis-San Francisco Rwy. | Management | |
| Chicago Union Station Co. | Pennsylvania RR and two Chicago railroads | Management | |
| Denver & Rio Grande Western RR Co. | Allegheny Corp. (indirectly) and Western Pacific RR | Pyramiding and Minority | Probably controlled by the Van Sweringen and other interests |
| Lehigh Valley RR Co. | Pennsylvania RR (indirectly) | Management | |
| N.Y., New Haven & Hartford RR Co. | Pennsylvania RR and Pennroad Corp. | Management | |
| Reading Co. | B & O RR and N.Y. Central RR | Management | |
| Spokane, Portland & Seattle Rwy. Co. | Great Northern Rwy. and Northern Pacific Rwy. | Management | |
| Central Public Service Co. | A.E. Pierce & Co., and holding company | Minority and Pyramiding | Possibly Family |
| Midland United Co. | 5 other public utility companies | Pyramiding and Management | Probably controlled by the Insull interests |
| North American Light & Power Co. | North American Co. and Middle West Utilities Co. | Pyramiding | Possibly Management |

**Table A-1** (*cont.*)

| Control Category, according to Berle and Means | Family Identification and Other Pertinent Information, according to Berle and Means | Ultimate Type of Control, according to Berle and Means | Author's Evaluation When Different |
|---|---|---|---|
| Public Service Corp. of N.J. | United Gas Improvement Co. and United Corp. | Management | |
| *Control by a Legal Device:* | | *Legal Device* | |
| American Tobacco Co. | None | Nonvoting common stock | Possibly Management |
| Cliffs Corp. | None | Voting trust and pyramiding | Probably controlled by the Eaton and Mather families |
| Crown Zellerbach Corp. | None | Voting trust | Probably controlled by the Zellerbach family |
| General Theatre Equipment, Inc. | None | Pyramiding, nonvoting common stock, and voting trust | Possibly Management |
| Internatl. Match Corp. | None | Pyramiding | Possibly Management |
| Liggett & Myers Tobacco Co. | None | Nonvoting common stock | Possibly Management |
| R.J. Reynolds Tobacco Co. | None | Nonvoting common stock | Probably controlled by the Reynolds and Gray family interests |
| Shell Union Oil Corp. | None | Pyramiding | Possibly Management |
| Union Oil Associates | None | Pyramiding | Possibly Family |
| United Stores Corp. | None | Pyramiding, special stock, and voting trust | Possibly controlled by the Morrow interests |
| Alleghany Corp. | None | Pyramiding | Probably controlled by the Van Sweringen interests |
| American Commonwealths Power Corp. | None | Nonvoting common stock | Possibly Management |

| | | *Ultimate Type of Control, according to Berle and Means* | |
|---|---|---|---|
| American Water Works & Elec. Co. | None | Voting trust | Possibly Management |
| Assoc. Gas & Elec. Co. | None | Nonvoting common stock | Possibly Management |
| Cities Service Co. | None | Special vote-weighted preferred stock | Possibly Management |
| Interborough Rapid Transit Co. | None | Voting trust | Possibly Management |
| Phila. Rapid Transit Co. | None | Pyramiding | Possibly Management |
| Tri-Utilities Corp. | None | Pyramiding | Possibly Management |
| United Light & Power Co. | None | Nonvoting common stock | Probably controlled by Cyrus S. Eaton |
| U.S. Elec. Power Corp. | None | Pyramiding and special stock | Possibly Management |
| Utilities Power & Light Corp. | None | Nonvoting common stock and voting trust | Possibly Management |

*Presumably Management Control:*

| | | | |
|---|---|---|---|
| American Can Co. | None | | Probably controlled by the Moore family interests |
| American Car & Foundry Co. | None | | |
| American Locomotive Co. | None | | |
| Amer. Radiator & Standard Sanitary Corp. | None | | |
| American Sugar Refining Co. | None | | |
| American Woolen Co. | None | | |
| Anaconda Copper Mining Co. | None | | |
| Armour & Co. (Ill.) | None | | Possibly controlled by the Armour family |
| Baldwin Locomotive Works | None | | |
| Bethlehem Steel Corp. | None | | |

**Table A-1** *(cont.)*

| Control Category, according to Berle and Means | Family Identification and Other Pertinent Information, according to Berle and Means | Ultimate Type of Control, according to Berle and Means | Author's Evaluation When Different |
|---|---|---|---|
| Borden Co. | None | | Possibly controlled by the Milbank interests |
| Chrysler Corp. | None | | |
| Drug, Inc. | None | | |
| Eastman Kodak Co. | None | | |
| Firestone Tire & Rubber Co. | None | | Probably controlled by the Firestone family |
| B.F. Goodrich & Co. | None | | |
| Internatl. Harvester Co. | None | | Probably controlled by the McCormick family |
| Internatl. Paper & Power Co. | None | | |
| Kennecott Copper Corp. | None | | Possibly controlled by the Guggenheim and Morgan interests |
| P. Lorillard Co. | None | | |
| Montgomery Ward & Co. | None | | |
| National Biscuit Co. | None | | Probably controlled by the Moore family interests |
| Natl. Dairy Products Corp. | None | | |
| Phila. & Reading Coal & Iron Corp. | None | | |
| Pullman, Inc. | None | | Possibly controlled by the Mellon and Morgan interests |
| Pure Oil Co. | None | | Possibly controlled by the Dawes family |
| Richfield Oil Co. | None | | |

|  | | |
|---|---|---|
| Sears, Roebuck & Co. | None | Possibly controlled by the Rosenwald family |
| Sinclair Consol'd. Oil Corp. | None | Possibly controlled by the Sinclair family |
| Studebaker Corp. | None | Possibly controlled by the Studebaker family |
| Swift & Co. | None | Probably controlled by the Swift family |
| Texas Corp. | None | |
| Union Carbide & Carbon Corp. | None | |
| United Fruit Co. | None | |
| United Shoe Machinery Corp. | None | Possibly controlled by the Brown and Barbour interests |
| Westinghouse Elec. & Mfg. Co. | None | |
| Wilson & Co. | | |
| F.W. Woolworth Co. | None | Possibly controlled by the Woolworth and other family interests |
| Youngstown Sheet & Tube Co. | None | |
| Brooklyn Manhattan Transit Co. | None | |
| Consol. Gas, Elec. Light, & Power Co. of Baltimore | None | |
| Edison Elec. Illum. Co. of Boston | None | |
| Internatl. Tel. & Tel. Corp. | None | |
| Southern Calif. Edison Co., Ltd. | None | |

*Management Control:*

| | | |
|---|---|---|
| General Electric Co. | Very small percentage holding, G.E. subsidiary | |

**Table A-1** *(cont.)*

| Control Category, according to Berle and Means | Family Identification and Other Pertinent Information, according to Berle and Means | Ultimate Type of Control, according to Berle and Means | Author's Evaluation When Different |
|---|---|---|---|
| U.S. Steel Corp. | Very small percentage holding, G.F. Baker | | |
| Atchison, Topeka, & Sante Fe Rwy. Co. | Very small percentage holdings, Mills family and Rockefeller Fdtn. | | |
| Baltimore & Ohio RR Co. | Very small percentage holdings, Union Pacific RR and Alien Property Custodian | | |
| Chicago, Milwaukee, St. Paul & Pacific RR Co. | Very small percentage holdings, E.S. Harkness and Dir. Gen. of Rds. | | |
| Chicago & North Western Rwy. Co. | Very small percentage holdings, Union Pacific RR and Vanderbilt family | | |
| Delaware & Hudson Co. | Very small percentage holdings, B.P. Trenkman and Home Ins. Co. | | |
| Great Northern Rwy. Co. | Very small percentage holdings, A.C. James and G.F. Baker, Jr. | | |
| Missouri-Kansas-Texas RR Co. | Very small percentage holdings, company and reorg. mgrs. | | |
| New York Central RR Co. | Small percentage holdings, Union Pacific RR and Vanderbilt family | | Possibly controlled by the Vanderbilt and other interests |
| Northern Pacific Rwy. Co. | Very small percentage holdings, A.C. James and E.B. Kennedy | | |

| Company | Holdings | Notes |
|---|---|---|
| Pennsylvania RR Co. | Very small percentage holdings, W.M. Potts and employees assn. | |
| St. Louis-San Francisco Rwy. Co. | Small percentage holdings, two companies | |
| Southern Pacific Co. | Very small percentage holdings, Dodge family and A.C. James | Possibly controlled by the Milbank interests |
| Southern Rwy. Co. | Very small percentage holdings, Milbank and Springs families | Probably controlled by the Harriman interests |
| Union Pacific RR Co. | Very small percentage holdings, Harriman family and Dutch concern | |
| A.T.&T. | Very small percentage holdings, Sun Life Assur. Co. and G.F. Baker | |
| Boston Elevated Rwy. Co. | Very small percentage holdings by one company and one broker | |
| Consol. Gas Co. of N.Y. | Very small percentage holdings, United Corp. and Sun Life Assur. Co. | |
| Electric Bond & Share Co. | Very small percentage holdings, company and employee stock purchase plan | |
| Western Union Tel. Co. | Very small percentage holdings, two companies | |
| *Special Situations:* | | |
| Chicago & Alton RR Co. | In hands of receiver | |
| Wheeling & Lake Erie Rwy. Co. | Bulk of stock held by trustee | Pyramiding |
| Chicago Railways Co. | In hands of receiver | |

*TNEC Study*

The TNEC study list of the largest 200 nonfinancial firms, on the other hand, appears to have been compiled without serious error or omission. In one respect, it wisely deviated from Berle and Means' selection procedure in that it excluded all companies in bankruptcy or receivership (as of January 31, 1940). Unfortunately, it too adhered to a rather unrealistic rule with reference to the amount of stock ownership necessary (50 percent or more, unless the value of the subsidiary's stock exceeded $60,000,000) to establish a subsidiary or other closely affiliated relationship. As a result, there were about 22 such nonautonomous concerns in the overall TNEC study sample.

The stock ownership data were derived, for the most part, from questionnaires submitted to the above corporations, and seem to be quite accurate. Judging from the assembled data, the TNEC staff was also able to take all apparently pertinent family relationships into account.

The TNEC's four main categories of control were as follows: majority control (defined logically as the ownership of over 50 percent of the voting stock in a concern), predominant minority control (defined as the ownership of from 30 to 50 percent of such stock), substantial minority control (the holding of from 10 to 30 percent of the voting shares), and small minority control (ownership of less than 10 percent, but also generally speaking more than 3 percent of the voting stock in a firm). However, since the author was uncertain as to whether stock ownership of 4 or 5 percent was really sufficient, as a rule, to establish working control at that time, he has chosen to describe (in the third column of the following table) most of these "small minority ownership" firms merely as possibly under family (or outside) control.[6] Because of certain pyramiding or stock ownership relationships, the author also listed (in the aforementioned third column) 22 other concerns as possibly under family control, although most of them were categorized in the TNEC study as being under either managerial or corporate interest group control.[7] According to this report, control could be exercised by one or more families, one or more corporate interest groups, or by a combination of the two.

---

[6] Because of certain stock ownership and directorship data (such as the holding of something like 7 or 8 percent of the voting stock and marked family representation on the board of directors), the author did classify five of these concerns—the American Can Co., Crown Zellerbach Corp., Lone Star Gas Corp., National Biscuit Co., and Swift & Co.—as probably under family control.

[7] In this special tabulation, two companies have been taken out of the TNEC's corporate interest group category, these concerns being the General Motors Corp. (which the author felt was definitely under family control) and the International Hydro-Electric System (which was under the control of the most likely family dominated International Power and Paper Co.). The International Paper & Power Co. was taken out of the jointly family and corporate interest group category because the Phipps interests owned 10.9 percent of the voting stock and had three representatives on its board of directors. In addition, the author believes that the Republic Steel Corp. and Pullman, Inc. should be classified as probably under family control because of substantial family stock ownership and marked family representation on their boards of directors.

A company-by-company breakdown of the TNEC's control status findings (along with the author's own evaluation when different) appears in Table A-2.[8]

Overall then, according to the author's calculations, at least 63 (or, to put it in relative terms, 52.5 percent) and perhaps as many as 74 (or approximately 62 percent) of the TNEC's top 120 industrial concerns could be considered family controlled companies.[9] Similarly, he estimated that at least 74 (or 37 percent) and possibly as many as 96 (or 48 percent) of the 200 largest nonfinancial firms could be classified as being under family control.[10] With reference to the 29 railroads incorporated in the TNEC's top 200 list, the author believes that a minimum of about 14 percent (and perhaps as many as 24 percent) could be identified as being under family control.[11] And in the public utility area he found that no less than 16 percent (and perhaps as many as almost 30 percent) of the 51 public utilities included in the TNEC study could be described as family controlled.

---

[8] See U.S. Temporary National Economic Committee, Monograph No. 29, *The Distribution of Ownership in the 200 Largest Nonfinancial Corporations*, pp. 1488-1504. All concerns designated by an asterisk were also in the top 108 industrial firms, ranked according to assets as of 1965, the year the author picked for corporate ranking and analysis.

[9] The total of 120 industrial firms used by the author in the above tabulation does not coincide, by the way, with the TNEC's aggregate of 126 manufacturing and other assorted concerns (96 of the former and 30 of the latter). This is because the author transferred six communications companies to the public utility category, making a sum of 51 such concerns. All told, this now somewhat revised TNEC industrial category includes 12 merchandising firms, 3 amusement companies, 2 specially classified transportation companies (the Hudson & Manhattan RR Co. and the General American Transportation Corp.), one publishing company (Hearst Consolidated Publications, Inc.), one agricultural concern (the United Fruit Co.), and one unclassified concern (the Koppers United Co.). Again, the more tentative higher totals in the above summary statements were arrived at by adding all companies described as possibly under family control in Table A-2 to all corporations classified as probably under family control.

[10] The former lesser figure does not differ too much from Robert Gordon's estimate that less than one-third of the total TNEC companies (exclusive of subsidiaries) were actually controlled by a small, close-knit group of individuals possessing the power to change management. See Robert A. Gordon, *Business Leadership in the Large Corporation* (Washington, D.C.: The Brookings Institution, 1945), p. 43.

[11] The more tentative higher totals in the above four summary statements were arrived at by adding all companies described by the author as possibly under family control in Table A-2 to all corporations classified there as probably under family control.

**Table A-2**

**Company-by-Company Listing and Analysis of the Top 200 Nonfinancial Concerns Classified, as of the late 1930s, under Various Types of Control by the U.S. Temporary National Economic Committee, together with Author's Evaluation**

| Control Category, according to the TNEC Study | Family Identification and Other Pertinent Information, according to the TNEC Study | Author's Evaluation When Different |
|---|---|---|
| *Majority Ownership by a Single Family:* | | |
| Ford Motor Co.* | 100% of voting stock held by the Ford family and family endowed foundation | |
| Great Atlantic & Pacific Tea Co. | 100% of voting stock held by the Hartford family | |
| Gulf Oil Corp.* | 70.2% of voting stock held by the Mellon family | |
| Hearst Consol'd. Publications, Inc. | 100% of voting stock held by William Randolph Hearst | |
| Koppers United Co. | 52.4% of voting stock held by the Mellon family | |
| S.H. Kress & Co. | 79.5% of voting stock held by the Kress family and family endowed foundation | |
| Sun Oil Co.* | 69.4% of voting stock held by the Pew family | |
| Duke Power Co. | 82.6% of voting stock held by the Duke family and family endowed foundation | |
| Federal Water Service Corp. | 100% of stock held by the Utility Operators Co., of which C.T. Chenery and family owned 18.7% of the stock | |
| *Majority Ownership by Two or More Families:* | | |
| American Cyanamid Co.* | 28.7% of voting stock held by W.B. Bell (an associate of late James B. Duke?) and another 27.2% held by Darby, Cooper, O'Daniel and Duke family interests | |
| Anderson, Clayton & Co. | 41.2% of common stock and over 40 per cent of the preferred stock (both voting) held by the Anderson and Clayton families | |

| Coca-Cola Co.* | 39.1% of voting stock held by the Coca-Cola Internatl. Corp., in which the Woodruff, Nunnally and Candler families represented the dominant interests (these and other families owned also over 10% of the stock directly) |
| --- | --- |
| Singer Mfg. Co.* | 54.7% of voting stock owned by the Clark, Bourne and Singer families |
| Virginian Rwy. Co. | 10.8% of the common stock and 52.1% of the preferred stock (both voting) held by the Rogers and Hyams families (particularly the former) |
| Long Island Lighting Co. | 59.3% of voting stock owned by the Phillips, Olmstead and Childs families |

*Predominant Minority Ownership by a Single Family:*

| Aluminum Co. of America* | 35.2% of voting stock held by the Mellon family and foundation |
| --- | --- |
| Crane Co. | 32.6% of common stock held by the Crane family |
| Cudahy Packing Co. | 48.7% of voting stock held by the Cudahy family |
| Deere & Co.* | 35.8% of the common stock and 25.8% of the preferred stock (both voting) held by the Deere family |
| E.I. du Pont de Nemours & Co.* | 43.9% of voting stock held by the du Pont family |
| Firestone Tire & Rubber Co.* | 35.5% of voting stock held by the Firestone family |
| International Harvester Co.* | 32.2% of the common stock and 23.4% of the preferred stock (both voting) held by the McCormick family |
| S.S. Kresge Co. | 44.2% of voting stock held by the Kresge family and family endowed foundation |

**Table A-2** *(cont.)*

| Control Category, according to the TNEC Study | Family Identification and Other Pertinent Information, according to the TNEC Study | Author's Evaluation When Different |
|---|---|---|
| R.H. Macy & Co. | 38.7% of voting stock held by the Straus family | |
| National Steel Corp.* | 29.0% of voting stock held by the Hanna family (through ownership of about 80% of the M.A. Hanna Co.) | |
| Pittsburgh Coal Co. | 50.1% of the common stock and 33.9% of the preferred stock (both voting) held by the Mellon family | |
| Pittsburgh Plate Glass Co.* | 35.3% of voting stock held by the Pitcairn family | |
| Western Pacific RR | About 40% of voting stock held by Arthur Curtiss James and family | |

*Predominant Minority Ownership by Two or More Families:*

| | | |
|---|---|---|
| Climax Molybdenum Co. | 31% of voting stock held by the Loeb, Hochschild, Sussman and Schott families | |
| Jones & Laughlin Steel Corp.* | 48.9% of voting stock held by the Jones and Laughlin families | |
| Marshall Field & Co. | 39.5% of the common stock and 96.9% of the preferred stock (both voting) held by the Field, Simpson, and Shedd-Reed families | |
| R.J. Reynolds Tobacco Co.* | 30.5% of voting stock held by the Reynolds, Gray, Lasater and Williams families | |
| Schenley Distillers Corp. | 37.6% of voting stock held by the Rosenstiel, Jacobi, Schwartzhaupt and Gerngross families | |
| Weyerhaeuser Timber Co.* | 34% of voting stock held by the Weyerhaeuser, Bell-Thatcher-Norton, Clapp, and McKnight families | |

*Substantial Minority Ownership by a Single Family:*

| | |
|---|---|
| Colgate-Palmolive-Peet Co.* | 17% of voting stock held by the Colgate family |
| Gimbel Bros., Inc. | 20.7% of voting stock held by the Gimbel family |
| New Jersey Zinc Co. | 20.1% of voting stock held by the Palmer family |
| Ohio Oil Co.* | 18.7% of voting stock held by the Rockefeller family and family endowed foundations |
| Owens-Illinois Glass Co.* | 16.8% of voting stock owned (indirectly) by the Levis Family |
| Sears, Roebuck & Co. | 14.0% of voting stock held by the Rosenwald family |
| Socony-Vacuum Oil Co., Inc.* | 16.3% of voting stock held by the Rockefeller family |
| Standard Oil Co. of Calif.* | 12.3% of voting stock held by the Rockefeller family and family endowed foundations |
| Standard Oil Co. of Indiana* | 11.4% of voting stock held by the Rockefeller family and family endowed foundations |
| Standard Oil Co. of N.J.* | 13.5% of voting stock held by the Rockefeller family and family endowed foundations |
| U.S. Gypsum Co. | 15.3% of the common stock and 10.4% of the preferred stock (both voting) held by the Avery family |
| U.S. Rubber Co.* | 15.7% of the common stock and 6.5% of the preferred stock (both voting) held by the du Pont family |
| North American Co. | 10.7% of common stock held by an investment company controlled by Harrison Williams |

*Substantial Minority Ownership by Two or More Families:*

| | |
|---|---|
| General American Transportation Corp. | 14.5% of voting stock held by the Mellon and Epstein families |
| General Foods Corp.* | 12.1% of voting stock held by the Davies and Woodward families |

**Table A-2** *(cont.)*

| Control Category, according to the TNEC Study | Family Identification and Other Pertinent Information, according to the TNEC Study | Author's Evaluation When Different |
|---|---|---|
| Inland Steel Co.* | 7.4% of voting stock held by the Block family and 6.4% of the stock held by the Mather-dominated Cliffs Corp. | |
| Internatl. Business Machines Corp.* | 10.2% of voting stock held by the Watson, Ford, Hewitt and Smithers families | |
| International Shoe Co. | 19.3% of voting stock held by the Johnson, Rand and Peters families | |
| Liggett & Myers Tobacco Co. | 23.5% of the common stock held by the Widener-Elkins, Dula, Ryan, and Duke family interests | |
| National Supply Co. | 11.2% of the common stock and 5.1% of the $2.00 preferred stock (both voting) held by the Hillman family and allied interests | |
| Phelps Dodge Corp.* | 11.0% of voting stock held by the A.C. James family and 9.8% held by the Dodge family and family endowed foundations | |
| Procter & Gamble Co.* | 10.9% of the common stock and 13.1% of the 8% preferred stock (both voting) held by the Procter and Gamble families | |
| Safeway Stores, Inc. | 19.2% of voting stock held by the Merrill and Lynch family interests | |
| Standard Brands, Inc. | 10% of the common stock and 6.1% of the preferred stock (both voting) held by the Fleischmann and Holmes families | |
| Wheeling Steel Corp. | 14.4% of the common stock and 11.5% of the preferred stock (both voting) held by the Whitaker-Wagner family, the Glass family, and the Mather-dominated Cliffs Corp. | |
| F.W. Woolworth Co. | 18.8% of voting stock held by the Woolworth-McCann-Betts-Donahue and Kirby families | |

| Company | Ownership | Notes |
|---|---|---|
| Youngstown Sheet & Tube Co.* | 12.8% of voting stock held by the Mather and Pickands family interests | |
| Atlantic Coast Line RR | 27% of common stock held (indirectly) by the Walters, Jenkins and Newcomer families | |
| Engineers Public Service Co. | 25.7% of voting stock held by the Stone and Webster family interests | |
| Pacific Lighting Corp. | 13.8% of common stock held by the Schilling, Miller and Volkmann families | |

*Small Minority Ownership:*

| Company | Family | Notes |
|---|---|---|
| American Can Co.* | Moore family | Probably family since 7.4% of the common stock and 0.7% of the preferred stock (both voting) held by the Moore family |
| Chrysler Corp.* | Chrysler and Bache families | Possibly family since 2.8% of voting stock held by the Bache and Chrysler families |
| Crown Zellerbach Corp.* | Zellerbach family | Probably family since 8.5% of voting stock held by the Zellerbach family, which had at least 3 seats on the board of directors |
| National Biscuit Co. | Moore family | Probably family since 7.4% of common stock held by the Moore family |
| Natl. Dairy Products Corp.* | Breyer, Rieck and McInnerney families | Possibly family since 3.8% of voting stock held by the Breyer, Rieck and McInnerney families |
| National Lead Co.* | Cornish family | Possibly family since about 8% of the voting stock was held by the Cornish family (which had no representatives on the board of directors) |
| J.C. Penney Co. | Penney, Sams and Hyer families | Probably family since 7.4% of voting stock held by the Penney, Sams and Hyer families |
| Phillips Petroleum Co.* | Phillips and du Pont families | Possibly family since 4.8% of the voting stock held by the Phillips family |

**Table A-2** (*cont.*)

| Control Category, according to the TNEC Study | Family Identification and Other Pertinent Information, according to the TNEC Study | Author's Evaluation When Different |
|---|---|---|
| Swift & Co.* | Swift family | Probably family since 5.2% of voting stock held by the Swift family, which had 6 out of the 9 seats on the board of directors |
| United Shoe Machinery Corp. | Woodward, Barbour, Hurd and Winslow families | Possibly family since 3.2% of the common stock and 1.9% of the preferred stock (both voting) was held by the Woodward, Barbour, Hurd and Winslow families |
| Warner Bros. Pictures, Inc. | Warner family | Possibly family since 4.2% of the voting stock held by the Warner family |
| Cities Service Co.* | Doherty interests | Possibly family since 5.1% of the common stock was held by the Doherty interests |
| Lone Star Gas Corp. | Crawford family | Probably family since 9.7% of the voting stock held by the Crawford family, which had at least 2 seats on the board of directors |
| *Minority Ownership by Family and Corporate Interest Groups:* | | |
| American Metal Co., Ltd.* | Hochschild family and Selection Trust, Ltd. | Possibly family since 11.9% of voting stock held by the Hochschild family (although 23.7% held by Selection Trust, Ltd.) |
| Allied Chemical & Dye Corp.* | Principal holdings those of "outside" corporate interests | |
| Consolidated Oil Corp.* | Petroleum Corp. of America and Rockefeller family | Possibly controlled by the Sinclair family interests |
| General Telephone Corp.* | Principal holdings those of various corporate interests | |
| Internatl. Paper & Power Co.* | Phipps interests and Chase Natl. Bank | Probably family since 10.9% of common stock held by the Phipps interests (although 9.3% also held by the Chase Natl. Bank) |

*Majority Ownership by a Single Corporate Interest Group:*

| | | |
|---|---|---|
| Armour & Co. (of Del.)* | Armour & Co. (of Illinois) | |
| Shell Union Oil Corp.* | Royal Dutch Shell Co. subsidiary | |
| Central RR of New Jersey | Reading Co. | |
| Louisville & Nashville RR | Atlantic Coast Line RR Co. | Probably family since controlled by the Atlantic Coast Line RR, which most likely was under the control of several families |
| New York, Chicago & St. Louis RR | Chesapeake & Ohio Rwy. | Possibly family since 57% of voting stock held by the Chesapeake & Ohio Rwy., which may be controlled by Robert R. Young and associates |
| Central & South West Utilities Co. | Middle West Corp. | |
| Cincinnati Gas & Elec. Co. | Columbia Gas & Elec. Corp. subsidiary of the United Corp. | |
| Cleveland Elec. Illum. Co. | North American Co. | Possibly family since controlled by the North American Co. (in which Harrison Williams held a substantial interest) |
| Consumers Power Co. | Commonwealth & Southern Corp. | |
| Duquesne Light Co. | Philadelphia Co. | |
| Electric Power & Light Corp. | Electric Bond & Share Corp. | |
| Empire Gas & Fuel Co. | Cities Services Corp. | Possibly family since controlled by the Cities Service Corp. (of which 5.1% of the common stock was held by the Doherty interests) |
| Internatl. Hydro-Electric System | Internatl. Paper & Power Co. | Probably family since 100% of the common stock and 4.6% of class "A" stock (both voting) was owned by the most likely family dominated Internatl. Paper & Power Co. |
| Kansas City Power & Light Co. | United Light & Power Co. | |
| New England Gas & Elec. Assn. | Associated Gas & Electric Co. | |

**Table A-2** *(cont.)*

| Control Category, according to the TNEC Study | Family Identification and Other Pertinent Information, according to the TNEC Study | Author's Evaluation When Different |
|---|---|---|
| New England Power Assn. | Internatl. Hydro-Electric System | Possibly family since Phipps interests held 5.3% of the voting stock |
| New England Tel. & Tel. Co. | American Tel. & Tel. Co. | |
| Pacific Tel. & Tel. Co. | American Tel. & Tel. Co. | |
| Philadelphia Co. | Standard Gas & Electric Co. | |
| Philadelphia Electric Co. | United Gas Improvement Co. | |
| United Gas Corp. | Electric Bond & Share Co. subsidiary | |
| West Penn Electric Co. | American Water Works & Electric Co. | |
| *Predominant Minority Ownership by a Single Corporate Interest Group:* | | |
| General Motors Corp.* | E.I. du Pont de Nemours & Co. | Probably family since 23% of voting stock owned by the family dominated E.I. du Pont de Nemours & Co. |
| Glen Alden Coal Co. | Lehigh & Wilkes-Barre Corp. | |
| Texas Gulf Sulphur Co. | Gulf Oil Corp. | Possibly family since 33.9% of voting stock held by the family dominated Gulf Oil Corp. |
| Chesapeake & Ohio Rwy. | Alleghany Corp. | Possibly family since 30.8% of common (voting) stock was held (indirectly) through the Alleghany Corp., which may have been controlled by Robert R. Young and associated interests |
| Illinois Central RR | Union Pacific RR Co. | |
| Norfolk & Western Rwy. | Pennsylvania RR Co. | |
| Pere Marquette Rwy. | Chesapeake & Ohio Rwy. | Possibly family since controlled by the Chesapeake & Ohio Rwy. which may have been in turn, dominated by the Alleghany Corp. and Robert R. Young and associated interests |
| Western Maryland Rwy. | Baltimore & Ohio RR Co. | |

| American & Foreign Power Co. | Electric Bond & Share Co. | |
| American Power & Light Co. | Electric Bond & Share Co. | |
| National Power & Light Co. | Electric Bond & Share Co. | |
| Northern States Power Co. | Standard Gas & Electric Co. | |
| Public Service Corp. of N.J. | United Corp. | |
| Standard Gas & Elec. Co. | Standard Light & Power Corp. | |

*Substantial Minority Ownership by a Single Corporate Interest Group:*

| Phila. & Reading Coal & Iron Corp. | Baltimore & Ohio RR Co. | |
| Tide Water Associated Oil Co.* | Mission Corp. | |
| American Gas & Electric Co. | Electric Bond & Share Co. | |
| Brooklyn Union Gas Co. | Koppers Co. | Possibly family since 23.9% of voting stock held by the Mellon-dominated Koppers Co. |
| Columbia Gas & Elec. Corp. | United Corp. | |
| Pacific Gas & Electric Co. | North American Co. | Possibly family since 18% of voting stock held by the North American Co. (in which Harrison Williams had a substantial interest) |
| United Gas Improvement Co. | United Corp. | |

*Majority Ownership by Two or More Corporate Interest Groups:*

| Lehigh Valley RR | Pennsylvania RR and subsidiary | |
| Reading Co. | Baltimore & Ohio RR and New York Central RR | |
| Niagara Hudson Power Co. | United Corp., Alcoa, and Niagara Share Corp. | |
| United Light & Power Co. | Koppers Co., Harrison Williams interests, and J. & W. Seligman interests | |

*Predominant Minority Ownership by Two or More Corporate Interest Groups:*

| Richfield Oil Corp.* | Cities Service Co. and Consol'd. Oil Corp. | Possibly family since 35.4% of voting stock owned by the Cities Service Co. and Consolidated Oil Corp. |

**Table A-2** *(cont.)*

| Control Category, according to the TNEC Study | Family Identification and Other Pertinent Information, according to the TNEC Study | Author's Evaluation When Different |
|---|---|---|
| Kansas City Southern Rwy. | Paine, Webber & Co. and Dutch concern | |
| Detroit Edison Co. | North American Co. | Possibly family since controlled by the North American Co. in which Harrison Williams held a substantial interest (although the American Light & Traction Co. also owned 20.3% of the stock) |
| Middle West Corp. | 1st Natl. Bank of Chicago, Bankers Trust Co., Chicago Corp., and other concerns | |
| *Substantial Minority Ownership by Two or More Corporate Interest Groups:* | | |
| Lehigh Coal & Navigation Co. | Internatl. Utilities group and other corporate interests | |
| Republic Steel Corp.* | Cliffs Corp. | Probably family since Mather family-dominated Cliffs Corp. had 8.3% of the common stock and 3 representatives on the board of directors |
| American Water Works & Electric Co. | Sanderson and Porter interests and United Corp. interests | |
| Commonwealth Edison Co. | 17 Chicago and New York banks | |
| Commonwealth & Southern Corp. | American Superpower Corp. and United Corp. | |
| Peoples Gas Light & Coke Co. | 7 Chicago and New York banks | |
| *Presumably Management Control* (according to TNEC, no apparent dominant stockholding): | | |
| Allis-Chalmers Mfg. Co.* | Small holdings, Falk family and Mellon interests | |
| American Car & Foundry Co. | Dutch concern | |
| Amer. Radiator & Std. Sanitary Corp. | Small holding, J.B. Pierce Fdtn. | |

| Company | Ownership |
|---|---|
| American Rolling Mill Co.* | Small holding, C.S. Payson |
| Amer. Smelting & Refining Co.* | Dutch concern |
| American Sugar Refining Co.* | Small holding, du Pont family |
| American Tobacco Co.* | Elkins-Widener interests |
| American Woolen Co. | |
| Anaconda Copper Mining Co.* | Dutch concern |
| Armour & Co. (of Ill.)* | Small holding, Armour family |
| Atlantic Refining Co.* | Small holdings, J.W. Van Dyke, A.R. Prentice, Union Pacific RR, and Dutch concern |
| Bethlehem Steel Corp.* | Dutch concern and Mellon and E.G. Grace interests |
| Borden Co.* | Small holdings, Borden family and Milbank interests |
| California Packing Corp. | Small holdings, Anderson and Armsby families |
| Continental Can Co.* | Small holding, F.C. Fox |
| Continental Oil Co.* | Small holding, Dutch concern |
| Corn Products Refining Co.* | Small holding, Sun Life Assurance Co. |
| Eastman Kodak Co.* | Small holdings, Strong family and Univ. of Rochester |
| General Electric Co.* | Small holdings, Sun Life Assur. Co. and GE sub. |
| B.F. Goodrich Co.* | Small holding, Raymond family |
| Goodyear Tire & Rubber Co.* | Small holding, Sears, Roebuck & Co. |
| Kennecott Copper Corp.* | Small holding, Dutch concern |
| Loew's, Inc. | Small holding, trustees of M.I.T. |
| Mid-Continent Petroleum Corp. | Dutch concern |
| Montgomery, Ward & Co. | Small holdings, Avery, McLennan, Ward and Thorne families |
| Natl. Distillers Products Corp.* | Small holding, Levis family |
| Paramount Pictures, Inc. | Small holdings, Allied Owners Corp. and Balaban family |

**Table A-2** *(cont.)*

| Control Category, according to the TNEC Study | Family Identification and Other Pertinent Information, according to the TNEC Study | Author's Evaluation When Different |
|---|---|---|
| Pullman, Inc. | Mellon interests | Probably family since 10.1% of voting stock held by the Mellon interests |
| Pure Oil Co.* | Small holding, Dawes family | |
| Radio Corp. of America* | Small holding, Dutch concern | |
| Texas Corp.* | Small holding, M.S. Hill | |
| Union Carbide & Carbon Corp.* | Small holding, Acheson family | |
| Union Oil Co. of Calif.* | Small holdings, employees provident fund and Stewart family | |
| United Fruit Co. | | |
| U.S. Smelting, Refining & Mining Co. | Small holding, trustees of M.I.T. | |
| U.S. Steel Corp.* | Small holding, Dutch concern | |
| Westinghouse Elec. & Mfg. Co.* | Small holding, Mellon interests | |
| Wilson & Co. | Dutch concern | |
| Atchison, Topeka & Sante Fe Rwy. | Small holding, Dutch concern | |
| Baltimore & Ohio RR | Small holdings, Swiss and Dutch concerns and Union Pacific RR | |
| Boston & Albany RR | Small holding, John Hancock Mutual Life Ins. Co. | |
| Carolina, Clinchfield & Ohio Rwy. | 10% of stock held by New York Life Ins. Co. | |
| Delaware & Hudson Co. | Small holding, M.J. Hicks | |
| Delaware, Lackawanna & Western RR | Small holding, Vanderbilt family | |
| Great Northern Rwy. | Small holding, A.C. James and wife | |
| Hudson & Manhatten RR | 10% of common stock and 7.6% of preferred stock (both voting) held by the Chase Natl. Bank | |

| | |
|---|---|
| Missouri-Kansas-Texas RR | Small holdings, Dutch concern and Reynolds family |
| Morris & Essex RR | Small holding, Metro. Life Ins. Co. |
| New York Central RR | Small holdings, Union Pacific RR and Delaware & Hudson Co. |
| Northern Pacific Rwy. | Small holding, A.C. James interests |
| Pennsylvania RR | Small holding, Union Pacific RR |
| Southern Pacific Co. | Small holding, Dutch concern |
| Southern Rwy. | Small holding, Milbank family |
| Union Pacific RR | Small holdings, Dutch concern and Harriman family |
| American Tel. & Tel. Co. | Small holding, Sun Life Assur. Co. |
| Boston Edison Co. | Massachusetts Utilities associates |
| Consol'd. Gas, Elec. Light & Power Co. of Baltimore | Small holding, General Electric Co. |
| Consol'd. Edison Co. of New York | Small holding, Niagara Hudson Power Co. |
| Internatl. Tel. & Tel. Corp.* | Small holding, Sun Life Assurance Co. |
| Southern Calif. Edison Co., Ltd. | Small holding, Sun Life Assurance Co. |
| Western Union Telegraph Co. | Small holdings, D.G. Geddes and Vanderbilt family |

# Appendix B

Analysis of Corporate Control Findings of Robert Larner (September 1966 *American Economic Review* article and 1970 monograph entitled *Management Control and the Large Corporation*); Robert Sheehan (15 June 1967 *Fortune* survey); and Other Persons Investigating this Subject in the Post-World War II Period

# Appendix B

As indicated earlier in the text, the two articles by Larner and Sheehan were the first studies in the post-World War II period to give much concrete evidence as to the reported decline in family control of large corporations in America.[1] Since these two articles were published at about the same time and claim to be fairly thorough and systematic research efforts which, despite their various differences in interpretation or emphasis, show that the managerial revolution is indeed a fact rather than a beguiling theory, their overall findings, sources of information, and methodology need to be subjected to close examination and comparative analysis.

First, as to conclusions, it should be noted that, according to Larner's calculations, 21 of the 117 industrials on his list (which were ranked by assets as of 1963) were controlled by either majority or minority interests.[2] However, nine of these

[1] See Robert J. Larner, "Ownership and Control in the 200 Largest Nonfinancial Corporations: 1929 and 1963," *American Economic Review* (September 1966), pp. 777-87 and Robert Sheehan, "Proprietors in the World of Big Business," *Fortune* (15 June 1967), pp. 178-83. Larner's recently published monograph, *Management Control and the Large Corporation* (New York: Dunellen Publishing Co., 1970) will be discussed in a later part of this appendix because of certain differences and changes that were made between his 1966 article and 1970 book.

[2] Of the 24 largest transportation companies on Larner's top 200 list, four were considered controlled, directly or indirectly, by various outside interests. However, in the author's opinion only one of these concerns, the New York Central RR, could definitely be classified as controlled by family forces. Two of these transportation companies, the Atlantic Coast Line RR and its affiliate or subsidiary, the Louisville & Nashville RR, were effectively controlled by the Mercantile Safe Deposit & Trust Co. of Baltimore, which (although Larner presented no data to indicate that this was a family controlled firm) may in turn have been dominated by the late Thomas Baldwin Butler. As stated earlier, the author also feels that Trans World Airlines, Inc. should probably be viewed as a management controlled corporation since there is no evidence that even a substantial minority of the banks and insurance companies holding, at least temporarily, Howard Hughes' former 78 percent stock ownership interest were dominated by outside or family forces (for identification of these institutions, see *Fortune*, May 1965, pp. 106-07). Furthermore, as shown in Table 4-1, the author believes that there were five other railroads on Larner's list (the Union Pacific RR, Chesapeake & Ohio Rwy., the Chicago, Milwaukee, St. Paul & Pacific RR, Chicago, Rock Island & Pacific RR, and the Illinois Central RR) which were controlled by family or outside forces, and three others (the Pennsylvania RR, Norfolk & Western Rwy., and the Southern Rwy) which may have been dominated by such interests in 1963. Finally, it should be pointed out that one of the railroads on Larner's list (the New York, Chicago & St. Louis RR) was not in the top 50 transportation ranking in 1965, having been merged into the Norfolk & Western Rwy. in 1964.

The author's less systematically and carefully established findings as to the locus of control in the nation's largest public utilities are contained in footnote 4 of Chapter 2 (in gross summary rather than detailed tabular form) and agree pretty much with those arrived at by Mr. Larner, except that the author is convinced that the Texas Eastern Transmission Corp. was controlled by the Brown brothers of Houston and that the Pacific Lighting Corp. may have been dominated by the Miller family of San Francisco.

117 companies (including three corporations dominated by certain outside interests)[3] were actually retail trade concerns rather than industrial enterprises, and therefore have been deleted from the following summary tabulation (Table B-1) in order to make it categorically comparable with the *Fortune* survey by Robert Sheehan. In effect, then, Larner presented an aggregate of 18 manufacturing and mining companies (or approximately 17 percent of the top 108 such firms, and roughly the same percentage of the 100 largest industrial enterprises) which could be classified, on the basis of his collected data, as being under family control. According to Sheehan, on the other hand, only about 11 percent of the 100 biggest industrial concerns in the country (ranked by volume of sales as of 1966) were dominated by family or entrepreneurial interests.

A breakdown of the biggest industrial firms which were identified in these two articles as being under family or other outside control is shown in Table B-1. As this table shows, a number of corporations which, according to Larner's evidence, appeared to be family firms were not so classified by Sheehan.[4] These companies included the Singer Co., the Dow Chemical Co., the Gulf Oil Corp., the Olin Mathieson Chemical Corp., the Aluminum Co. of America (Alcoa), and W.R. Grace & Co.

Yet when viewed from a family control standpoint, Larner's data are in need of some correction or modification too, for his study was simply conceived as an appraisal of the extent of management versus both majority and minority interest control. In order to translate Larner's findings into family control percentage totals, the author was compelled to eliminate two (and some would argue it should have been three) companies.[5] One of these concerns—the Minnesota

---

[3]These three firms were the Great Atlantic & Pacific Tea Co. (which Larner classified as majority controlled), the May Department Stores Co., and Sears, Roebuck & Co. (both of which Larner considered to be minority controlled). As indicated in Table 4-1, the author disagrees with the first and third designations and also Larner's classification of Federated Department Stores, Inc., Safeway Stores, Inc., and the F.W. Woolworth Co. as management dominated.

[4]Overall, there were 15 industrial concerns on Sheehan's list which were not on Larner's list of the 108 largest manufacturing and mining enterprises. (Three of these 15, marked "d" in Table B-1, were subsequently identified in Larner's 1970 expanded analysis as minority-controlled corporations.) Conversely, there were 20 such firms on Larner's list (including the two concerns marked "c" in Table B-1) which did not appear in the *Fortune* ranking used by Sheehan. All this was due largely to the fact that the two lists were compiled on different bases (sales versus assets) rather than because of the three-year time interval. It should also be pointed out that, in keeping with the long-established practice of *Moody's* manuals, Larner classified one concern, the General Telephone & Electronics Co., as a public utility, whereas Sheehan and *Fortune* considered it basically a manufacturing firm.

[5]In his (then) unpublished appendix Larner simply stated that the directors of the Minnesota Mining & Mfg. Co. owned about 20 percent of the voting stock. However, this could conceivably have been some kind of huge management holding, for Larner did not indicate whether there were any substantial family interests involved. Moreover, with reference to Deere & Co., Larner found that two individuals (L.E. Kennedy and V.V. Miller) served as cotrustees for 14 percent of the common stock, but because the author has been unable to determine whether these gentlemen represented either family or management forces, he decided that he should not, on the basis of the evidence presented, attempt to make any reclassification of this concern.

**Table B-1**

**Summary of Sheehan and Larner Article Findings as to Family Controlled Firms in the Top 100 and 108 Industrial Corporations as of the Mid-1960s, together with Author's Evaluation**

| Larner findings (contained in *American Economic Review*, September 1966)[a] | | Sheehan findings (contained in *Fortune*, 15 June 1967) | | Author's Evaluation When Different (in one or both cases) |
|---|---|---|---|---|
| Family or Outside Controlled Firms (out of 108 largest industrials, based on assets as of 1963) | Dominant Family or Outside Interests | Family or Entrepreneurially Controlled Firms (out of 100 largest industrials, based on volume of sales as of 1966) | Dominant Family | |
| Ford Motor Co. | Ford | Ford Motor Co. | Ford | |
| E.I. du Pont de Nemours & Co. | du Pont | E.I. du Pont de Nemours & Co. | du Pont | |
| Firestone Tire & Rubber Co. | Firestone | Firestone Tire & Rubber Co. | Firestone | |
| General Tire & Rubber Co. | O'Neil | General Tire & Rubber Co. | O'Neil | |
| Reynolds Metals Co. | Reynolds | Reynolds Metals Co. | Reynolds | |
| Pittsburgh Plate Glass Co. | Pitcairn | Pittsburgh Plate Glass Co. | Pitcairn | |
| Sun Oil Co. | Pew | Sun Oil Co. | Pew | |
| Deere & Co. | (unidentified)[b] | Deere & Co. | Deere | same as Sheehan |
| | | Ralston Purina Co.[d] | Danforth | |
| | | Carnation Co.[d] | E.H. Stuart | |
| | | McDonnell Aircraft Corp.[d] | James S. McDonnell, Jr. | |
| Minnesota Mining & Mfg. Co. | (unidentified)[b] | | | McKnight, Ordway and other families |
| Dow Chemical Co. | Dow | | | |
| Singer Co. | Clark, Kircher and associated interests | | | primarily the Clark family |
| Gulf Oil Corp. | Mellon | | | |

**Table B-1** *(Cont.)*

| Larner findings (contained in *American Economic Review*, September 1966)[a] | | Sheehan findings (contained in *Fortune*, 15 June 1967) | | Author's Evaluation When Different (in one or both cases) |
|---|---|---|---|---|
| Family or Outside Controlled Firms (out of 108 largest industrials, based on assets as of 1963) | Dominant Family or Outside Interests | Family or Entrepreneurially Controlled Firms (out of 100 largest industrials, based on volume of sales as of 1966) | Dominant Family | |
| Aluminum Co. of America (Alcoa) | Mellon, Hunt and Davies *(sic)* family interests | | | primarily the Mellon family |
| Olin Mathieson Chemical Corp. | Olin, Hanes and Nichols interests | | | primarily the Olin family |
| W.R. Grace & Co. | Grace, Pyne and Rupley interests | | | primarily the Grace family |
| Kaiser Industries Corp.[c] | Kaiser | | | |
| Schenley Industries, Inc.[c] | L. Rosentiel and associates | | | |
| American Metal Climax, Inc. | Selection Trust Ltd. | | | Selection Trust Ltd. or the Hochschild and possibly other American families |

[a]For confirmation of these findings, see Robert J. Larner, *Management Control and the Large Corporation*, pp. 70-88.
[b]See Footnote 5 (this chapter)
[c]See Footnote 4 (this chapter)
[d]See Footnote 4 (this chapter)

Mining & Mfg. Co.—was deleted because it was not specifically identified as a family-dominated corporation. The second company—American Metal Climax, Inc.—was dropped because the author was not sure whether control actually rested with the Selection Trust Ltd. (an apparently management run British investment and securities firm which owned about 12 percent of the stock) or with the Hochschilds and possibly other American families. At the same time, however, the author believes that there were three other corporations Larner classified as controlled by a pyramiding legal device which could also be described as being family dominated. These are as follows:[6]

Tidewater Oil Co.—according to Larner's note on page 780, his evidence indicated that this company was under the control of majority interests, which his (then) unpublished appendix identified as J. Paul Getty.

Joseph E. Seagrams & Sons, Inc.—Larner's then unpublished appendix showed that the Bronfman family owned 39 percent of Seagrams' parent company, Distillers Corp.-Seagrams Ltd.

Kaiser Aluminum & Chemical Corp.—Larner's then unpublished appendix revealed that 41.5 percent of the stock was held by Kaiser Industries and its subsidiary, the Henry J. Kaiser Co., which Larner had already described as being under majority (in this case family) control.

What is more, on the basis of the author's evidence presented in Table 3-1, it would appear that there were, in all, about 16 other manufacturing and mining firms on Larner's list and as many as 24 other such concerns on Sheehan's list which should have been classified as being under family control (plus a lesser number of other firms on both lists that may also have been under possible family control), but which were not so designated for one reason or another.[7]

Finally, from the standpoint of methodology, it should be observed that Larner relied very heavily on corporate proxy statements to arrive at his findings, although, as indicated earlier (see Chapter 2), these sources of information frequently fail to list large family (or other outside) shareholdings. He also claimed to have used stock ownership information submitted annually to (but

---

[6]All told, there were five industrial concerns classified as controlled by a legal device. The other two were the Coca-Cola Co., which Larner described as ultimately controlled by management forces, and the Shell Oil Co., which Larner's then unpublished appendix revealed to be under the indirect control of certain outside (foreign) interests. The author has no information indicating that this latter firm was family controlled and therefore did not include this company in this category. The data in Larner's unpublished appendix indicated (directly or indirectly) that the other concerns—Tidewater, Seagrams, and Kaiser Aluminum & Chemical—should all be considered family controlled concerns.

[7]Larner did qualify his findings however by noting on page 785 that there were four other industrial concerns (the Inland Steel Co., IBM, the Weyerhaeuser Co., and J.P. Stevens & Co.) which seemed to be controlled or at least very strongly influenced by a single family within the managerial ranks, even though the family involved owned only a small percentage of the overall voting stock. But since Larner did not view these concerns—or the one merchandising company in this category, Federated Department Stores, Inc.—as being dominated by outside interests (because he considered them management, albeit family management firms), he did not include them in the minority controlled category.

not published by) the Securities and Exchange Commission on its Form 10-K.[8] Yet in his (then) unpublished appendix, Larner referred repeatedly to the corporate proxy statements and cited the SEC's 10-K reports only twice. Moreover in one of these two cases, that of the Aluminum Co. of America (Alcoa)—the 10-K report stated that the Mellon, Hunt and Davies *(sic)* families owned a total of 8.2 percent of the outstanding shares, whereas the annual proxy statement maintained that they owned 12.4 percent of the stock (and perhaps indirectly another 14 percent), a differential which would seem to indicate that the SEC's Form 10-K is most likely not a very good source of reliable data.[9]

While Sheehan, on the other hand, did not identify any sources of information in his *Fortune* article, the fact that he did not designate either Gulf Oil or Alcoa as being under family control raises a very serious question concerning the validity of his data or methodology.[10] For example, just four months after the publication of Sheehan's article, *Fortune* itself stated (through another staff writer) that approximately 25 percent of the stock of the Gulf Oil Corp. and 30 percent of the stock of Alcoa was owned, directly or indirectly, by members of the Mellon family, the latter figure revealing that even the above Alcoa proxy statement percentage was on the low side.[11]

As indicated earlier, the publication of Larner's expanded findings in 1970 in a monograph entitled *Management Control and the Large Corporation* did not do much, unfortunately, to improve the quality of his economic analysis. One of the primary reasons for this is that Larner continued to rely largely on corporate proxy statements and selected annual reports submitted to the Federal Power Commission and Interstate Commerce Commission as his principal sources of stock ownership information.[12] As a result, while Larner extended his analysis

---

[8]In addition, on seven occasions he drew upon data contained in Standard & Poor's *Standard Listed Stock Reports*, but the author has found this to be a source of limited or questionable value.

[9]With regard to railroad and utility companies, Larner relied to a considerable extent on the annual reports which these firms must submit to the Interstate Commerce Commission and Federal Power Commission. The author, unfortunately, has not had access to these records and therefore cannot really comment on the adequacy of their control stock data, but in the case of the ICC reports he is inclined to believe, because of the discrepancy between his findings (see the second section of Table 4-1) and those of Larner, that they frequently fail to reveal much about the locus of power in such concerns.

[10]In the process of reporting that Richard K. Mellon owned about 3 percent of the stock of Alcoa and nearly 1.8 percent of the stock of the Gulf Oil Corp., Sheehan did stress the fact that this enormously wealthy individual wielded considerable influence in the affairs of these two companies, but apparently did not have any additional information as to the (Gulf Oil or Alcoa) holdings of other members of the Mellon family and therefore did not include these concerns in the family controlled category.

[11]See Charles J.V. Murphy, "The Mellons of Pittsburgh," *Fortune* (October 1967), p. 121.

[12]Here Larner did make somewhat greater use of the so-called 10-K reports submitted to the SEC than he did in his 1966 *American Economic Review* article (citing this source a total of 15 times in analyzing nonfinancial concerns ranked in the top 201 to 500 corporate bracket, in contrast to just twice for the first 200), but as far as the author has been able to determine, this source of share ownership information is no better than those listed above. Larner also utilized the various *Moody's* manuals on more frequent occasion, though the number was still limited to about a dozen because these directories do not ordinarily contain much pertinent stock ownership data.

to the 500 largest nonfinancial concerns in the country (as of 1963) and did change the control status of two companies in the top 200, the overall management versus family or outside control percentages arrived at in his study must still be viewed as quite deficient.[13]

For example, with regard to manufacturing and mining enterprises, there are at least 38 major industrial corporations of the 290 on Larner's top 500 list which, as a look at Table 3-1 will plainly show, should have been classified as family controlled firms.[14] These 38 companies (and their rankings in these two studies) are shown below.[15]

| Rank in Larner's List | Name of Company (and Rank in Author's Table 3-1) |
| --- | --- |
| 19. | International Business Machines Corp. (#9) |
| 24. | Chrysler Corp. (#6) |
| 60. | International Paper Co. (#40) |
| 61. | R.J. Reynolds Tobacco Co. (#58) |
| 80. | Inland Steel Co. (#63) |

[13] The two companies which were switched from a management to a minority controlled category were the Consolidation Coal Co. and the National Steel Corp., the discovery of additional information (the source of which was not revealed) having led Larner to alter his previous corporate control classification (see p. 120). The only other significant change in overall findings or rankings was the addition of the Erie-Lackawanna RR to the top 200 nonfinancial concerns (an inadvertent omission from Larner's original top 200) and the incorporation of the Missouri-Pacific RR (which was listed 47th in the unpublished appendix of his 1966 article) under its parent organization, the Mississippi River Fuel Corp. (#459 in Appendix A of his 1970 book).

[14] Furthermore, as may be seen by a glance at Table 3-1, there were also 18 other industrial concerns which the author felt should be described as possibly under family control because of considerable evidence pointing in this direction, generally in the form of inside or outside representation on the board of directors.

[15] At the same time it should be noted that, according to Larner, there were several other companies which he claimed were under outside control, but which the author ultimately classified, in the absence of any significant signs of family influence, as management dominated concerns. These included the Shell Oil Co., Lever Bros. Co., the General Aniline & Film Corp. (which was under federal government control), and the Kellogg Co. (a little over half of whose stock was held by the apparently management-dominated W.K. Kellogg Foundation). Larner also described the Grinnell Corp. as a minority controlled firm on the basis of unrevealed confidential data, whereas the author, not having access to this source of information and having no evidence to the contrary, felt compelled to place this company in the management dominated category. The reason for the difference between Larner's classification of the Wheeling Steel Corp. as a management controlled concern and the author's designation of the company as a family dominated firm stems from the fact that this corporation passed from a management to family control status in the latter part of 1964 when Norton Simon purchased a very substantial stock ownership interest. There would, however, seem to be a real discrepancy in the manner in which Larner treated the Coca-Cola Co., for on page 11 he maintained that the available evidence suggested that this corporation was effectively management controlled, while in Appendix A (p. 87) he asserted that this company was ultimately under minority control.

Moreover, there were two other companies on Larner's top 500 list for which he could obtain no stock ownership information, but which he felt likely to be under outside control (see Larner, *Management Control*, p. 16). However, according to *Forbes* (15 June 1968, p. 20), one of these enterprises, the above-listed Potlatch Forests, Inc., was approximately 50 percent owned by the Weyerhaeuser interests. The other company for which Larner could find no pertinent data (but believed was probably privately owned) was the Boise Cascade Corp., which the author classified as possibly under family control on the basis of a stock ownership statement contained in *Forbes* (1 April 1966, p. 30).

| Rank in Larner's List | Name of Company (and Rank in Author's Table 3-1) |
|---|---|
| 110. | U.S. Rubber Co. (#49) |
| 112. | Brunswick Corp. (#196) |
| 131. | Weyerhaeuser Co. (#92) |
| 132. | Marathon Oil Co. (#125) |
| 143. | St. Regis Paper Co. (#99) |
| 167. | Kimberly-Clark Corp. (#113) |
| 182. | Minneapolis-Honeywell Regulator Co. (#89) |
| 188. | Armour & Co. (#25) |
| 198. | J.P. Stevens & Co. (#86) |
| 208. | Philip Morris, Inc. (#142) |
| 214. | United Merchants & Manufacturers, Inc. (#120) |
| 228. | Litton Industries, Inc. (#85) |
| 271. | West Virginia Pulp & Paper Co. (#197) |
| 278. | Merck & Co., Inc. (#214) |
| 280. | General Mills, Inc. (#117) |
| 284. | Champion Papers, Inc. (#157) |
| 291. | Libbey-Owens-Ford Glass Co. (#258) |
| 304. | Colorado Fuel & Iron Corp. (#285) |
| 305. | Union Bag-Camp Paper Corp. (#238) |
| 314. | Mack Trucks, Inc. (#200) |
| 321. | Kerr-McGee Oil Industries, Inc. (#248) |
| 328. | Ingersoll-Rand Co. (#170) |
| 333. | Koppers Co., Inc. (#178) |
| 344. | McLouth Steel Corp. (#257) |
| 363. | Rockwell-Standard Corp. (#167) |
| 382. | International Shoe Co. (#174) |
| 389. | Genesco Inc. (#108) |
| 394. | Quaker Oats Co. (#160) |
| 395. | Grumman Aircraft Eng'rg. Corp. (#106) |
| 425. | Pillsbury Co. (#136) |
| 462. | Philadelphia & Reading Corp. (#270) |
| 473. | Potlatch Forests, Inc. (#311) |
| 492. | Ling-Temco-Vought, Inc. (#186) |

In addition, there are probably about a half-dozen other concerns on Larner's list but not on the author's, such as the (indirectly) Eaton-dominated Cleveland-Cliffs Iron Co., which reliable evidence indicates are most likely under family control.[16] Thus, although Larner admits at one point (p. 21) that he may have

---

[16]See, with reference to the Cleveland-Cliffs Iron Co. and its probable parent company, the Detroit Steel Corp., *Business Week* (15 January 1955), p. 112, SEC *Official Summary* (July 1960), p. 9, and the 1965 *Moody's Industrial Manual*, p. 1446.

classified some concerns incorrectly, it would seem that there are actually a very significant number of manufacturing and mining firms which he erroneously identified as management controlled companies.

Larner's record of corporate analysis proved to be somewhat better with regard to the 24 merchandising concerns found in the top 201 to 500 ranking. As may be seen in the first section of Table 4-1, only three of these companies—the First National Stores, Inc. (#19), Rapid-American Corp. (treated in conjunction with the McCrory Corp., #23), and R.H. Macy & Co. (#22)—could definitely be considered under family or entrepreneurial control.[17] There were also two other firms—Marshall Field & Co., and the City Products Corp.—which were classified as possibly family controlled because of certain recurrent patterns of corporate executive leadership or directorship service.[18]

Similarly, with regard to the 15 transportation companies on both the author's (or *Fortune's*) top 50 list and Larner's 201 to 500 ranking, only one, the Reading Co., was probably under (in this case indirect) family control according to the author's calculations.[19] And of the six transportation companies on Larner's list but not on the author's (in large measure because of the difference in the manner of selection), again only one was in all probability controlled by outside or family forces. This concern was the Delaware & Hudson Co., which has for many years been controlled (like the Union Pacific RR) by the Brown Brothers Harriman interests.[20]

Finally it should be pointed out that of the 120 public utilities on Larner's top 500 list only two—the Duke Power Co. and Hillman-dominated Texas Gas Transmission Corp.—were, according to his computations, controlled by outside forces. However, in looking over this set of very important public utilities, the author found several others which were probably under family or entrepreneurial control. These include the Texas Eastern Transmission Corp. (see *Business Week*, 25 May 1957, p. 106), the Arkansas Louisiana Gas Co. (see *Fortune*, May 1959, pp. 149 66 and Standard & Poor's *Corporation Records*, Vol. A-B, December 1967-January 1968, p. 5885), and the General Waterworks Corp. and International Utilities Corp., both of which were controlled by the Butcher family interests and allies of Philadelphia (see *Forbes*, 15 December 1965, pp. 24-26 and the SEC *Official Summary*, June 1966, p. 20).

In contrast to all of the above works, which point very much toward managerial dominance of the world of big business, two other studies published in the

[17]Larner claims, though he presents no real evidence to support this assertion, that the Western Auto Supply Co's. parent company, the Beneficial Finance Co., is itself minority controlled, but since the author has no information to this effect, he classified both firms as management dominated concerns.

[18]Of the 12 companies on Larner's top 500 list which fell into a general service or miscellaneous category, the author feels that only one was misclassified, this company being the American Broadcasting system, which has probably been dominated by the E.J. Noble interests over the years (see the first part of Chapter 2).

[19]Four others—United States Lines, Denver & Rio Grande Western RR, Delta Airlines, and Eastern Airlines—were possibly under family control.

[20]See *New York Times* (23 April 1968), p. 65 and (27 April 1968), p. 65.

post-World War II period have purported to show that such indeed was not the case. One of these was Don Villarejo's analysis, "Stock ownership and the control of corporations," a fairly detailed article which appeared in the Autumn 1961 issue of a rather obscure journal known as *New University Thought*. Villarejo, who was at that time a graduate student in physics at the University of Chicago, attempted to ascertain the amount of concentrated stock ownership in the 250 largest industrial companies as of 1959 (using the July 1960 *Fortune* ranking which was based on the volume of sales). By thumbing through the SEC's *Official Summary* from apparently 1947 to 1961 and tapping certain other sources of information, Villarejo put together a mass of what he described as "usable" data for 232 of the concerns in this top 250 category. Using a stock ownership standard of 5 percent or more as a measure of "working" control (provided, it should be added, that it represented the largest single interest), Villarejo found that about 60 percent of these 232 firms had this specified degree of concentrated stock ownership. However, as far as the author has been able to determine from Villarejo's share ownership tables, only about 85 (or roughly 37 percent) of these particular (232) concerns could be classified as being under family control.[21] Thus, despite Villarejo's seemingly very impressive array of statistics, the author does not put a great deal of stock in these figures, for many prove upon closer examination to be of a distinctly doubtful nature. In a number of cases, for instance, Villarejo relied largely on TNEC data, which were more than 20 years old and no longer therefore very reliable. Moreover, in checking Villarejo's various SEC *(Official Summary)* citations, the author found a rather sizable percentage to be in error. Hence the author is not prone to place too much weight on Villarejo's findings.

The other study having any appreciable amount of information on this important subject was Ferdinand Lundberg's 1968 best-seller entitled *The Rich and the Super-Rich*. Relying largely on just 10 issues (or roughly 2 1/2 months coverage) of *The Value Line Investment Survey* (a handy secondary source of stock ownership statistics) and only secondarily on various issues of the SEC's *Official Summary*, Lundberg compiled some data which showed that 39 of 92 big industrial concerns (that is, those which fall in the top 300 category) listed in the text

---

[21] Villarejo excluded six companies (Shell Oil, Lever Bros., J. Seagrams & Sons, General Aniline & Film, Chemstrand, and Western Electric) from his top 250 industrial analysis because they were controlled by either foreign, governmental, or other parent corporate interests. Of the other twelve companies in this special category, Villarejo actually found that seven were controlled by various private interests. These concerns were the Norton Co., Springs Cotton Mills, the American-Marietta Co., Anheuser-Busch Inc., the Carnation Co., the Kaiser Steel Corp., and Eli Lilly & Co. Of the other five firms in this category, the author would classify three—the McLouth Steel Corp., Time, Inc., and the Weyerhaeuser Co.—as probably under family control on the basis of the evidence assembled in Table 3-1. (The other two probably management dominated firms were the Lone Star Steel Corp. and the Sherwin-Williams Co.).

In addition, it should be pointed out that of the 91 corporations which Villarejo did not think were controlled by outside or family forces, the author would list five as probably under family control according to his calculations in Table 3-1. These five companies are the Colorado Fuel & Iron Corp., Libbey-Owens-Ford Glass Co., Philip Morris, Inc., R.J. Reynolds Tobacco Co., and the U.S. Rubber Co.

of his study could be considered under family control, if one used a stock ownership standard of 5 percent or more as a means of determining such matters.[22] But in the author's opinion these figures are extremely misleading, since these firms were not selected in any systematic fashion (not representing anything like the 92 largest industrial corporations in the country), and many big companies controlled by family interests were missed in Lundberg's rather haphazard survey.

In addition, in his Appendix B Lundberg presented a tabular analysis of the extent to which the 202 top nonfinancial concerns (ranked according to 1964 assets) were dominated by one or more wealthy familes as of, apparently, the mid- or late 1960s. The author, however, has many serious doubts about the accuracy or validity of these reported findings, particularly since no real information was provided to support them. Instead Lundberg merely inserted a general claim at the head of the third and last column that such family dominance designations were based on some unspecified (1960-65?) SEC source or the now very much outdated TNEC records. All told, of the 121 mining and manufacturing firms listed in his Appendix B, Lundberg concluded that 86 (or approximately 71 percent) were dominated by various family groups. This, it should be noted, is an inordinately high and probably inaccurate percentage if the author's assembled data (see Table 3-1) are at all close to correct, and one which must be viewed as strongly suspect.

[22]See Ferdinand Lundberg, *The Rich and the Super-Rich* (New York: Lyle Stuart, Inc., 1968), pp. 220-45. Only about 25 of the 100 largest industrial concerns were listed in this very unevenly selected sample, much too small a number to use as a basis for generalization. Overall, Lundberg examined, in unsystematic and superficial manner, something like 270 fairly sizable industrial concerns, about 20 merchandising firms, a like number of transportation companies, 2 financial institutions, and about a half-dozen miscellaneous corporations. On. the basis of these data, Lundberg went on to claim (on p. 248) that it has now ". . . been abundantly shown that the members of a small coterie, comparable in relative size to the owning class of the Banana Republics and other unbenign polities, own and control all important economic enterprises in the United States," an assertion which the author finds close to incredible.

# Appendix C

Company-by-Company Corporate
Control Analysis of Manufacturing and
Mining Concerns Ranked from 301 to
500 on *Fortune's* 1965 Industrial List

**Table C-1**

**Company-by-Company Corporate Control Analysis of Manufacturing and Mining Concerns Ranked from 301 to 500 on *Fortune's* 1965 Industrial List**

Abbreviation and Explanation Key:

PF – probably family

F? – possibly family

PM – probably management

I-BD – significant family representation as inside members of the board of directors

O-BD – significant family representation as outside members of the board of directors

I & O-BD – significant family representation as both inside and outside members of the board of directors (though not necessarily at the same time; in those relatively few instances where significant gaps have occurred, the author has used the designation I or O-BD)

By the phrase "over the years" the author means from at least roughly 1955 to 1965, by the term "in recent years" less than the last five to eight years of this time period (although in both cases there may be some gaps in certain years)

NYT – *New York Times*

S & P – Standard & Poor's

SEC OS – SEC's *Official Summary of Securities Transactions and Holdings*

| 1965 Rank (based on 1964 volume of sales) | Name of Company | Type of Control | Evidence or Comments |
|---|---|---|---|
| 301. | Federal Mogul Corp. | F? | Muzzy family?—see I-BD over the years |
| 302. | Interchemical Corp. | PM | |
| 303. | Peabody Coal Co. | PF | As of 1965 the Kelce family owned more than 14% of the stock (see *Fortune*, September 1965, p. 52); also I & O-BD in recent years |
| 304. | Lear Siegler, Inc. | PM | |
| 305. | Beech-Nut Life Savers, Inc. | PF | Probably controlled by the Arkell and Noble family interests, in recent years most likely the latter (see *Time* 18 June 1956, pp. 92-93); also I-BD over the years |

| No. | Company | PM | PF | F? | Notes |
|---|---|---|---|---|---|
| 306. | Dan River Mills, Inc. | | PF | | As of the early 1960s at least 9.2% of the stock owned by the Iselin and Jefferson interests (see SEC *OS*, May 1961); also O-BD in recent years |
| 307. | West Point Mfg. Co. | | PF | | Probably controlled by the Lanier family (see *Forbes*, 1 March 1966, p. 63); also I-BD over the years |
| 308. | Carborundum Co. | | PF | | As of 1967 the Mellon family owned 20% of the stock (see *Fortune*, October 1967, p. 122); also O-BD over the years |
| 309. | Frito-Lay, Inc. | | PF | | As of 1964-65 H.W. Lay had at least 8.3% of the stock (see SEC *OS*, April 1964); also I-BD over the years |
| 310. | Electric Storage Battery Co. | PM | | | |
| 311. | Potlatch Forests, Inc. | | PF | | Approximately 50% of the stock owned by the Weyerhaeuser interests (see *Forbes*, 15 June 1968, p. 20); also O-BD over the years |
| 312. | Castle & Cooke, Inc. | | | F? | Castle and Cooke interests?–see I or O-BD over the years |
| 313. | Evans Products Co. | | PF | | As of 1965 the Norton Simon interests had 9.3% of the stock (see *Fortune*, June 1965, p. 149 and *Forbes*, 1 December 1966, p. 33); also I & O-BD in 1965 |
| 314. | Iowa Beef Packers, Inc. | | PF | | Up to late 1965 founders A.D. Anderson and C.J. Holman together owned 12.5% of the stock (see SEC *OS*, December 1965); also I-BD in recent years |
| 315. | Foster Wheeler Corp. | | PF (indirectly) | | Probably controlled (through a pyramiding relationship) by the Olmstead and Johnston-Lemon interests of Washington, D.C. (see SEC *OS*, October 1963; the 1965 *Moody's Bank & Finance Manual*, p. 891, and the 1965 *Moody's Industrial Manual*, p. 1288); also O-BD over the years |

**Table C-1** *(cont.)*

| 1965 Rank | Name of Company | Type of Control | Evidence or Comments |
|---|---|---|---|
| 316. | Richardson-Merrill, Inc. | PF | As of the late 1950s and early 1960s the Richardson family had at least 3.4% of the stock (see SEC *OS*, March 1957, November 1962, and April 1964); also I & O-BD over the years |
| 317. | Fairmount Foods Co. | PM | |
| 318. | Continental Motors Corp. | PF | As of the mid-1960s T.C. Ryan (of San Diego, Calif.) had at least 37.9% of the stock of the Ryan Aeronautical Co., which in turn owned 44.8% of the stock of the Continental Motors Corp. (see the 1965 *Moody's Industrial Manual*, p. 503 and SEC *OS*, January 1967); also I-BD in 1965 |
| 319. | Diamond Alkali Co. | PF | As of the early 1960s the Evans family (of Cleveland) had at least 5.8% of the stock (see SEC *OS*, April 1962); also I & O-BD over the years |
| 320. | A.E. Staley Mfg. Co. | PF | As of 1967 the Staley family owned 53% of the stock (see *Fortune*, 15 June 1967, p. 180); also I & O-BD over the years |
| 321. | Merritt-Chapman & Scott Corp. | PF | As of the mid-1960s the Wolfson family (of Florida) had about 30% of the stock (see *NYT*, 19 October 1966, p. 63); also I-BD over the years |
| 322. | Gerber Products Co. | PF | As of the late 1960s the Gerber family had 23.1% of the stock (see *Finance*, July 1969, p. 52); also I & O-BD over the years |
| 323. | Amsted Industries, Inc. | PM | |
| 324. | Ex-Cell-O Corp. | F? | Andreae family?– see O-BD over the years |
| 325. | American Enka Corp. | PM (foreign) | Majority of stock owned by probably management dominated Algemene Kunstzijde Unie N.V. of Holland (see the 1965 *Moody's Industrial Manual*, p. 278); also O-BD over the years |

| | | | |
|---|---|---|---|
| 326. | Pittsburgh Steel Co. | PF | As of the mid-1960s the family-controlled J.H. Hillman & Sons Co. owned 19% of the voting stock (see the 1965 *Moody's Industrial Manual*, p. 839); also I & O-BD over the years |
| 327. | Blaw-Knox Co. | PM | |
| 328. | Chemetron Corp. | PM | |
| 329. | Bell & Howell Co. | PM | |
| 330. | Bemis Bros. Bag Co. | PF | As of the late 1960s the Bemis family had at least 6.4% of the stock (see SEC *OS*, October 1968, April 1969, May 1969, and June 1969); also I-BD over the years |
| 331. | Cincinnati Milling Machine Co. | PF | As of 1971 the Geier family still had more than 25% of the stock (see *Business Week*, 20 November 1971, p. 46); also I-BD over the years |
| 332. | Rockwell Mfg. Co. | PF | As of 1967 the Rockwell family (of Pittsburgh) owned 20% of the stock, with another 20-25% in the hands of their allies (see *Fortune*, June 1967, p. 101); also I-BD over the years |
| 333. | Eastern Gas & Fuel Associates | PF(I) | As of the mid-1960s S.H. Scheuer had 20.6% of the stock (see SEC *OS*, June 1965 and *Fortune*, February 1969, pp. 123 & 154); also O-BD in recent years |
| 334. | Outboard Marine Corp. | PF | As of the late 1950s S.F. Briggs had 22.9% of the stock and R. Evinrude had another 18.7% (see *Fortune*, July 1958, p. 192); also I-BD over the years |

**Table C-1** *(cont.)*

| 1965 Rank | Name of Company | Type of Control | Evidence or Comments |
|---|---|---|---|
| 335. | Schenley Industries, Inc. | PF(I) | According to the December 1965 SEC *OS*, L.S. Rosenstiel had 18.2% of the stock–according to the 1965 *Moody's Industrial Manual* (p. 1570), L.S. Rosenstiel had 11.7% of the voting stock and his associates had another 12.8%; also I-BD over the years |
| 336. | Hupp Corp. | PM | |
| 337. | Colt Industries, Inc. | PM | |
| 338. | Anchor Hocking Glass Corp. | F? | As of the early 1960s the Fulton family had at least 6.2% of the stock (see SEC *OS*, May 1961 and February 1962); also I & O-BD over the years |
| 339. | General Baking Co. | PM | |
| 340. | Amerada Petroleum Corp. | PM | |
| 341. | Ward Foods, Inc. | PF(I) | As of the mid-1960s probably controlled (through the Noma Corp.) by the Bluhdorn and Yaeger interests (see *NYT*, 11 July 1963, p. 37 and SEC *OS*, December 1963); also O-BD in recent years |
| 342. | Jim Walter Corp. | PF | As of the mid-1960s James Walter had at least 8.0% of the stock (see SEC *OS*, April 1964); also I-BD over the years |
| 343. | Granite City Steel Co. | PM | |
| 344. | Purex Corp., Ltd. | PF | As of the mid-1960s the Pelletier-Precourt family had 18% of the stock (see *Forbes*, 15 February 1967, p. 32); also I-BD over the years |
| 345. | Pabst Brewing Co. | PM | |

| No. | Company | | | Notes |
|---|---|---|---|---|
| 346. | Sharon Steel Corp. | | PF | Probably controlled by the Roemer family (see *Forbes*, 1 June 1961, p. 32); also I-BD over the years |
| 347. | Indian Head Mills, Inc. | | PF(I) | As of the mid-1960s J.E. Robison owned about 18.9% of the stock (see SEC *OS*, December 1964); also I-BD over the years and *Forbes*, 15 November 1964, p. 31 |
| 348. | McCall Corp. | | PF | As of 1965 Hunt Foods & Industries, Inc., controlled by Norton Simon, owned 28.4% of the stock (see the 1965 *Moody's Industrial Manual*, p. 2109); also O-BD in recent years |
| 349. | Curtiss-Wright Corp. | PM | | |
| 350. | Interstate Bakeries Corp. | PM | | |
| 351. | Simmons Co. | | PF | As of 1971 the Simmons family still had about 4.2% of the stock (see *NYT*, 8 August 1971, Sect. 3, p. 7); also I-BD over the years and *Forbes*, 15 March 1966, p. 41 |
| 352. | Stanley Warner Corp. | | PF | As of the mid-1960s the Fabian family indirectly owned 17.8% of the stock (see *NYT*, 22 July 1967, p. 28); also I-BD over the years |
| 353. | American Petrofina, Inc. | PM (foreign) | | Subsidiary of probably management dominated Petrofina S.A. of Belgium (see 1965 *Moody's Industrial Manual*, p. 1264) |
| 354. | Square D Co. | F? | | Magin family?:—see I-BD over the years |
| 355. | Universal-Cyclops Steel Corp. | | PF | As of the early 1960s the Reeves interests (of Ohio) had at least 5.6% of the stock (see SEC *OS*, June and September 1961); also O-BD in recent years |
| 356. | Rayonier, Inc. | PM | | |
| 357. | Standard Packaging Corp. | PM | | |

**Table C-1** *(cont.)*

| 1965 Rank | Name of Company | Type of Control | Evidence or Comments |
|---|---|---|---|
| 358. | Murphy Oil Corp. | PF | As of the mid-1960s the Murphy family (of Arkansas) owned 55% of the stock (see *Forbes*, 1 November 1967, p. 75); also I-BD over the years |
| 359. | Cutler-Hammer, Inc. | PF | As of the mid-1960s the Fitzgerald family had about 10% of the stock (see *Forbes*, 1 July 1964, p. 16); also I or O-BD over the years |
| 360. | Thomas J. Lipton, Inc. | PM (foreign) | Subsidiary of probably management dominated Unilever N.V. (see the 1965 *Moody's Industrial Manual*, p. 2702) |
| 361. | U.S. Pipe & Foundry Co. | F? | Colgate family?– see O-BD over the years |
| 362. | Kern County Land Co. | PM | |
| 363. | Kendall Co. | PF | During the 1960s the Kendall family owned between 28% and 29.3% of the stock (see SEC *OS*, March and April 1961 and *NYT*, 9 September 1971, p. 61); also I or O-BD over the years |
| 364. | Allied Mills, Inc. | PM | |
| 365. | National Can Corp. | PM | |
| 366. | Chicago Bridge & Iron Corp. | PF | As of the late 1960s the Horton family (of Chicago) had at least 8.2% of the stock (see SEC *OS*, August 1969 and *Forbes*, 15 February 1968, p. 38); also I-BD over the years |
| 367. | Packaging Corp. of America | PF | Probably controlled by the Carey family and W. Young, the latter having 4.0% of the stock as of the mid-1960s (see SEC *OS*, June and October 1963); also I & O-BD over the years |
| 368. | Pennsalt Chemicals Corp. | PM | |

| | |  |  |  | |
|---|---|---|---|---|---|
| 369. | Mohasco Industries, Inc. | | | PF | As of the mid-1960s the Shuttleworth family had at least 3.0% of the stock (see SEC *OS*, March 1965 and March 1967); Ewing family also probably involved; also I-BD over the years |
| 370. | Beaunit Corp. | PM | | | |
| 371. | Hart, Schaffner & Marx | | | PF | As of the mid- or late 1960s the Schaffner family had at least 3.4% of the stock (see SEC *OS*, May 1965 and March 1968); also O-BD over the years |
| 372. | The Stanley Works | PM | | | |
| 373. | Pacolet Industries, Inc. | | | PF | As of the mid-1960s a large majority of the stock was held by the privately owned Deering-Milliken, Inc. (see *Fortune*, 15 July 1966, p. 225); also I & O-BD over the years |
| 374. | Ampex Corp. | | F? | | Mellon family? (see *Fortune*, October 1967, p. 127); also I-BD over the years |
| 375. | Falstaff Brewing Co. | | | PF | As of 1965 the Griesedieck family had at least 4.5% of the stock and as of 1960 H.A. Beffa had 7.1% (see SEC *OS*, August 1965, October 1965, November 1965, August 1971, and November 1960; *NYT*, 12 June 1966, Sect. 3, p. 3; *Forbes*, 1 May 1965, p. 37; and *Dun's Review*, August 1966, pp. 38-40); also I & O-BD over the years |
| 376. | Curtis Publishing Co. | | | PF | As of the late 1960s the Curtis-Bok interests had 32% of the common stock and 22% of the preferred stock (see *NYT*, 7 February 1969, p. 49); also I-BD over the years |
| 377. | Fairchild Camera & Instrument Corp. | | | PF | As of 1965 S.M. Fairchild had 19% of the stock (see *Forbes*, 15 June 1965, p. 30); also I-BD over the years |
| 378. | Vulcan Materials Corp. | | | PF | As of 1960 the Ireland family had about 41% of the stock (see *Fortune*, January 1960, p. 148); also I & O-BD over the years |

**Table C-1** *(cont.)*

| 1965 Rank | Name of Company | Type of Control | Evidence of Comments |
|---|---|---|---|
| 379. | Polaroid Corp. | PF | As of the mid-1960s the Land family had 19.4% of the stock (see *Forbes*, 15 June 1964, p. 19); also I-BD over the years |
| 380. | Consolidated Cigar Corp. | PF | As of early 1959 the Silberman family owned 12.4% of the stock and as trustees or executors controlled another 12.5% (see the 1961 *Moody's Industrial Manual*, p. 799); also I-BD over the years and *NYT*, 24 September 1964, p. 18. |
| 381. | Baldwin-Lima-Hamilton Corp. | PM | |
| 382. | Trane Co. | PF | As of the mid- and late 1960s the Hood and Trane families had at least 11.3% of the stock (see SEC *OS*, July 1965, May 1966, and May 1968); also I & O-BD over the years |
| 383. | The New York Times Co. | PF | As of the mid-1960s the Ochs-Sulzberger family had over 60% of the stock (see *Forbes*, 15 August 1967, p. 20); also I & O-BD over the years |
| 384. | Witco Chemical Co. | PF | As of 1965 the Wishnick family owned 34% of the stock (see the 1965 *Moody's Industrial Manual*, p. 1951); also I-BD over the years |
| 385. | Hanna Mining Co. | PF (indirectly) | As of 1965 46.5% of the stock held by the probably family dominated M.A. Hanna Co. (see the 1965 *Moody's Industrial Manual*, p. 1850, *Forbes*, 1 November 1965, p. 16, and *NYT*, 5 April 1964, Sect. 3, p. 1); also I & O-BD over the years |
| 386. | Fieldcrest Mills, Inc. | PF (indirectly) | As of 1965 53.8% of the stock was held by the Amoskeag Co., of which the Dumaine family owned 30.5% of the shares (see the 1965 *Moody's Industrial Manual*, p. 881 and SEC *OS*, July 1965); also O-BD over the years |

| | | | |
|---|---|---|---|
| 387. | Armstrong Rubber Co. | PM (indirectly) | About 10% of the stock owned by the probably management dominated Sears, Roebuck & Co. in the mid-1960s (see SEC *OS*, February 1967); also O-BD in recent years |
| 388. | American Chain & Cable Co., Inc. | PM | |
| 389. | Universal American Corp. | PF(I) | As of 1965 H.E. Gould and F.S. Levien had 31% of the stock (see SEC *OS*, July 1965); also I-BD over the years |
| 390. | Great Western Sugar Co. | F? | Thacher-White interests?—see O-BD over the years |
| 391. | Cowles Magazines & Broadcasting, Inc. | PF | As of the mid-1960s the Cowles family had at least 20.6% of the stock (see SEC *OS*, September 1966); also I & O-BD over the years |
| 392. | Di Giorgio Corp. | PF | As of the late 1960s the Di Giorgio family owned 20% of the stock (see *Forbes*, 1 August 1968, p. 48); also I & O-BD over the years |
| 393. | Stewart-Warner Corp. | PM | |
| 394. | KVP Sutherland Paper Co. | PM | |
| 395. | Keystone Wire & Steel Co. | PF | During the 1960s the Sommer family had at least 3.3% of the stock (see SEC *OS*, May 1961, February 1962, August 1966, August 1967, March 1968, and August 1968); also I & O-BD over the years (in fact, a majority of the officers and directors were members of the family in 1965) |
| 396. | Ruberoid Co. | PF | As of the mid-1960s the Milstein family had at least 5.5% of the stock (see SEC *OS*, September 1963); also I-BD in recent years and *Forbes*, 15 March 1971, p. 21 |
| 397. | Certain-teed Products Corp. | PM | |

**Table C-1** *(cont.)*

| 1965 Rank | Name of Company | Type of Control | | Evidence or Comments |
|---|---|---|---|---|
| 398. | Western Publishing Co. | | PF | Probably controlled by the Wadewitz, Benstead, and Johnson interests (of Wisconsin), which held at least 12.5% of the voting stock as of the mid- and late 1960s (see SEC *OS*, February 1966, July 1966, December 1966, and September 1970); also I-BD over the years |
| 399. | Eagle Pitcher Co. | PM | | |
| 400. | Inland Container Corp. | | PF(I) | As of 1970 H.C. Krannert still had at least 9.3% of the stock (see SEC *OS*, September 1970); also I-BD over the years |
| 401. | I-T-E Circuit Breaker Co. | | PF | Up to 1967 probably controlled by the Scott family (see *Forbes*, 15 March 1970, p. 51); also I-BD over the years |
| 402. | American Biltrite Rubber Co. | | PF | As of the mid-1960s the Marcus family had at least 15.6% of the stock (see SEC *OS*, August 1964)—Bernstein family also probably involved—according to S & P *Corporation Records* (Vol. A-B, December 1970-January 1971, p. 1934), Bernstein family had 35.3% of the stock; also I & O-BD over the years |
| 403. | Jonathan Logan, Inc. | | PF | As of 1965 the Schwartz family had at least 20.7% of the stock (see SEC *OS*, January and March 1965); also I-BD over the years |
| 404. | Rohr Corp. | | F? | Rohr family? (see SEC *OS*, January 1962); also I-BD over the years |
| 405. | Riegel Paper Corp. | | PF | As of the late 1960s the Riegel family had between 30% and 35% of the stock (see *Forbes*, 1 September 1968, p. 39); also I & O-BD over the years |
| 406. | Joy Manufacturing Co. | PM | | |
| 407. | Hammermill Paper Co. | PM | | |

| No. | Company | | | | Notes |
|---|---|---|---|---|---|
| 408. | Maremont Corp. | PF | | | As of the late 1950s the Maremont-Wolfson family (of Chicago) had at least 6.7% of the stock (see SEC *OS*, November 1967 and February 1970); also I-BD over the years |
| 409. | Endicott Johnson Corp. | | PM | | |
| 410. | United Biscuit Co. of America | | PM | | |
| 411. | Lone Star Cement Corp. | | PM | | |
| 412. | Chesebrough-Pond's, Inc. | | PM | | |
| 413. | Colorado Milling & Elevator Co. | PF | | | As of 1965 probably controlled by the Thacher-White family (see *Time*, 16 August 1968, p. 65 and *Business Week*, 19 October 1968, p. 179) |
| 414. | Ideal Cement Co. | PF | | | As of the mid-1960s the Dobbins-Boettcher interests had 11.4% of the stock (see SEC *OS*, December 1966); also I-BD over the years |
| 415. | Hewlett-Packard Co. | PF(I) | | | As of 1965 David Packard and W.R. Hewlett owned 63.8% of the stock (see the 1965 *Moody's Industrial Manual*, p. 1479); also I-BD over the years |
| 416. | SCM Corp. | | | F? | Mead-Kleinschmidt and Smith families (of Syracuse)?—see I & O-BD over the years |
| 417. | Maytag Co. | PF | | | As of the early 1960s the Maytag family had 57% of the stock (see *Time*, 18 August 1961, p. 70); also I & O-BD over the years |
| 418. | Champion Spark Plug Co. | PF | | | As of about 1950 the Stranahan family had 86.4% of the stock (see *Forbes*, 15 May 1959, p. 37); also I-BD over the years |

**Table C-1** *(cont.)*

| 1965 Rank | Name of Company | Type of Control | Evidence or Comments |
|---|---|---|---|
| 419. | Kellwood Co. | PM (indirectly) | Possibly controlled by the probably management dominated Sears, Roebuck & Co., which owned 21.4% of the stock (see the 1965 *Moody's Industrial Manual*, p. 170); also O-BD in recent years |
| 420. | Harsco Corp. | PM | |
| 421. | Woodward Iron Co. | PF | As of the late 1950s the Woodward family had at least 19.1% of the stock (see SEC *OS*, December 1957); also I-BD over the years |
| 422. | Cessna Aircraft Co. | PF | As of the mid-1960s the Cessna-Wallace family had at least 4.4% of the stock (see SEC *OS*, June 1964 and *Forbes*, 15 October 1960, p. 22); also I-BD over the years |
| 423. | Fibreboard Paper Products Corp. | PM | |
| 424. | Southern States Cooperative, Inc. | PM | |
| 425. | Control Data Corp. | F? | Wm. C. Norris? (see SEC *OS*, June 1964); also I-BD since establishment in 1957 |
| 426. | Wm. Wrigley, Jr. Co. | PF | As of the mid-1960s the Wrigley family had at least 25.4% of the stock (see SEC *OS*, October 1966 and November 1966); also I-BD over the years |
| 427. | Houdaille Industries, Inc. | PM | |
| 428. | E.W. Bliss Co. | PM | |
| 429. | Lukens Steel Co. | PF | As of the late 1950s the Lukens and Huston families owned nearly 40% of the stock (see *Time*, 22 April 1957, p. 97)—as of 1970 the Huston family still owned 36.7% of the stock (see S & P *Corporation Records*, Vol. L-O, October-November 1970, p. 3729); also I & O-BD over the years |

| No. | Company | PM | PF | Notes |
|---|---|---|---|---|
| 430. | Collins & Aikman Corp. | | PF | As of the late 1960s the McCullough family had 10% of the stock (see *Forbes*, 1 September 1969, p. 41); also I-BD in recent years |
| 431. | Calumet & Hecla, Inc. | PM | | |
| 432. | Internatl. Pipe & Ceramics Corp. | | PF | As of the mid-1960s the Hirsh family had at least 7.4% of the stock (see SEC *OS*, April 1965 and August 1966); also I & O-BD over the years |
| 433. | National Sugar Refining Co. | | PF | As of 1965 the Havemeyer interests had a little over 26% of the stock (see the 1965 *Moody's Industrial Manual*, p. 2137); also I-BD over the years |
| 434. | Rheem Manufacturing Co. | PM | | |
| 435. | American Optical Co. | PM | | |
| 436. | Handy & Harman | | PF(I) | As of 1965 C.W. Handy had 10.7% of the stock (see SEC *OS*, December 1965); also I-BD over the years |
| 437. | Miles Laboratories, Inc. | | PF | As of the early 1960s the Beardsley-Miles family owned about 50% of the stock (see *Forbes*, 15 November 1961, p. 30); also I & O-BD over the years |
| 438. | Wyandotte Chemicals Corp. | | PF | As of the late 1960s the Ford-Knight family (of Detroit and Toledo) owned about 60% of the stock (see *Business Week*, 8 November 1969, p. 50); also I & O-BD over the years |
| 439. | Copperweld Steel Co. | PM | | |
| 440. | Reichhold Chemicals, Inc. | | PF(I) | As of the early 1960s H.H. Reichhold owned 29% of the stock (see *Forbes*, 1 September 1962, p. 15); also I-BD over the years |

**Table C-1** *(cont.)*

| 1965 Rank | Name of Company | Type of Control | Evidence or Comments |
|---|---|---|---|
| 441. | Ekco Products Co. | PM | |
| 442. | Canada Dry Corp. | PF | As of 1965 the Norton Simon interests had 24.8% of the stock (see *Fortune*, June 1965, p. 148); also O-BD in 1965 |
| 443. | Grolier Inc. | PF | As of the mid- and late 1960s the Murphy family (of New York City) had at least 28.9% of the stock (see SEC *OS*, March 1967 and November 1969); also I-BD over the years |
| 444. | Union Tank Car Co. | PM | |
| 445. | Cabot Corp. | PF | As of 1965 the Cabot family owned 64% of the stock (see the 1965 *Moody's Industrial Manual*, p. 303); also I-BD over the years |
| 446. | Koehring Co. | PM | |
| 447. | Standard Pressed Steel Co. | PF | As of 1965 the Hallowell family had at least 21.2% of the stock (see SEC *OS*, February 1965); also I-BD over the years |
| 448. | Harbison-Walker Refractories Co. | PM | |
| 449. | Royal McBee Corp. | PF | Probably controlled by the Ryan family of New York City (see *Forbes*, 1 May 1962, p. 28); also I-BD over the years |
| 450. | Crowell-Collier & MacMillan, Inc. | F? | As of the mid-1960s may have been controlled by A.G. Erpf (see *NYT*, 3 February 1971, p. 40); also I-BD over the years |
| 451. | Arvin Industries, Inc. | PM | |
| 452. | Chicago Pneumatic Tool Co. | PM | |
| 453. | Clevite Corp. | PM | |

| No. | Company | Class 1 | Class 2 | Notes |
|---|---|---|---|---|
| 454. | Island Creek Coal Co. | F? (indirectly) | | May have been controlled by the probably family dominated Cleveland Trust Co.—see I or O-BD over the years |
| 455. | Warwick Electronics, Inc. | PM (indirectly) | | As of 1965 84.5% of the stock owned by the probably management dominated Sears, Roebuck & Co. (see the 1965 *Moody's Industrial Manual*, p. 2558); also I or O-BD over the years |
| 456. | Air Products & Chemicals, Inc. | | PF | As of the mid-1960s the Pool family had at least 4.7% of the stock (see SEC *OS*, September 1963 and March 1964); also I-BD over the years |
| 457. | Botany Industries, Inc. | | PF | As of the mid-1960s the Daroff family owned 25.2% of the stock (see *Finance*, September 1967, p. 34C); also I & O-BD in recent years |
| 458. | Olivetti Underwood Corp. | | PF (foreign) | Controlled by the probably family dominated Olivetti & Co., S. p. A. of Italy (see *Business Week*, 19 November 1960, p. 76 and *Fortune*, September 1964, p. 60); Agnelli (Fiat) and Pirelli families may also be involved; also I & O-BD in recent years |
| 459. | St. Joseph Lead Co. | PM | | |
| 460. | U.S. Industries, Inc. | PM | | |
| 461. | Geo. D. Roper Corp. | PM (indirectly) | | As of 1965 59% of the stock owned by the probably management dominated Sears, Roebuck & Co. (see the 1965 *Moody's Industrial Manual*, p. 2557); also O-BD in recent years |
| 462. | U.S. Shoe Corp. | | PF | As of the mid- and late 1960s the Stern family had at least 6.6% of the stock (see SEC *OS*, May 1964 and September 1968); Stix family may be involved too; also I-BD over the years |
| 463. | Wagner Electric Corp. | PM | | |
| 464. | Howe Sound Co. | PM (foreign) | | As of 1965 49% of the stock owned by Pechiney Enterprises of France (see the 1965 *Moody's Industrial Manual*, p. 1888); also O-BD in recent years |

**Table C-1** *(cont.)*

| 1965 Rank | Name of Company | Type of Control | | Evidence or Comments |
|---|---|---|---|---|
| 465. | Miehle-Goss-Dexter, Inc. | PM | | |
| 466. | Beech Aircraft Corp. | | PF | As of the latter part of 1965 Mrs. Olive A. Beech and her daughters owned 15.5% of the stock (see the 1966 *Moody's Industrial Manual*, p. 195); also I-BD over the years |
| 467. | Gardner-Denver Co. | PM | | |
| 468. | Commonwealth Oil Refining Co. | F? (indirectly) | | As of the mid-1960s approximately 20% of the stock was was owned by the First Boston Corp., New England Petroleum Corp., State Street Research & Management Co. (of Boston), and the Pitcairn Co., some of which are probably family controlled (see *NYT*, 17 May 1964, Sect. 3, p. 3); also O-BD over the years |
| 469. | Superior Oil Co. | | PF | As of about 1960 the Keck family owned 51% of the stock (see *Fortune*, August 1959, p. 47); also I & O-BD over the years |
| 470. | Bell Intercontinental Corp. | | PF (indirectly) | As of 1965 50.1% of the stock owned by the Equity Corp., of which D.M. Milton had roughly 20% of the stock (see the 1965 *Moody's Industrial Manual*, p. 2169, *Forbes*, 15 June 1965, p. 29, and *NYT*, 2 February 1966, p. 43); also I & O-BD over the years |
| 471. | Universal Match Corp. | PM | | |
| 472. | Rex Chainbelt, Inc. | PM | | |
| 473. | Clark Oil & Refining Corp. | | PF | As of 1967 the Clark family (of Milwaukee) owned 26% of the stock (see *Fortune*, 15 June 1967, p. 182); also I-BD over the years |
| 474. | Cooper-Bessemer Corp. | PM | | |
| 475. | Farmers Union Central Exchange | PM | | |

| | Company | Type | Notes |
|---|---|---|---|
| 476. | Hobart Manufacturing Co. | PF | Probably controlled by the Meeker and Johnston families (of Troy, Ohio), the latter owning at least 7.7% of the stock as of the mid-1960s (see SEC *OS*, July 1962); also I-BD over the years |
| 477. | Bucyrus-Erie Co. | PM | |
| 478. | International Silver Co. | PF | As of 1965 C.W. Engelhard (of Engelhard Hanovia, Inc.) owned 5.2% of the stock (see *Forbes*, 1 August 1965, p. 20); also O-BD in recent years |
| 479. | Needham Packing Co. | PF | As of 1967 the Needham family owned 25% of the stock (see *Fortune*, 15 June 1967, p. 181); also I-BD over the years |
| 480. | Pepperell Manufacturing Co. | PM | |
| 481. | Electrolux Corp. | PF (foreign indirectly) | Controlled by ASEA, a Swedish concern dominated by the Wallenberg family (see *Business Week*, 25 February 1967, p. 116); also, with regard to ASEA, see I-BD in recent years |
| 482. | Harnischfeger Corp. | PF | As of 1965 H. Harnischfeger owned 59.7% of the stock (see SEC *OS*, January 1965); also I-BD over the years |
| 483. | Schering Corp. | PM | |
| 484. | Raybestos-Manhattan, Inc. | PF | As of 1971 the Simpson family still had at least 16.8% of the stock (see SEC *OS*, January 1971); also I-BD over the years |
| 485. | Alberto-Culver Co. | PF | As of 1965 L.H. Lavin owned 44.8% of the stock (see the 1965 *Moody's Industrial Manual*, p. 1248); also I-BD over the years |
| 486. | Seaboard Allied Milling Co. | PF | As of 1965 the Bresky family had 91% of the stock of the Seaboard Flour Corp. which, in turn, owned 71% of the stock of the Seaboard Allied Milling Co. (see the 1965 *Moody's Industrial Manual*, p. 2283); also I & O-BD over the years |

**Table C-1** *(cont.)*

| 1965 Rank | Name of Company | Type of Control | Evidence or Comments |
|---|---|---|---|
| 487. | Harris-Intertype Corp. | PM | |
| 488. | Federal Paper Board Co., Inc. | PF | As of the late 1960s the Kennedy family (of New Jersey) had at least 11.6% of the stock (see SEC *OS*, July 1967, April 1968, May 1968, and July 1968); also I-BD over the years |
| 489. | The Black & Decker Mfg. Co. | PF | Probably controlled by the Black and Decker families (see *Fortune*, November 1964, p. 44); also I & O-BD over the years |
| 490. | H.H. Robertson Co. | PM | |
| 491. | Reeves Bros., Inc. | PF | As of the mid-1960s the Reeves family (of New York City) had at least 45.3% of the stock (see SEC *OS*, May 1965, September 1965, and October 1966); also I-BD over the years |
| 492. | Nebraska Consolidated Mills Co. | PF(I) | As of the mid-1960s R.S. Dickinson and J.A. Mactier had 9.2% of the stock (see SEC *OS*, September 1966 and March 1967); also I-BD over the years |
| 493. | Bibb Manufacturing Co. | F? | Lane and Turner families?–see I & O-BD over the years |
| 494. | Todd Shipyards Corp. | PF | As of the mid-1960s the Reilly family had 14.9% of the stock (see SEC *OS*, May 1966); also I & O-BD over the years |
| 495. | Ceco Steel Products Corp. | PF | As of the early 1960s probably controlled by the Ochiltree family and M.L. Meyer interests (of Chicago), the latter having 18.0% of the stock (see SEC *OS*, July 1962); also I & O-BD over the years |

| | | | | | Evidence or Comments |
|---|---|---|---|---|---|
| 496. | Glen Alden Corp. | | | PF | As of 1965 49.7% of the stock was owned by the McCrory Corp. which was indirectly controlled, in turn, by M. Riklis (see the 1965 *Moody's Industrial Manual*, p. 2568, *Fortune*, February 1962, p. 123, and *Forbes*, 15 January 1969, p. 43); also I-BD in 1965 |
| 497. | Pitney-Bowes, Inc. | | F? | | Bowes family interests?—see I-BD over the years |
| 498. | Lily-Tulip Cup Corp. | PM | | | |
| 499. | Detroit Steel Corp. | | | PF | As of early 1968 (but not thereafter), 13% of the stock was held by the Cyrus Eaton-Daley interests (see *NYT*, 27 March 1968, p. 59); also I & O-BD over the years and *Business Week*, 15 January 1955, p. 112 |
| 500. | Draper Corp. | PM | | | |
| | Totals | 76 | 16 | 108 | |

Notes: For the above list of corporations in the 301-to-500 range of *Fortune's* 1965 industrial ranking, see "The Fortune Directory," *Fortune* (July 1965), pp. 160-67. All divisional computations based on SEC *Official Summary* data were done by slide rule, which it was felt was sufficiently accurate for purposes of this study. In many instances a number of monthly SEC stock ownership citations are listed in the "Evidence or Comments," column, none of which may refer to the holdings of the family or families identified as controlling a particular concern. In such cases there is, as a rule, only one large stock ownership figure listed in each of the company's monthly entries, and the reader can usually assume that the person holding these shares is related to the firm's economically dominant family, a fact which can frequently be corroborated through the use of *Who's Who in America* or some other reliable source of biographical information.

**Table C-2**
**Privately Owned Companies Large Enough to be Incorporated in the 301-to-500 Range of the 1965 *Fortune* Industrial Ranking**

| Name of Company | Estimated Annual[a] Volume of Sales (as of the mid-1960s) | Controlling Family |
|---|---|---|
| P. Ballantine & Sons | $140,000,000 (1964) | Badenhausen family |
| C.F. Braun & Co. | $100,000,000+ (1964) | Braun family of Alhambra, Calif. |
| California & Hawaiian Sugar Refining Corp., Ltd. | $170,000,000 (1964) | Probably various interrelated large plantation-owning families in Hawaii |
| Daniel Construction Co. | $100,000,000+ (1964) | Daniel family of South Carolina |
| Encyclopaedia Britannica, Inc. | $125,000,000 (1964) | Benton family of New York City |
| Great Lakes Carbon Corp. | $125,000,000 (1965) | Skakel family |
| Hallmark Cards Inc. | $150,000,000 (1964) | Hall family of Kansas City, Mo. |
| Theo. Hamm Brewing Co. | $135,000,000 (1964) | Hamm family of St. Paul |
| S.C. Johnson & Son, Inc. | $150,000,000 (1964) | Johnson family of Racine, Wisc. |
| J.A. Jones Construction Co. | $100,000,000+ (1964) | Jones family of Charlotte, N.C. |
| Peter Kiewit Sons Inc. | $200,000,000 (1964) | Kiewit family of Omaha, Neba. |
| Reader's Digest Assn., Inc. | $150,000,000 (1964) | De Witt and Lila Wallace |
| Rock Island Oil & Refining Co. (now known as Koch Industries, Inc.) | Probably over $129,000,000 | Koch family of Wichita, Kansas |
| F.&M. Schaefer Brewing Co. | $120,000,000+ (1965) | Schaefer family of New York City |
| E.W. Scripps Co. | $200,000,000+ (1965) | Scripps and Howard families of Cincinnati |
| Simpson Timber Co. | $135,000,000+ (1965) | Reed family of Seattle |
| Triangle Publications, Inc. | $150,000,000 (1964) | Annenberg family of Philadelphia |

[a]See *Forbes* (1 February 1965), p. 34, *Fortune* (15 July 1966), pp. 328-48, and *Forbes* (1 August 1968), p. 41.

# Index

181

193

## About the Author

**Philip H. Burch** received the Ph.D. degree from Rutgers University, where he is currently associate research professor at the Bureau of Government Research. His book, *Highway Revenue and Expenditure Policy in the United States*, was published by the Rutgers University Press in 1962. He is the author of numerous other monographs and articles. His current research activity includes studies of water pollution control and of educational policy and finance. Born in Trenton, New Jersey, in 1930, Mr. Burch is the father of four children.